PRUNELLA

The Authorized Biography of Prunella Scales

Teresa Ransom

BBC
LARGE
PRINT

First published 2005
by
John Murray (Publishers)
This Large Print edition published 2006
by
BBC Audiobooks Ltd
by arrangement with
John Murray (Publishers)
A division of Hodder Headline

UK Hardcover ISBN 1 4056 4805 8
UK Softcover   ISBN 1 4056 4809 0

British Library Cataloguing in Publication Data available

Printed and bound in Great Britain by
Antony Rowe Ltd., Chippenham, Wiltshire

For Vicky, Andrew and Edward

Contents

Illustrations

Looking for Victoria
49. Outside Buckingham Palace, with
      Timothy, after being awarded the CBE
50. Prunella and Timothy celebrating their
      fortieth wedding anniversary in 2003

The author and publishers would like to thank the following for permission to reproduce illustrations: plates 1 and 15, Betty Turner; 2, 3, 8, 13, 14 and 16, Tim Illingworth; 4, 9, 11, and 12, Peter Dobb; 24, 31, 32 and 37, BBC; 26, D. C. Thomson & Co. Ltd.; 39, Merchant Ivory Productions; 43, Robert C. Kelly, Wayne Harrison and Ross Mollison; 44, Tesco; 50, Nobby Clark. Photographs 6, 7, 10, 17–23, 25, 27–30, 35, 36 and 40–2 are from Prunella Scales's own collection. Photographs 5, 46, 47 and 48 were taken by the author.

Acknowledgements

Prunella Scales and her family have been endlessly hospitable and helpful over the last few years. Pru has patiently answered numerous questions, allowed me to accompany her while she has been working, fed me, given me a bed when necessary, and tried to initiate me into the mysteries of compost-making.

I am grateful to her husband, Timothy West, not only for giving me a revealing insight into the business, but also for checking my facts. Their sons, Samuel and Joseph West, were equally helpful, as were other members of the family, Juliet Jones, Tim Illingworth, Peter Dobb and David Scales.

Many thanks to all those who let me watch Pru working, including Louise Osmond, the director of the BBC's *Looking for Victoria*, who kindly gave me permission to watch much of the filming of the show, and Lucy Skilbeck, the director of *Too Far to Walk*, who let me sit in on rehearsal. The Actors Centre allowed me to attend some of Pru's workshops.

I watched the making of Tesco commercials, thanks to Robin Gray, and a rehearsal for *An Evening with Queen Victoria*, when I met Katrina Hendrey, Richard Burnett, Ian Partridge and Nicholas Curry, who told me about touring with the show.

Other friends and contemporaries of Pru who were generous with their time included: Richard Briers, John Cleese, Richard Cotterell, Geraldine

McEwan, Andrew Sachs, George Hall, Robert Tanitch and Vernon Dobtcheff. Also many thanks to Heather Bell, one of Pru's schoolteachers, and to her early flatmates, Enid Pound, Miranda Mackintosh and the Hon. Margaret van Koetsveld.

In Bucks Mills, Mr and Mrs Rathmell allowed me to visit the Old School House and Rachel and Paul King and Peggy Braund helped with background information.

Lastly I'm extremely grateful to Caroline Knox and Gordon Wise for their always positive help, advice and encouragement, and, as always, to my agent, Sara Menguc.

'Love the art in yourself, not yourself in the art'
Konstantin Stanislavsky

Preface

'I haven't got a clear idea of myself, which is why I'm diffident about a biography. Maybe it's my puritan upbringing. I was taught that "I, me, my, mine" are the four least important words in the language. I remember Ma saying occasionally "I, I, I, I," in a reproachful way. My parents were always very supportive though; they were pleased when I got good school certificate results, and they were glad when I got into drama school. They were very positive about achievements, but also particular about behaviour and manners.'

*   *   *

I am to write Prunella Scales's biography, and while I wait at Clapham Junction for her to collect me the situation suddenly seems a little unreal. Her car pulls up and she flings open the door: 'Lovely to see you. Get in!' As this will be the first of many such visits, I'm not quite sure what to expect, although I feel it will be less daunting for Prunella, who has given innumerable interviews.

We arrive at the four-storey Victorian house in Wandsworth; the pale yellow front is festooned with white wisteria, while an arch in the small front garden supports yellow roses. At the top of the steps the front door opens into a narrow hall hung with prints, where I leave my coat. Books line two walls of the library cum music-room where we are to do this first interview; mostly about the theatre, they are arranged into categories. The low shelves on the third side of the room all contain music and voice tapes; above them the wall is crowded with faded photographs. A small grand piano fills a sunny corner. Music stands are dotted about. Apart from those on the shelves, books are everywhere, not to mention tapes, CDs and videos. This is a work-room.

My first impression of Prunella is of someone very small, with huge eyes. She is quick, both in speech and movement, and very alert. She speaks fast, and sometimes so softly that it is hard to catch what she is saying. Physically very active, she is always jumping to her feet either to find a book to illustrate a point she is making, or to show me a photograph of one of her ancestors. The conversation, too, tends to become fragmented as she switches from one channel to another. It is like trying to interview a humming-bird.

*   *   *

The front of the house faces out over the busy South Circular road, and looking out of the window while I wait for her to find some photographs, I see that the small front border is a knot garden full of herbs. Prunella tells me she used to grow vegetables there, but while she was away on tour people waiting at the nearby bus stop always pinched the beans and strawberries, so she gave up. She doesn't mind if they take bits of the herbs.

I am introduced to her two cats, Colman and Sardou. Prunella and her husband, the actor Timothy West, have always had cats. 'When Lion, our first cat, died we had two rather confused neutered toms called Lily and Baylis (after the famous manager of the Old Vic theatre, Lilian Baylis). We thought our cats ought to have theatrical names. Many years later, after they died, we got two kittens, black and white brothers, and called them Garrick and Colman, after the eighteenth-century actor-managers. Garrick disappeared quite early on—Tim said he had gone on tour—so we got another one we called Cibber after an even older poet and writer, who also disappeared. We then chose one of our French daughter-in-law's kittens, a beautiful grey fluffy one, which of course had to be named after a French playwright. We thought that calling him Feydeau after the famous *farceur* might make Colman feel inferior, so we called him Sardou, but in spite of this Colman has never quite brought himself to accept Sardou, he considers him an intruder. Every morning he endures a daily licking all over, and then turns round and hits him. Underneath it all they're really quite friendly.' Colman and Sardou, who have been sleeping in the sun, stare at me with complete indifference.

*   *   *

I am to write Prunella's story because, she says, she can't do it. We first got in touch when I contacted her about Fanny Trollope—mother of Anthony and the subject of my first biography, which Prunella recorded for Clipper Audio. When I tentatively suggested I would like to write her biography, she very politely refused my request; she thought she ought to try to write the story herself. Two years later I received a phone call asking me if I was still interested. Today's meeting is the result of that phone call.

As the weeks of interviews go on I begin to realize that Prunella is more than modest about her work. Always warm and welcoming, she seems happy to be interviewed, but when we talk about what she has achieved she sometimes seems almost embarrassed by her success. At one of our meetings she says, 'I am the most boring person in the world, that's partly why I wanted to be an actress. Putting on the whole persona, another persona, gives you a sense of freedom and release. Being yourself, on the whole, doesn't.' John Cleese, who worked with her in *Fawlty Towers*, says she is very self-effacing and not really comfortable with any kind of compliment, but he thinks this is probably because she feels she doesn't have anything worth saying—a view certainly not shared by others.

This apparent lack of self-esteem disappears when she's acting. Immensely versatile, in the guise of another character she can switch from virago to shy secretary, Sybil Fawlty to HM the Queen, Tesco's Dottie, Miss Mapp, Queen Victoria, to mention just a few, and will be different, believable, and almost unrecognizable in each character. Now in her early seventies, Prunella has quite astonishing energy, and keeps a schedule which would exhaust many younger actors. She works in theatre, television and radio; makes documentary voice-overs, reads audio books, teaches, and gives recitals with her husband. Journalist Merrill Ferguson wrote about her in the 1980s: 'She teaches drama, she votes left wing, she worries about the bomb, reads voraciously, believes in the equality of women, and argues with a fluency that would do credit to most politicians. Prunella is something of a theatrical phenomenon in that she is a serious actress and a serious woman, has played in everything from Greek tragedy to French farce, from American drama to Shakespeare, films and television; and played, almost without exception, with a considerable amount of distinction.'

Because she is still almost constantly in work, it is not easy for Prunella to find time for interviews. She agrees that in order to keep up with her, and to try to understand more about how she approaches a part, I should go with her on location, whether it be rehearsing a play, filming a BBC docu-drama, teaching a masterclass, or making a commercial. Over the months, as I interview her, travel with her, and slowly begin to get to know her, a clearer picture begins to emerge of this generous, complicated, brilliant and intensely private woman. What began, I thought, as a straightforward biography, has become anything but that; it has become a fascinating search for a very elusive person who feels most comfortable when wearing another persona. As she says herself, 'I don't know who the hell I am.'

1

'The possessor of a good
sense of humour'

'Prunella was late in arriving,' according to her brother Timothy Illingworth, 'and our mother, tired of the constant enquiries, thought she would play a trick on the village. Dressing up our very small cook in a bonnet and shawl, she helped her into the large old-fashioned pram and asked the nanny to push the pram around the village to see wha..t happened. There was considerable excitement. "Has the baby arrived?" "Can we have a look?" "Of course," said Nan Patterson, stepping back as they crowded around. "Come and see." '

The beaming cook, thus, arguably, became Prunella's first understudy.

*   *   *

Prunella Margaret Rumney Illingworth was born on 22 June 1932 at the Forge, in Sutton Abinger, Surrey. The Forge, an old timbered house with the smithy beside it, is situated at a road junction between the villages of Abinger Common, Holmbury Saint Mary and Abinger Hatch, and when a working concern would have been well situated for passing trade. The house overlooks a narrow road edged with high banks, and on the far side of the road a wide green field sweeps down into the valley with a small stream separating it from the public house on the far side.

1

Prunella spent most of her childhood in this part of Surrey; the Forge, Broomhills and Kempslade have all been her homes, and her parents remained in the area for most of their lives. One day she drove me round and showed me various places where she had once lived. As we headed through long green avenues of arching trees dense enough to shut out the sun, what struck me forcibly was the timeless quality of the area. The roadway is carved so deeply into the ground by generations of travellers and traffic that the tree roots jutting out along the edges have bound it into an earthen-walled tunnel roofed with green. From the tunnel of trees we emerged between high grassy banks tall enough to obscure the view before plunging back into the cool greenness. Prunella says she almost recognizes the individual trees because she has been around long enough to watch them grow. As we drove past, she pointed out neat little houses and cottages hidden in the woods. This part of the world seems to belong to a different generation—those who were brought up with Christopher Robin, Violet Needham, and *Swallows and Amazons* as role models. It feels remote from the frantic pace of today, a safe place steeped in nostalgia and tradition. This is where Prunella grew up.

*   *   *

Prunella's father's family came from Kendal in Westmoreland, where they owned the Illingworth Tobacco factory, purveyors, in earlier times, of Rumney scented snuff. Her paternal grandfather, Charles Rumney Illingworth, trained as a doctor before being appointed as house surgeon at the Peterborough Hospital. His particular interest was in community health and the prevention of infective diseases; in 1894 he applied for a position as Medical Officer of Health in London and became a senior health adviser in the borough of Tooting. He and his wife, Jessie Richardson, had four children: Sydney Royston (Roy), Philip Noel, Jessie Winifred, and the youngest, Prunella's father, John Richardson, who was born in Tooting on 25 June 1895.

Prunella's paternal grandparents died before she was born. 'To me they are just photographs on the wall of the sitting-room. Apparently my grandfather was hopeless at managing money and died in debt, whereupon Jessie became a Christian Scientist. I wonder if that was her protest against the medical profession in general, or perhaps just my grandfather's inability to earn a good income from it.' Their financial situation was so difficult that Jessie wrote to her brother-in-law, James Illingworth, back in Kendal, to ask for money to educate her four children.

John, who went to Latymer School, left when he was only sixteen. Prunella isn't sure why but thinks it was probably for financial reasons—being the youngest child, it is possible that the Kendal money had run out. Three years later, in the summer of 1914, the beginning of the First World War, he enlisted in the Artists' Rifles. He was invalided home after the battle of Ypres with a 'blighty'—the name given to a wound severe enough to send a soldier back to England. Prunella remembers that he always had a slight hole in his thigh and believes that the leg wound was the reason he survived, for he never returned to the Western Front. When he recovered he was despatched to India in the Wiltshire Regiment, seconded into the Indian Army and sent to the North West Frontier. He served in Signals, was promoted to

Major, and remained there from 1918 until 1920. A skilful rider, one of his jobs was to lay telephone lines, galloping on horseback with a hook in one hand, with which he would lift the cables over the hedges. When he was discharged, or axed, as so many were in 1920, he stayed on in India and got a job with the English cotton firm Tootal Broadhurst Lee.

Of John's siblings, his elder brother, Noel, became a merchant seaman and was known in the family as 'wicked uncle Noel', though no one can remember why. Roy died young, and his sister, Jessie Winifred, married Walter Dobb, a captain in the regular army during the First World War. After leaving the army he became general manager for Remington Typewriters in London.

*   *   *

Prunella's mother, Catherine Scales, also the youngest of four children, was born in Bradford on 8 May 1901. According to family archives, Prunella's great-great-grandfather, the Reverend Thomas Scales, was an influential Congregational minister, a schoolmaster, and a leading light in the fight against slavery. His son, Henry Christian Scales, founded a successful wool company in Bradford. A textile converter, he bought woollens and worsteds from factories in Yorkshire and Lancashire and cottons from India—they had an office in Bombay. These he stored in his Bradford warehouse before cutting, dyeing and crating the different materials, then despatching the finished products to fulfil orders from around the world. Prunella's grandfather, Walter, was born on 20 November 1850. When he was sixteen he began working in various local wool firms to learn the business, and when he was twenty-one, according to his diaries, he travelled to France, spending several days in Lille, Paris, Tours, Angers, Bordeaux and Nîmes. He repeated these trips over the next four years, each time being away for several weeks, and also travelled to Italy and Portugal as part of his work in the textile business. An excellent linguist, he spoke five languages fluently. Walter inherited his father's wool business in 1875 when he was only twenty-five, and later became an ardent Nonconformist, a governor of the London Missionary Society, a keen cricketer and an active member of the local Liberal party. Though Prunella never knew any of her grandparents they have, perhaps, left her a legacy of altruism and liberal thinking.

*   *   *

In 1887 Walter married twenty-six-year-old Edith Birkinshaw, who Prunella believes 'wore very tight boots', and whose family came from Sligo in Ireland. Walter and Edith had four children. The eldest, Winifred, known as Freda, was born in 1888. Then in 1890, came Cuthbert (Cus), who read medicine at Edinburgh and served as a doctor in the Royal Army Medical Corps. He won a Military Cross in 1918 and again in 1919, for bravery under fire while leading his stretcher-bearers out to collect hundreds of wounded from no man's land. He was in charge of the hospitals in Malta during the Second World War, became a Brigadier and later worked in India. The third child, Alexander (Alec) was born in 1893 and lastly, eight years later, came Catherine in 1901. Nicknamed the *bambino* before she was born, this was shortened to *bimbo*, in the Italian fashion, and then to Bim.

5

Thirteen years separated Freda and Bim.

Walter, whose three sisters ran a dame school in Bradford, believed in a good education for his children, including his daughters. The eldest, Freda, Prunella's aunt and godmother, went to Bradford Grammar School and then to a finishing school in Switzerland, but, according to Prunella, 'never completely lost her northern accent and always said "und" instead of "and" '. Bim, the youngest, was sent as a boarder to Moira House, a progressive girl's school in Eastbourne, where Prunella would later be a pupil.

Walter suffered heart failure in early April 1914 and died on the 22nd while on holiday in the Isle of Wight, where he and Edith had been going every winter to get away from the northern chills. Although he had apparently not been well for some years, his death at sixty-three must have been a terrible blow for his family. He was buried at the Salem Congregational Church in Bradford, where he had been Senior Deacon. Because Cuthbert had already chosen a career in medicine, the second son, Alec, inherited the wool business, but when war was declared on 4 August he volunteered for the West Yorkshire Regiment and was sent to France with the 6th Battalion. In his absence, Walter's nephew, Fred, already working in the company, took over the management of the firm. When her father died, Bim was still at Moira House; Walter had written a loving letter to his daughter, arranging to collect her from Victoria Station on 6 April when her term finished, but in the event he was too unwell to leave the Isle of Wight. Bim, as the baby of the family, had a special relationship with her father and must have missed him greatly.

Moira House had been founded in 1875 by Charles

Ingham, who in 1908 handed over the management of the school to his theosophist daughter, Gertrude, headmistress when Bim was there and still teaching thirty years later when Prunella became a pupil. The regular curriculum included science, an unusual subject for girls at that time, and there was considerable emphasis on sport, drama, speech and music. Team games were mandatory, and Bim, who was skilled at most sports, became captain of cricket, hockey and tennis. The students didn't sit public examinations: both Gertrude Ingham and her father believed that they put the wrong emphasis on education, and thought it better that each girl should be allowed to develop her own potential.

The creative teaching at Moira House had a profound and lasting effect on Bim's outlook, and she flourished in the stimulating atmosphere. She became involved in every aspect of school life; according to one of the senior teachers, Mona Swann, she was not particularly academic, but the school appreciated her creative ability and her strong leadership qualities. She played a leading role in founding a scout group; initially the group met for discussions, picnics and to put on plays, but with the onset of the First World War they spent their free time making swabs for Eastbourne Hospital to help with the war effort. Their leader was a junior mistress, Emily Cummings, known affectionately as Cummy, who became a lifelong friend to Bim and was later to play an important part in Prunella's childhood.

In February 1918 the whole school was involved in a play, *The Quest for the Holy Grail*, devised by Mona Swann, in which Bim played Sir Galahad. It was about then (possibly influenced by the Arthurian legends) that she helped create a system known as the League,

7

in which school monitors were romantically classified as Squires and Knights. Bim became one of the first Knights. The League was still in existence when Prunella went to Moira House, but had expanded into Pages and Service Squires of three different categories, Squires, Standard Bearers and Knights. Prunella, who was a Standard Bearer, says, 'It could sound a bit pretentious, but actually it worked very well. As the whole school took part in the elections one got used to the obligation of voting. It was extremely unconventional at the time.'

In the bitter conflict being slowly played out in Europe, many families lost sons and brothers. On 6 January 1918, in Bim's last year at school, her adored elder brother Alec was killed in action. Two years earlier he had survived being wounded and had been awarded a Military Cross. On his death the wool mill went to cousin Fred, who had been managing it during the war; but without the experienced Walter in charge the business began to lose money and the family's financial future became less secure.

Bim left school determined to become an actress, and went to the Royal Academy of Dramatic Art (RADA), where according to the family she stayed for only one term. Perhaps there were financial reasons for this; certainly in about 1920 her mother, Edith, moved from their large house at 18 North Park Road, Heaton, Manningham, to live in more modest accommodation at Harrogate. There she became ill, and, as was expected at that time, Bim, the unmarried daughter, stayed at home to look after her. Prunella thinks they sold the English home and went to live for a while in Italy. 'My understanding is that they stayed in an Italian boarding house because it was cheap.' While in Harrogate, Bim appeared with the Halifax

Thespians, a local amateur group, in what Prunella describes as 'a play of startling sentimentality' by Laurence Housman and Harley Granville Barker called *Prunella, or Love in a Dutch Garden*. A whimsical verse play, it followed the fortunes and adventures of a troupe of travelling mummers and was immensely popular at the time; the text underwent numerous reprints and adaptations. 'Ma fell in love with the leading man, whom she didn't marry, but she kept the heroine's name for me. One of my early boyfriends used to call me "love in a Dutch garden" when he was cross with me.'

Her performance deemed a success, Bim became even more determined to act professionally. When Edith died, aged sixty-two, in December 1925 from heart problems, twenty-four-year-old Bim was free to join the Liverpool Playhouse, one of the most prestigious regional repertory companies. Starting as an acting student, doing backstage work and playing occasional small parts, she gradually worked her way up to become a permanent member of the company, working with some of the leading actors of her time. She played Hermia in a production of *A Midsummer Night's Dream*, with Robert Donat as Oberon and Diana Wynyard as Titania, and was in a J.M. Barrie play, *A Kiss for Cinderella*. She received good notices and was 'discovered' by Esmé Percy, a well-known actor who was making a guest appearance at the Liverpool Playhouse and was about to play the lead in *Byron* at the Criterion Theatre in London. He offered Bim a small part; she accepted, and left Liverpool for the excitement and challenge of working in London. When she left she was presented with a book of Galsworthy plays; tucked inside it Prunella found a letter signed by most of the company, including

9

Robert Donat, Diana Wynyard and Majorie Fielding: 'To Catherine Scales, with best wishes for your future success and happiness.' Although *Byron* flopped, Bim got a good review in *The Times* for her performance, and a letter of encouragement from Robert Donat: 'Darling, your performance was outstanding. I do miss you.'

Prunella says her mother was quite creative, though always hopeless with any kind of working machinery. However, in spite of having had what was for those times a liberal education, she had quite a conservative outlook. According to her old teacher, Mona Swann, she was a good companion. 'She had a deep engaging chuckle which stemmed from three dominant characteristics: a buoyant sense of humour, a boundless interest and delight in people, and an unflagging *joie de vivre* both in the everyday world around her and in the fertile world of her imagination.'

While in London Bim shared a flat in Ecclestone Street with a friend from Moira House, Eileen Healing, and it was here that she met John Illingworth, now employed by Tootal's head office as a sales manager. John had first met Eileen at an army dance during his time as an officer in India, and had got in touch with her when he returned to England. Timothy Illingworth, Prunella's brother, was told that Eileen had sent a note to Bim: 'There's a funny little man from the Indian Army, who is coming home and I'm dead scared about him. Will you come to dinner and chaperone me?' Bim went; she and John got on well and began to see more of each other. He went to see her in *Byron* at the Criterion and she was beguiled by a bouquet he sent her on the first night, an unusual and inventive arrangement of cabbages. After *Byron* closed, Bim worked for a while at Amersham Repertory Theatre. But she was in love, and when, within six months of their meeting, she became engaged to John, she resolved to give up professional acting.

John Illingworth was a dapper, good-looking man with a small moustache. He wasn't very tall, only about five foot seven, but then neither was Bim, at only five foot three. John's nephew, Peter Dobb, remembers him as being courteous and well-dressed. He was the only person Peter had ever known who wore a silk cravat with his pyjamas. His son, Timmo, says he was always impeccably dressed, particularly in London, where he wore a bowler hat, carried a tightly rolled umbrella, and wore spats in winter to protect his highly polished shoes. His grandson, Sam, remembers that even as a much older man John always looked good; 'He wore nice narrow ties and grey herringbone tweed jackets.'

Freda, who had become a surrogate mother to her much younger sister, offered to organize the wedding. She had been married for some years to a wealthy baronet, Sir Gordon Kaye, the owner of a wool mill in Huddersfield, both title and mill inherited from his father. Gordon had served in the Royal Flying Corps during the First World War until he was invalided out, after which he returned to Huddersfield to run the mill and joined the Territorials in the King's Own Yorkshire Light Infantry. The Kayes were living in the north, and Freda took over the wedding arrangements and issued the invitations. The director of the Liverpool Playhouse, William Armstrong, was one of those invited: 'Dearest Bim. I am writing to you and I hope you will pass the message on to your charming and Titled Sister. I believe Marjorie, and several of us are going to try and come down, but I can't answer for myself just at the moment, as our season opens the night before and I may have a great deal to do. Would we be able to get back all right for the evening performance? And what in the name of God do you want for a wedding present (anything up to 30/- but not a penny more), as I have just been to Corsica and am completely broke.'

Bim and John were married on 5 September 1930 at St Philip's church, Birchencliffe, Huddersfield, and Bim was given away by her brother-in-law, Sir Gordon Kaye. Prunella says, 'A week before the wedding they had been involved in a car accident in Eaton Square, not my father's fault apparently, but my mother injured her leg and it was still in plaster for the wedding.' The upset of the accident may have been one of the reasons that Bim never learnt to drive. Although she took numerous driving lessons, she never passed her test.

For the first year of their marriage Prunella's parents lived in London, in a small flat in Queen's Mansions, West End Lane, West Hampstead, but when Bim became pregnant they decided they needed to find a house in the country. They rented the Forge, in Sutton Abinger, from where John drove to London every day in his Tootal company car, a Hillman Minx.

It was at the Forge, in the upstairs bedroom, that Prunella was born at 9.30 p.m. on 22 June 1932, while her father waited downstairs, as all conventional fathers did. She was baptized C. of E., with Gertrude Ingham, the headmistress of Moira House, as one of the godmothers, Aunt Freda, another. Freda's son, cousin David, was a godfather, along with Harry Darbyshire, an ex-boyfriend of her mother who apparently continued to write to Bim for many years.

By this time Freda and Gordon Kaye had also moved down to Surrey with their three sons, Stephen, David and Brian, and Prunella grew up looking on the boys as her quasi older brothers. The move meant that Bim continued to have Freda's close support.

Timothy Illingworth, born in Hampstead on 19 March 1934, was twenty months younger than Prunella. She remembers being exceedingly jealous of him, and when asked by a friend of the family if she had any brothers and sisters, she said crossly: ' "No. I've only got Timmy, with curls." I also remember saying to my mother in a tantrum, "I hate Timmy, I hate him, I want to cut off his arm." Good Freudian stuff, which of course nobody recognized in those days. I can remember my mother breastfeeding him, the fireguard, and the pattern the Valor paraffin stove made on the ceiling.' Prunella had straight hair, which she grew long and wore in plaits, probably as an overt protest against her brother's curls.

Her parents decided that with two children they should really buy a house of their own, and in 1937 they found a developer who was building what Prunella calls 'post-office Georgian' houses in Logmore Lane, just above Westcott, near Dorking. They had very little money but were able to borrow the freehold purchase price of £600 from Freda and Gordon. On one of my visits Prunella drove me past Broomhills, the first and only home her parents ever owned. The house is quite large and stands well back from the road at the end of a gravel driveway. She remembers that upstairs there were five bedrooms, a bathroom and a dressing-room; downstairs, a dining-room, sitting-room and kitchen. 'The big bedroom was the nursery and there was also a night nursery. Elsie's bedroom was at the end, also Ma and Pa's bedroom and Pa's dressing-room.' Like most houses of that time there was no central heating. 'It is incredible to think that my parents, who were quite hard up, could afford a cook and the mother's help, Elsie, who joined us after Nan Patterson left. She was blonde, very nice, and in her twenties. She helped to look after me. When I was five years old I started going to Stanway, the local primary school in Dorking. I was taken there on the bus by Elsie.' It was a half-hour journey. Her brother Timothy—now known as Timmo—remembers playing on his tricycle in the garden at Broomhills, Fred Morton, the gardener, who swore a lot, and being terrified by a frog.

After her first term at Stanway, Prunella's headmistress, Miss G.E. Short, reported that 'she is absolutely whole-hearted in all she undertakes. She is intelligent and her sense of humour and fun make her a delightful member of the group.' By the summer of 1938 her form-mistress noted that six-year-old Prunella's 'reading is quite exceptional. She is both enthusiastic and appreciative of what is done for her.' She was, however, rather untidy and 'is still fond of her own voice'. There is one more report for December 1938: 'She is the possessor of a good sense of humour and is able to appreciate the ridiculous. Prunella is a reliable, capable and happy little girl and enters fully into school life.'

Prunella, who has always loved words, remembers her first reading lesson. 'It's very vivid. Miss McGill taught us. She stood in front of the blackboard and told us a story. "There were Mr and Mrs Smith, and they lived in a house and they had a dog. And the dog was lying on the hearth rug and the dog went 'huh'," and she wrote an 'h' on the board. Then she said, "There was a baby in a cot by the fireplace, and the

14

baby went 'aa'," and she wrote an 'a' on the board. "On the mantelpiece above the fireplace was a clock and the clock went 'tt'," and she wrote a 't' on the board. 'Then Mrs Smith came down and she said, "Dear, have you seen my hat?" And there it was on the blackboard. That was the way they taught in those days.'

Although Bim no longer acted professionally, she had not completely given it up, and after her marriage she became an enthusiastic member of the local amateur dramatic society. Prunella, who thanks to Miss McGill learnt to read early, became involved with this too, and remembers, when only five, hearing her mother's lines for a pageant about the history of England written by E.M. Forster, who lived at Abinger. The village production of *England's Pleasant Land* was directed by Tom Harrison and performed in a field in Westcott. Prunella still has her mother's copy of the play. It is a story of the land, told by the two main characters, Jack and Jill. Bim played Jill.

Prunella also loved drawing and painting, and was very proud when one of her pictures won a competition. She remembers her excitement when she went on stage to collect the prize at the Embassy Cinema in Dorking and shook hands with the film star Leslie Howard. 'I was a fantasist as a child. I fantasized about the prince in the film of *Snow White*, which we saw when I was about seven, and I had a cut-out book of the story. We had a '78 gramophone record of it which I played a lot on the wind-up gramophone, but the cast all had American accents. The prince was my fantasy companion—I was the princess, of course.'

One of her most powerful and influential memories is of when she was six, and her parents took her to

Sadlers Wells to see the opera *Hansel and Gretel*, conducted by Sir Thomas Beecham. The curtain-raiser was a short ballet, *The Gods Go A'Begging*, based on a suite by Handel, and she was totally captivated. Fascinated by the ballerinas dancing on point, she decided to be a ballet dancer. Unfortunately the dream was an impossibility: there were no local ballet classes where they lived in Westcott, and absolutely nothing during the war when they evacuated to Devon. Prunella realized by the age of eight that she was too old to learn to dance professionally. 'I said to my mother, "All right, I'll be an actress then!" Ma was quite cross. "You should never do anything as second best." But having said that, she did give me every help and encouragement.' Prunella says possibly Bim's own interest in the theatre may have influenced her choice.

Bim herself had other outlets for her creativity. In 1938, a year before the onset of the Second World War, she published a children's book, *Gay Company*, and the next year another one called *Nugger Nonsense*. The books got good reviews, but the plates were lost in one of the air raids on London during the war, and they were never reprinted. To celebrate the publication of *Gay Company* Bim went to Paris with her friend Moubray Leigh, who had drawn the illustrations, and brought back a beautiful Parisian doll for Prunella—which she still has. 'I'm afraid I immediately christened her Edith—not a very suitable name for a Parisian doll. We have this menagerie on top of the wardrobe in our bedroom, starting with Blue Bear, whom I had when I was one-and-a-half. The most recent one is a huge white tiger given to me by the stage-door keeper at the Comedy Theatre when I was working there in *A Day in the Death of Joe Egg* in

16

2002.' Edith is part of the collection.

When war was declared in the autumn of 1939, John Illingworth was forty-four and too old to be called up. He tried working as a special constable for several months but wanted to take a more active part in the war, so volunteered for army service. He enjoyed the army; indeed, Prunella and her brother both think he much preferred it to civilian life. 'We've never known whether to describe this as patriotism, or a desire to get away from home.' Timmo says Bim was definitely the one in charge in the house, and the strong one in the marriage.

Broomhills was situated under an enemy flight path, which was frightening for them all. A time bomb was dropped in their garden and quickly deactivated by the local bomb disposal unit. There was talk of more bombing raids, however, and Surrey was understood to be a prime target. Many families, with the threat of invasion looming and the father about to go into the army, planned to get their children out of the country. Realizing that the location of their house was dangerous, the Illingworths wondered whether Bim should take the children to Canada. They put the house on the market in preparation for leaving, but it was a disastrous time to sell. They received only £400 for it, a loss of £200, and as a result John was never able to repay the loan from Gordon Kaye.

In 1940, after they had sold Broomhills, they stayed for a while with friends, Cyril and Nancy Atkinson, who lived nearby in Wotton. Cyril, known as Kins, was agent for the Wotton Estate in Abinger. To Timmo, the war seemed frighteningly close as the tanks rumbled down the Guildford road, past the cottage where they were staying, to take up positions on the North Downs in anticipation of an imminent German

17

invasion. Many children like Timmo, too young to understand what was happening, were affected by the often unspoken fears of those around them. So the family were quite pleased when Freda and Gordon, who because of the Surrey air-raids had already moved back to Yorkshire, invited them to stay. Bim took Prunella and Timmo there, while John, still working as a special constable, remained in Surrey but visited when he could get away at weekends.

Prunella says she began to realize as she grew older that uncle Gordon, 'or "Gorgie" as we used to call him, had little time for my father, although he was very fond of Ma and of us'. On one occasion, according to Timmo, when John was staying with Gordon and Freda at Grice Hall, he left some loose change lying on his dressing-table and it was subsequently stolen by one of the servants. The refugee cook was found to be the culprit, so had to be sacked, much to Gordon's fury. He despised John for being so careless. The loan on the house remained unpaid and may well have been another cause for his dislike. For his part John Illingworth found Gordon rather overbearing, and the two men were certainly at odds politically. Prunella thinks 'Gordon, who was a convinced Tory, probably distrusted my father, who voted Liberal. My mother wasn't very politically conscious, but as I grew up and became a student, I voted Labour.'

*　　　*　　　*

Gordon Kaye had bought Grice Hall, a vast Elizabethan country house within commuting distance of his mill in Huddersfield. It had an extensive garden, a tennis court, a home farm, and a large staff including

18

two gardeners and a farm manager. Bim invited Miss Cummings—Cummy, her old teacher from Moira House—to go to Yorkshire with them to help with the education of the children. She and Bim had remained close friends, and Cummy now took over the children's lessons and taught them around the morning-room table: Prunella says it was like having a governess. 'It was the sort of country life which we'd never experienced before. It was another world. There was a herd of cows which I learned to milk by hand, and the local hounds met in the courtyard. We were very lucky; although it was right out of my parents' league both financially and socially, it's been a useful resource, as an actress, to know what that kind of life involved.' Timmo loved it and spent most of his time out of doors helping the farm manager, Bob Peace.

The cousins, Stephen, David and Brian, were rarely at home. Stephen, the eldest, not accepted for the forces because his lungs had been affected by pneumonia, ran the mill with his father. Later, wanting to be more directly involved with the war, he became an Admiralty courier; however, he had always wanted to be an actor. After the war he took a postgraduate training at the Webber Douglas school, and by 1949 he had joined the Bristol Old Vic company. The two younger sons, David and Brian, joined up as soon as the war started. David, a doctor, went to Normandy and Arnhem with the Parachute Brigade; Brian, who had a first class law degree from Oxford, became a fighter pilot but his experiences in the war affected him so badly that he never went back to law.

Prunella remembers the first winter they were at Grice Hall, when the weather was very severe. 'There were six-foot-deep snowdrifts and we were collecting groceries from the village on a sledge. I got whooping cough and was very ill. Ma thought it was too cold up there and my dad wasn't very happy about being dependent on relations, so, in spite of the raids, we went back down to Surrey.' It was a difficult and unsettling time for the children. 'The Atkinsons took us in, though they had two children of their own and the house was much too small for all of us.' Prunella, who had not fully recovered from her whooping cough, contracted double pneumonia in May 1940 and nearly died. She was one of the first patients to be prescribed a new wonder drug, M & B, one of the earliest antibiotics. The doctor advised Bim that she should try to get her away to somewhere warmer.

On 12 July 1940 John got his eagerly awaited call-up notice to report to St Austell, in Cornwall, to take up an appointment as an instructor. Too old to go back to the infantry, he joined the Pioneer Corps and in May 1941 took over the command of 50th Company in Minehead. It seemed to Bim a good idea to follow the doctor's advice and move the whole family to the west country to be near John. Other friends of the Illingworths owned a cottage in a little fishing village called Bucks Mills on the north Devon coast, which they lent to Bim so that eight-year-old Prunella could recuperate. Because Bim couldn't drive, another friend, Nora Cundell, who owned an Austin Seven, bravely offered to drive them from Surrey to Devon. Bim loaded Timmo, Prunella and the luggage into Nora's tiny car, and they set off on an exhausting journey of over 300 miles, the last part of the journey down small winding country roads. Prunella, still recovering from pneumonia, was very weak, and the children were both car-sick. They made the whole nightmare journey in one day, stopping on the way

20

several times for petrol and food. Prunella can remember very little of the journey, but at one of the stops Timmo recalls that she left behind one of her dolls, and cried for hours. To cap it all, when they eventually arrived at Bucks Mills the cottage was not ready for them. Luckily the vicar, Mr Whitaker, who lived at the top end of the village close to the church and the school, kindly offered to put them all up for the night.

2

'Learning around the kitchen table'

'One eccentric old lady in the village, Mrs Saunders, had lost her husband and two sons in the First World War. She used to serve teas for visitors outside her house on six-foot-long tables and every night she insisted on turning the tables upside down, she said, "so that them Jerries wouldn't see 'em on their way to bomb Exeter". The complete blackout of all windows and doors was mandatory, and at night the ARP wardens would patrol the roads to make sure that the rules were being observed. One night when Ernest Braund was on duty he was passing Mrs Saunders's cottage when her door flew open, light streamed across the street, and she came out calling for her cat. "Pussy, pussy, where be you, my dear?" She had an enormous torch which she shone around and up into the sky. Ernest descended on her. "Put that there torch out. They'm Jerries up there!" Mrs Saunders, who was stone deaf, went back inside to fetch her large brass ear trumpet. When she came back Ernest bellowed into it again—"Put that there light out, they'm Jerries up there." Mrs Saunders turned to him in amazement. "Can they 'ear us then?" '

*   *   *

Bucks Mills is a small fishing village overlooking Bideford Bay. Most of the houses there are clustered

22

together towards the foot of the steep hill, on a low bluff overlooking the water. The seashore below the cottages is made up of huge pebbles and jagged rocks smashed down where the steep cliffs have crumbled; the beach itself is only accessible from the water, along the coastal paths, or by foot down a steep narrow path from the village. It can be rough walking on the rocky foreshore when the tide is high, but at low water there is a small sandy beach and a wide gully known as the Gut, opposite the now crumbling quay. One day when I was there the gusts of wind were so fierce I had to grab the railing along the steep path to keep upright. That part of the north Devon coast can be dangerous in wild weather when the wind and rain roar in off the Atlantic, beating up the valley, buffeting the exposed cottages bordering the narrow road.

The village has a unique history. Populated, according to the local story, by the descendants of seven brothers from Spain shipwrecked on the coast after the Armada, most of the families there were either called Braund or married to Braunds.

Almost all the Braunds have now gone, their cottages taken over by outsiders who come for holidays in the summer months. Living in Bucks Mills during the war, when it was still a working fishing village, had a profound effect on the children evacuated there. Ernest Braund was the senior fisherman, a great local character with memorably splendid whiskers and skin eruptions blistering his face, which the children were convinced were barnacles. His daughter Mamie always dressed like a Spaniard with a red flower in her hair; her claim to fame was that she had once been in a film. Mrs Reggie Braund, whose husband was the coastguard, ran the local shop, while Mrs Charlie Braund ran the boarding-house known as the Hotel, where the Illingworths stayed until they could move into the borrowed cottage. One day when Prunella had a scuffle in the street with other evacuees, Charlie Braund came out of his cow-shed near the hotel and told her, 'Tiddun proper for little maids to fight.' She remembers sitting on the doorstep howling, 'I want to be a boy. I want to be a boy.' The Braunds became like an extended family for Prunella and Timmo.

Soon after their arrival the Illingworths were able to move into the first of their temporary homes, and although they had to move several times during their stay, Bim coped magnificently. At St John's Cottage, where they stayed most of the time, conditions were fairly primitive: they washed in front of the fire, sitting in a tin bath filled by carrying cans of hot water from the smoky oil stove in the kitchen on which Bim did all the cooking. Timmo recalls one morning when, to his horror, he got up to find his new white cricket shirt and shorts, which Bim had just given him for his birthday, covered with black oily smuts. The unreliable Aladdin oil lamp had been turned up too high and 'smeeched'. All lighting was by oil lamps or candles. But to the children, who were too young to remember much else, it was all great fun and they thrived there.

Whenever Bim was too busy to play with him, Timmo would go and visit Grenville, Charlie Braund's son, who possessed an awe-inspiring vocabulary of swear words and who, as part of his living, trapped the numerous rabbits living in burrows on the steep slopes leading down to the village. Grenville taught Timmo how to milk his father's cows, and sometimes took him rabbiting using gin traps, which was how both children learnt to skin and gut rabbits, making a welcome

24

addition to the sparse meat rations. Bim, a leader as ever, organized the digging of a communal vegetable garden up above the village. She made sure all the children from the village helped, including the evacuees, and it proved very productive.

When they weren't at school the children were nearly always on the beach, or away exploring on their own, walking for miles along the cliff paths. All the children learnt to swim there, and spent much of their time in the Bunky Pool, a rock pool where they sailed boats and caught prawns. If it wasn't too rough they would also be allowed go out with the fishermen to catch herrings and mackerel on hand-lines. Peggy Braund, now in her eighties and living in Clovelly, remembers being taught to swim off her father's fishing boat at the age of three. Her father fixed a belt around her waist made up of lobster-pot corks threaded on a rope, tied Peggy and her four-year-old brother to his boat, and then dropped them over the side. They learnt to swim very quickly.

There were rules about picking up driftwood washed on to the beach. If it was piled up against the cliff, that meant it had been claimed. If Ernest saw the children approaching it he would tell them off. 'That's not yours.' However, Timmo says they did manage to find enough for their open fire in the cottage. Every week Bim and the children would walk up to a farm at the top of the valley to collect eggs, and sometimes cream, and in the summer they would help the farmer, Mr Turner, with his haymaking. On the way to the farm they passed the house of Josiah Braund, and further up the valley that of James Braund, who was rumoured to be mad. Timmo remembers: 'Sometimes in the dark evenings you would hear a horn being blown from the top of the valley, which meant that something awful was going to happen and we were all terrified. The locals said a spell had been put on someone unknown: it was all very spooky and mysterious.'

The family stayed in Bucks Mills for nearly two years, moving from one rented cottage to another. Like many other children, they saw virtually nothing of their father during the war. Shortly after their arrival John was posted from Minehead up to the Shetland Islands. This kind of random posting happened to many families, and usually, when the men moved, their wives and children stayed put and made a life for themselves in one place. It was almost impossible for John to come as far as Bucks Mills to see his family: he had very little leave and the distance was too great. In one of his letters to Prunella he wrote: 'Write to me and tell me all your doings. It's a long time since we met, and will be longer still I'm afraid.'

He did occasionally manage to get as far as Exeter, and then Bim would hire Charlie Braund's car and they would all be driven to Exeter station to collect him. And sometimes if he could get to London, Bim would make the slow and unpredictable train journey from Devon to see him. A family story tells how on one of these journeys she met a naval Captain called Worthington, who asked her where she lived and then bet her £5 that he would come and visit her there. She said, 'Impossible! Too rugged a coastline.' But as Timmo remembers, 'Sure enough, one bright summer's day a mine-sweeper came round Gallantry Bower Point and anchored in the bay. A rowing boat was dropped over the side, with the First Lieutenant on the oars and the Captain sitting in the stern. Here was Captain Worthington arriving at Bucks Mills and winning his five pounds.'

26

The family had some interesting neighbours. Next door lived Marjorie Frost, whose husband commanded a parachute battalion, and through her they were sometimes able to get news from the Front. Another neighbour who fascinated them was Helen Berg, a naturalist and skilled marksman appointed by the War Office to kill the peregrine falcons nesting in the steep cliffs, to prevent them attacking the carrier pigeons coming in from France carrying vital messages. Armed with a specially made sawn-off shotgun, she would be lowered over the side of the cliff on a rope and tackle system devised by Mark Braund, so that she could destroy the eggs in the nests and shoot the birds. It was dangerous work. Mark did all Helen's driving, and Timmo remembers him as amazingly good-looking, with deep blue eyes. He had two sons, friends of Timmo's, who made a box wagon with a rope attached to the front wheels to steer it. Into this all the boys would pile and rumble at breakneck speed from the top cottage, down the hill, grinding to a halt in the centre of the cliff that overlooked the beach.

When they were first at Bucks Mills, Prunella and Timmo went to the village school just above the church, a mile and a quarter's climb through the woods up a very steep hill. They were at the school for two terms, and learnt reading, copperplate writing, arithmetic and scripture, taught by Mr Whitaker. Mrs Thomas, who was Welsh, was the very strict headmistress. She would listen to their catechism, and if they talked in class, would cane them across the palms of their hands. Prunella sat next to Conrad James from the village, who knew his catechism better than she did. They had to stand up in turn to repeat it, and she learnt the words by heart from listening to

27

him. 'I always say I learnt my catechism in a broad north Devon accent, and my alphabet in cockney.' Shortly after Prunella and Timmo had started at the village school, about thirty evacuee children arrived, labelled, from Northfleet in East London. With the exception of Ernest, who was considered too old, most of the villagers had one or more evacuees billeted on them. Their arrival doubled the size of the school, but they came with their own teacher, Mrs Prudence, who took the younger children, including Prunella and Timmo. She taught them their cockney alphabet to the tune of 'Auld Lang Syne'. They began with the alphabet, followed by the verse:

> *And when the teacher claps her hands*
> *Quite silent we must be,*
> *And sit up nicely in our seats,*
> *And learn our ABC.*

Then came a repeat singing of the alphabet. Prunella remembers being quite indignant because she had, after all, learnt her alphabet at Stanway, and could already read.

Bim, academically ambitious for both her children, decided that because the teaching at the village school did not include the science or history which they would need in their future education, she must make other arrangements for their lessons. She invited Cummy, whose family originally came from north Devon, to come and live with them again so that she could take over their morning lessons. The little group included several other children from the village, and Cummy taught them English, arithmetic, history, music and geometry; Prunella says she taught the latter out of a book. Bim also taught the children herself, mainly in the afternoons, when she read stories in French or rehearsed plays with them. 'Ma believed that to be successful as an actress, you must read widely, especially history and the arts.' Prunella thinks the particular input from her mother may have had a lasting impact on the way she thinks about herself, and possibly constrained her in some ways. 'Perhaps it's something to do with being educated at home, where we were twenty-four hours a day with Ma until we went away to school. It was sort of learning around the kitchen table. I think of my mum's early teaching, "You are the least important person in the world." It was bad manners to talk about yourself and you got really inhibited about it.'

Timmo was part of this small school along with two other boys who were boarding with them, John Herrington and John Clay, whose parents wanted them to live somewhere safe in the country. Somehow Bim kept house for her own family, the two evacuee boys and her old friend Cummy, on £8 a week. Prunella is not quite sure about Cummy's relationship with Bim. She says Cummy adored her mother, which was why she loved being with them, and Bim was certainly fond of her, but 'I think my dad was uncomfortable with her around.' Timmo says he disliked Cummy and resented her friendship with his mother. He felt she had too much influence in the house because she always told them what to do. She was quite a domineering figure—he describes her as 'formidable' and remembers how he hated being surrounded by women. Timmo admits he could be a difficult child. He had a fierce temper, and sometimes when he got out of control Bim would just pick him up, carry him over her shoulder upstairs to his room, and lock him in until he had finished throwing the bedclothes out of the window and quietened down. Cummy remained a permanent fixture in their lives.

During the summer of 1941, while still at Bucks Mills, Bim directed a children's play to raise funds in aid of children in bombed areas. The play, *Fat King Melon and Princess Caraway*, by A. P. Herbert, was a great success and raised ten pounds. Roy from London played Fat King Melon; Prunella, Princess Caraway. Prunella remembers that the children in the cast had a wonderful mixture of accents, with the London evacuees' cockney, the middle-class children with middle-class accents and the local schoolchildren with their broad Devon. Bim always had a good ear for regional speech, a useful skill for an actor, and one which her daughter inherited. Prunella, who has a photographic memory, can still remember pages of the play and quote them on demand.

Because of the war, Prunella grew up among a great mixture of people from different backgrounds and different regions. Timothy West thinks this is a tremendous asset for an actor, because so much of English drama is about differences in class.

*   *   *

Eventually it was deemed time for the children to have a more formal education. Nine-year-old Prunella was a bright child, and Bim wanted her to go to her old school, Moira House, but it was a private school and Bim and John had no money with which to pay the fees. At the onset of war, because of the fear of air-raids, the school had been evacuated from Eastbourne to a temporary home at the Thurlestone Hotel near Plymouth. At that early stage in the war people believed that it would all be over very soon, and so the

30

staff had taken only enough books and equipment to last them for six months. When Plymouth became the target of bombs, the school had to move again, and this time they found a vacant hotel on Lake Windermere in the Lake District. The staff and children were installed in their new home in September 1940.

Bim had always kept in touch with the three senior staff: Gertrude Ingham, now partly retired but still a strong influence; her deputy, Edith Tizzard; and Mona Swann, who became headmistress at the beginning of the war. Edith Tizzard, or E.T. as she was known by everybody at the school, had family in Barnstaple and while staying with them came over to visit Cummy and Bim at Bucks Mills. Bim was determined that Prunella should go to the school where she had been so happy, and hoped that E.T. might be able to help. E.T. assessed some of Prunella's work and on the strength of this came up with a solution: Moira House would grant Prunella a scholarship, Timmo would be allowed to attend the school as a temporary measure until he was old enough to go to preparatory school, and Bim would be given the post of under-matron, which would give her both an income and a home for herself and the children. Prunella and Timmo went ahead to the Lake District for the first term so that they could settle in, while Bim and Cummy packed up in Devon before going on to Grice Hall. Bim would take up her post in September 1942 at the beginning of the school year.

*   *   *

In the summer of 1942, ten-year-old Prunella started her education at Moira House. She was excited, because she had loved Arthur Ransome's *Swallows and Amazons* and she knew the school was located somewhere near the setting for the book. She and Timmo travelled up to Windermere by train, an ordeal during the war, as strict blackout was enforced on stations and there was only one miserable light bulb in the carriage. Trains were irregular, and journeys were often interrupted by sirens and sometimes air-raids. Stations were so dimly lit it was hard to find the way out, and all the station names had been removed to confuse the Germans should they invade. The result just confused everybody.

It was a long journey. The children had to travel from Bucks Mills to Exeter, and then up to Huddersfield, where they stayed with Aunt Freda before going on to Windermere. Prunella remembers the cry, ' "Illingworth, passenger to Windermere, via Leeds and CarnFORTH," signifying a day of suitcases, trudging and terror, which may be the reason for my slightly agoraphobic fear of travel to this day'. Knowing that her parents had no real base, she says she had no sense of security. Travelling meant getting on a train and not knowing if, or when, the train would arrive. There was always the danger of air raids. Changing at Leeds and Carnforth, it took almost a whole day to reach the town of Windermere, but even that was not the end of the journey. The Ferry Hotel, where the school was now based, was on the opposite side of the lake from the railway station, so the children had to take a taxi to Bowness and from there catch the ferry across the lake to the school.

When Prunella first arrived she was put into a nine-bed dormitory called Rose—all the rooms were named after flowers or from Arthurian legends. It was the first time in her life she had ever been away from her mother and she was homesick, as were many of the others, who cried at night under the bedclothes. The war was a time of confusion and disruption for many people, but Prunella found the school routine very comforting, and remembers the seniors and staff as being generally kind and understanding. Timmo was in a room with two other boys, younger brothers who were allowed to be part of the school while waiting to go on to their prep schools.

Shortly after they left Bucks Mills Mr Whitaker sent Prunella a poem, dated 5 May 1942.

> My dear friend Pru, 'twas good of you
> to write to me, and so you see,
> I waste no time to send a rhyme,
> to tell you straight, the thought I hate,
> that for so long, you will be gone.
> That you and Tim, with mother Bim,
> will never come, as you have done,
> to hear me preach, be on the beach,
> play round St John's, eat lots of scones.
> Alas! Alack I wish you back.
> . . .
> My love to you, my love to all:
> and when you visit Bucks, please call.

Uncle Gordon was another who sent her poems at school. In March 1943 he wrote: 'I was glad that my small and admonitory verse proved of assistance in your fire drill. Do you slide down ropes in your night attire or is the weather too chilly for such goings on? You will be glad to know that Cummy is behaving in a most exemplary fashion, and often spends a "huffing" hour playing draughts with Brian.' Heather Bell, a young teacher at Windermere while Prunella and Bim were there, can remember the fire drill, when the girls

33

had to learn how to escape from the upper floors by climbing down ropes attached to the bedroom walls. The ropes were flung out of the upstairs windows and Timmo says it was terrifying scrambling down in the dark from three storeys up.

Prunella thinks that one of the reasons she loved boarding school so much was because it gave her a sense of belonging somewhere, which she desperately needed. 'I think I'm still a bit of an institution freak. I've always loved being part of a company, such as the Salisbury Arts Theatre, the Oxford Playhouse or the National Theatre. I love the sense of security one gets from being part of a big organization.' Heather Bell believes Moira House was a very happy school but in some ways a bit old-fashioned despite its progressive intentions. For example, when the children went to say goodnight to the teachers they always made a little curtsey. But the school was divided into sitting-rooms of mixed ages, so they were part of the general school community as well as working with their peers in the classrooms; and on Saturday and Sunday evenings they all gathered together while one of the teachers read aloud. Because of this intermingling of groups there was a general friendliness between the staff and the girls.

Wartime was a difficult time for everyone; people were uprooted from their homes, and many fathers were away. Although life was austere, the Lake District provided a safe refuge, reasonably remote from the miseries and fears of the war. The school, separated from Windermere itself by the lake, became a self-contained community. The children could go rowing on the lake, and there was swimming, mountain walking and rock climbing. As part of their war effort, the girls kept hens, worked on an allotment

34

and collected and cut wood for the fires. 'Dig for Victory' was the national catchphrase, and the children helped with the potato crops, haymaking and fruit harvesting. One of the staff, Miss Knott, knew the area well, and organized the climbing excursions. Two of the others took up ballroom dancing and gave classes for staff and students. Heather Bell taught Latin and modern history and wrote Latin plays for the girls to perform. Art and poetry flourished, as did the all-important drama organized by Mona Swann, occasionally helped by Bim. When Mona was producing *The Barretts of Wimpole Street*, one of the girls became ill at the last minute and Bim took her place, and for one production, Bim played Queen Victoria to Mona Swann's Albert.

One of Prunella's closest school friends was Veronica Goldschmidt, whose Jewish family had escaped from Germany just before the war. Veronica, who had two brothers, lived in Kent, and the girls often stayed with each other during the holidays. She and Prunella kept in touch for the rest of Veronica's life. They both enjoyed acting and were often in school plays together. Scenes between Queen Victoria and Prince Albert seem to have been a favourite subject in the school—on one occasion Prunella played Victoria to Veronica's Albert in scenes from Laurence Housman's play *Victoria Regina*.

French was taught by Henriette de Waligorski, a Frenchwoman, whom Prunella remembers as a brilliant teacher. There was always a special table in the dining-room where the girls were allowed to speak only French during the meal, and she became fluent in the language. The eclectic curriculum was a gift to Prunella, who with her retentive memory absorbed it all like a sponge. She was in a class of very bright girls who spurred each other on. They were a friendly group and worked well together. 'If you feel that you are being valued for what you can give, then it makes you feel very happy. It's a comfort thing.'

It wasn't so easy for Timmo, who was like a fish out of water. He missed his father, and he was in awe of Prunella's academic ability. Red-haired, with a furious temper, he hated Moira House. Living in an environment totally dominated by women, he rebelled in the only way he could. He got into trouble one night for fighting with another boy, John Daglish, hitting him so hard that he knocked his head against the iron bedstead. Timmo was warned that his behaviour was not appropriate for a girls' school. On another occasion he climbed a huge, forbidden yew tree in the school grounds to get away from everyone, but found that he desperately needed to pee. Always practical, he peed down through the leaves, but to his horror, and no doubt hers, one of the mistresses was lying in a deckchair directly below him. Timmo remembered she was wearing dark glasses. That was misdemeanour number two. The last and most serious of his crimes was when the three boys stuffed cotton waste into the main shaft of the ferry taking sixty girls over to the games field, located on the further shore. The boat came to a grinding halt in the middle of the lake. The boys triumphantly admitted to being the culprits. Timmo was sent for by Gertrude Ingham, known as G.A., the most senior of the staff, by then semi-retired, one of the founders of the school and one of Prunella's godmothers. She was an awe-inspiring figure. A theosophist who always dressed in the flowing clothes of the pre First World War period, with immaculate hair to match, G.A. seemed to the pupils to glide from one room to another like someone on a cloud, with one hand outstretched to lead her, and the other trailing behind. She told Timmo firmly that he would have to learn to control his behaviour. He can still remember her amazing eyes—'like God'. She gave him £5 to buy a viola before she told him he was now old enough to move on to the Craig, the boys' school on the other side of the lake at Bowness. He was delighted.

G.A. took English, music and bible history classes, and Prunella remembers: 'When she was teaching the Old and New Testaments and got to the rude bits, she would tell the class, "Now I want you to shut your bibles now, dearies, because I'm going to jump about a bit." The picture of the stately G.A. jumping about a bit made us giggle uncontrollably.'

When they were younger and always together, Prunella and Timmo, like most siblings, fought and argued. Timmo felt Prunella was very close to his mother, and, missing his father, he admits he sometimes felt excluded. They were very different temperamentally: Prunella was an avid reader, and Timmo much preferred being out of doors. Prunella was keen to master everything she attempted, and excelled academically; Timmo did not, and sometimes felt a bit left behind, though he was, Prunella says, a fine sportsman. However, once he went to the Craig, things were less competitive and 'we got on much better'.

After they had left Bucks Mills, the children spent most of their school holidays at Grice Hall. There was the large garden, looked after by Sam Taylor, a tennis court and an air-raid shelter, which fortunately they never had to use. The house was large enough for them each to have their own room and they were blissfully happy there. During the long summer

37

holidays Bim would organize a play for the local village in which Prunella and Timmo took part. Aunt Freda, who was small and pretty, was a great disciplinarian and morbidly obsessive about cleanliness. When she opened the morning post she dropped the envelopes on to the floor because she believed them to be covered in bugs and diseases and then, having read the letters, she would go to wash her hands before continuing with her breakfast. She also made the children wash their hands whenever they came into the house. They were both quite wary of her, though Timmo remembers she was incredibly generous. When the school holidays ended, Bim, as under-matron, had to go back to Moira House at least one day early to make sure all was in readiness for the returning students, and because the children hated having their holidays cut short, sometimes Aunt Freda would escort them on the train instead of Bim. Apparently this was almost worse than going back early. Aunt Freda was a terrible worrier and made them sit bolt upright for the whole train journey in case they got nits from the seat cushions—a fate so shameful that it must be avoided at all costs.

Sir Gordon could also be fierce, but it was usually for a good reason. On one occasion, inspired by the Arthur Ransome books, Timmo remembers that he and Prunella painted a large white skull-and-crossbones on many of the trees in the park around Grice Hall, and Prunella got so carried away that she even chalked another huge skull-and-crossbones on the front door. Prunella firmly denies all memory of this episode. Timmo thinks Prunella was not particularly mischievous as a child, but does remember that Sir Gordon was furious when he came home that evening, though he soon forgave them. The Kayes enjoyed having the children there during their holidays and, most importantly, gave them the closest they had at that time to the protection of a permanent home.

*   *   *

John Illingworth was part of the Normandy landing force. He was a Major in the Pioneer Corps Company that landed at Caen on D+4 and then fought their way through northern France to Belgium. Prunella remembers that he talked of his batman, Sarazani, who was so short that he almost disappeared under the waves and had to be helped to the beach. John wrote to Prunella in June 1944: 'On landing this side we didn't go ashore in the usual way, but waded through the surf! But the water only came up to my waist and I very soon dried during the long march we had to do afterwards. It is a very beautiful country, but of course when people are busy with war, it is not quite the time to come, so I can't invite you over for your summer holidays! Mummy told me in her last letter that you'd had some pictures (or 'a' picture) sent up to an exhibition in London. I hope it was liked by the people who saw it. Congratulations. Write to me and tell me all your doings. It is a long time since we met, and will be longer still I'm afraid.'

He wrote again on 19 June 1944, just before her twelfth birthday, to wish her many happy returns. 'I've been unable to buy you anything because of the difficulty of getting up to London before I left England, but I thought you'd like the enclosed to keep as a souvenir or to change at the bank.' He sent her a 100 franc note 'given to me before we sailed from England. It was in my wallet in my hip pocket and got soaked when I had to wade ashore, but it seems to have dried out all right. I got the first letters from you and Mummy since I left England and was very *very* glad to find them for me in the Company's mail bag. Letters mean an awful lot nowadays as you can imagine. I love your illustration of the fire drill: most graphic and I can well imagine Mummy being the life of the party! New experiences for both your parents—Mummy to go down a fire escape and Daddy to wade ashore in France. I think I prefer my experience as I hate heights! No more now my sweet. It's over six months since I saw you all. Well—time passes very quickly and I just look forward to the next time of meeting. My love and you're my very dear, Always, Daddy.' The 100 franc note, kept as a souvenir, is still safely tucked into the envelope.

John was sent home from Belgium towards the end of 1944 with a skin cancer on his ear which needed to be treated, and was then put in charge of a prisoner-of-war camp in England until he was demobbed in August 1945. With his return, Bim resigned from her post as under-matron at Moira House and set out to find somewhere for the family to live.

3

'I think they spent the next two years wondering why they had bothered.'

'Early in my training at the Old Vic School, we had to do an improvisation of getting up in the morning. When it was my turn I did waking up to the alarm; switching it off; lighting a candle; staggering across the room to light the Aladdin lamp; trimming the lamp; breaking the ice in the washbasin and washing. Michel St Denis was very impressed. "Very good, Prunella, very good, very inventive, very original." I didn't tell him that it wasn't original at all. It was actually what I did every morning.'

*   *   *

When Bim set out to find a house for the family her problem was where to go. Their Surrey house had been sold and they had no money to buy another. Bim wrote to their friend Kins Atkinson, estate manager of the Wotton Estate, to see if he had a cottage they could rent, and he offered them Kempslade, a remote, rambling old four-bedroom farmhouse near Leith Hill, in a valley surrounded by woods. The house was over two miles from the nearest bus stop, and though the location was idyllic, there was no electricity, gas or running water. All the water for the house came from the nearby Friday Street pond, via an unreliable pump—occasionally the water froze during the winter. Cooking was done on an old Aga range in the kitchen,

41

and oil lamps and candles provided the lighting. It certainly wasn't ideal, but at a rental of only £92 a year it was affordable.

At Kempslade they were in the depths of the country with plenty of places to explore. There was a lawn at the front of the house, surrounded by oak trees with a herbaceous border made by Bim and Timmo, an old granary near the house where the children played, stables used as toolsheds, and a barn where John kept his car.

Kempslade was surrounded by fourteen acres of grassland, and the garden was huge. Prunella says, 'We were almost self-supporting. Pa had a vegetable garden and grew strawberries to which the grey squirrels took a liking. He had hung nets over the beds to keep them away from the fruit, but he came in one day. "Come and look at those damn squirrels." When we went out we could see the squirrels were bouncing on the nets, and at the bottom of each bounce they would reach through the mesh and grab another strawberry.'

Timmo was paid 6d a tail by the gamekeeper for any grey squirrel he shot, as they were considered vermin; he and John also shot rabbits for the table. Timmo had a sheepdog called Larry, they had several cats, all named after kings and queens, and Bim had a passion for Pekinese. Sam West remembers two of them, Huang and Puffin, from a later era. Animals were always an important part of their lives. They kept hens, four ducks—Jacqueline, Jemima, Melinda and Jane—and two geese, a present to Timmo from Freda, which were kept in the old laundry.

After John was demobbed he returned to his pre-war job as sales manager at Tootal's main office in Cavendish Square. This meant leaving Kempslade by seven in the morning and getting home late in the evening. Timmo remembers his dad, wearing his bowler hat and carrying his briefcase and rolled umbrella, being chased by the gander as he went out to the garage in the morning. The gander also held the laundry boy at bay in his van, refusing to let him out to deliver the clean laundry, and on another occasion settled himself firmly in the front seat of a sports car belonging to a visiting friend, repelling all efforts to remove him. In the end John got so fed up with the gander's antisocial behaviour that, much to Timmo's fury, he shot him, leaving the poor goose without a mate.

Because John was away all day and Bim didn't drive, getting out of the house meant they had to walk or bicycle everywhere. The nearest bus stop was over two miles down country lanes, or they could walk the same distance through the woods to the Wotton Hatch pub to catch the bus to Dorking. After doing their shopping it had to be carried home, or, if too heavy, left at the pub for John to pick up in the evening.

Prunella tells of the day when her father shot her mother through the sitting-room ceiling. 'One morning when Dad was shaving in the kitchen he saw a pigeon in the elderberry tree eating the berries which we used for jam. He went into the sitting-room where his twelve-bore gun was hanging on meat hooks, loaded it, shot the pigeon through the kitchen window, and went back to hang up the gun again. He must have forgotten to unload the second barrel, because when he hung it up, his thumb, still covered in shaving soap, slipped on the hammer, and he inadvertently pulled the trigger. The shot blew an enormous hole in the sitting-room ceiling. Ma's bedroom was above and he thought he had shot her.

The noise woke me up, and when I went into Ma's room there was powdered plaster coming up through the floorboards and a white-faced Dad in the doorway saying, "Are you all right?" '

Bim was in charge of the family finances: she had to be. John was not good at managing money and there was only just enough to cover expenses if they were careful. She had inherited some railway shares and a little money from her family, and every month the housekeeping money of £25 in cash arrived in a registered envelope. The children vividly remember their mother sitting at the kitchen table and sorting the money into envelopes for coal, oil, food, rates and housekeeping. This would be kept aside to pay the essential bills. There was little left over for extras.

Gordon and Freda Kaye had now moved back to Surrey too, and were living not far from Kempslade. As Prunella's godmother, Aunt Freda helped pay the fees for Moira House, and was always very generous to her sister and the children, with presents and sometimes clothes. As Timothy West explains, 'Pru's background wasn't privileged at all. Even after the war her parents never had any money. They never again had a house of their own, and for a lot of the time, especially in their later years, Pru was supporting them.'

Although money was so scarce, Lily from the village would come in to help Bim with the cleaning. Up in the woods, not far from Kempslade, was a large ammunition dump, and some time after the war it blew up—no one knew why. Lily, who also served behind the bar at the local pub, said to Bim, 'It was funny, I was drying the glasses behind the bar, and not one of the glasses was broken, but all the curlers in me hair flew out!'

Timmo remembers that both his parents had a great sense of humour. John, like Bim, was always very generous, though so hopeless at his own accounts that Bim had to take over. He was articulate and wrote beautifully; he was also musical and could play the piano by ear. He loved to take the children up to London, separately, for their own special day out. Timmo would be taken to Victoria Station, where he was allowed to help stoke the boiler of the *Golden Arrow* then watch it being shunted backwards on to the carriages; then off they would go to Lord's to watch a test match, or, if that was boring, go on to the zoo instead. For Prunella's special day she would be taken to an art gallery, where her father would talk to her about the paintings, and sometimes on to the ballet or a play. John knew London very well: not only had he been brought up there, but as London sales manager for Tootal's he had driven around the city every day. However, Timmo believes that Bim was always the strong one in the marriage. 'She never really got angry with us but would just say firmly, "I don't think that is quite right." '

*   *   *

Both Bim and John wanted the best education they could find for their children. Prunella, with a scholarship and the help of Aunt Freda, was securely established as a boarder at Moira House, now once again based at Eastbourne. Somehow her parents managed to scrape enough money together for Timmo's fees at the Craig, and later at Dauntsey's, a school in Wiltshire founded for the sons of farmers, where sport featured high on the curriculum. Timmo had always wanted to work on the land, and there was a farm attached to the school.

During the term, while the children were away, Bim was by herself during the long days in the isolated farmhouse. Because she liked company she offered a home to a French girl, Jacqueline Oudin, who had managed to escape when her house in France had been taken over by the Germans during the war. Jacqueline stayed with them at Kempslade for about two and a half years, taught at the Stanway school in Dorking, and, when Prunella and Timmo were at home, helped them with their French, while Bim taught her English.

To Prunella, who had just returned to Moira House, Bim wrote: 'The house seems very silent. Jacky and I have gardened quite a lot, and the postman (Sandy Whiskers) cheered my heart by presenting me with a bundle of wallflowers—so we'll have a gay garden in the spring . . . Heaps of love darling. Take your tonic and enjoy the term. Be courageous—but quietly, and don't create revolutions. All big things are achieved quietly and slowly in the beginning. I miss you.'

Another memorable friend of their parents from Prunella and Timmo's childhood was Louis Connick, an ex-US Marine who read law at King's College, Cambridge. While Louis was at Cambridge, Bim invited him to live with them during the holidays and help with some of the heavy work in the garden. Timmo remembers the excitement, at thirteen, of being collected from Dauntsey's by Louis, driving his Cadillac.

Prunella still enjoyed school. With an excellent memory and a thirst for information, she learnt fast; as well as the regular curriculum, she had piano lessons and excelled at speech and drama. Moira House was one of the first girls' schools to incorporate Dalcroze eurythmics into the curriculum. The dictionary defines eurythmics as 'the art of interpreting in graceful bodily movements the rhythm of musical compositions'. In the early days of Moira House they used to give demonstrations in London, but when Prunella was there, Mona Swann had added to the basic eurythmics something called choral speech; a way of redefining poetry in which the poet's words, spoken by various choral groups, combined text and movement to interpret the poem or play.

It was a wonderful way of absorbing a wide range of poems for the students, though Prunella fears it may have been less wonderful for the parents who came to watch performances. She was in many of the plays at Moira House, and because of her eclectic background and good ear she was good at regional accents and was usually given character parts, especially male ones. She must have sometimes written to her mother for advice, for on one occasion Bim replied: 'Ophelia—I think that the essential quality is a sort of shut away stillness in the beginning—like a young (very young) nun—then the wild stir up after. Think of how she would *think* of Hamlet—and how Hamlet would affect her and her love and feelings for him. But I haven't really studied the poem and you're probably bursting with ideas yourself.'

Although after her marriage Bim never again acted professionally, she still enjoyed it and joined the Westcott Players, a local and very active amateur theatre group under the direction of Greville Poke, also editor of *Everybody's Magazine*. Here she both acted and directed. John was also involved, as was Prunella when she was at home; she would hear Bim's lines and occasionally played a part. Timmo kept well

47

away; he says it wasn't his scene. Because Bim couldn't drive she had to rely on her friends to get her to and from rehearsals, which proved a particular restriction when she tried to join the BBC's radio drama department after the war, giving up when she realized the impossibility of getting to London for rehearsals or performances.

Towards the end of her time at Moira House, Prunella was asked to be a bridesmaid by Jacqueline Oudin's sister, Anne-Marie, who was to be married in Rennes Cathedral. She stayed with Jacqueline's parents, who had become family friends. Another family who were influential all through her life were the Reverend Anthony Otter and his wife, Dorothy. It was through Tony Otter that Louis Connick had been introduced to the family. The Otters had lived in the flat next to Bim and John in London when they were first married; Tony Otter was Timmo's godfather and Prunella's first boyfriend was his half-brother, John, educated at Marlborough, who opted to go down the mines for his National Service. She remembers he took her to a rugger ball: 'He was a lovely person and we stayed good friends all our lives.' She is afraid that one of the reasons they split up may have been because he was too much in awe of her academic achievements. 'I got 8 As in my school certificate and John Otter was appalled.' A ninth distinction was added when she took music in December that year. In recognition of her achievement, in July 1948 she was presented with a book token as 'Prize for 1st place, Oxford School Certificate, Moira House'. Uncle Gordon wrote a poetical tribute to Prunella's School Certificate success:

Hang out the banners, and flaunt the washing too,

For Prunella Illingworth has gotten through.
Blow, blow the trumpet, the clashing cymbals clang,
Prunella Illingworth's got through with a bang.
Eight blooming Alphas she took in her stride—!
All Moira house is bursting stays with pride—
As are Old Miss Ingham and Swannee River too
Grin with delight at A.Talfas Pru!

There was considerable pressure on her from the school to sit for Oxford or Cambridge entrance, but she wanted to act, and decided to apply for a place at the prestigious Old Vic School in London, at the theatre of the same name near Waterloo. This drama school was run by a distinguished triumvirate: Michel St Denis, George Devine and Glen Byam Shaw. Before the war, Michel St Denis had founded the London Theatre Studio (Peter Ustinov was among the many illustrious students there) with the idea of introducing an innovative approach to acting. Its aim was to go back to first principles: to work without scenery, using the imagination, and to give classes which included mime, masks, singing, movement, juggling and acrobatics. When the Theatre Studio, which had influenced many leading actors from John Gielgud to Peggy Ashcroft and directors such as Tyrone Guthrie, closed with the onset of war, Michel St Denis remained in England and became the head of Radio Free France. One of his tasks was to coach Winston Churchill for the speeches he made in French. After the war, St Denis was invited to take over the bomb-damaged building in Waterloo Road as a drama school and the base for a children's theatre company (the Young Vic), while the Old Vic company, run by Laurence Olivier, Ralph Richardson and John Burrell, moved temporarily to the New Theatre (now the Albery) in St Martin's Lane. The Old Vic School, continuing the London Theatre Studio's innovative and idealistic approach, opened in 1946.

When seventeen-year-old Prunella auditioned for the two-year course in 1949, she had a letter of commendation from Mona Swann, who had already worked with Michel St Denis at the London Theatre Studio. The first audition was taken by John Blatchley, and she'd chosen a chorus from *Henry V* and a piece from Thornton Wilder's *Our Town*. The second audition was for Michel St Denis and Glen Byam Shaw, who admitted her, awarded her a scholarship, and then, she says, 'spent the next two years wondering why they had bothered. I had very thick glasses, hair in plaits and I think must have seemed distinctly unfanciable and academic.'

The scholarship took care of the tuition fees, and she applied for a grant from Surrey County Council to cover her living and travelling expenses. 'I was interviewed by the Surrey Grants Board. They sat behind a table and looked carefully at my school certificate results. Then the Chairman spoke. "Miss Illingworth: two writers, Shakespeare and Shelley. What would you say was the difference between them?" "Well," I replied, rather surprised by the question. "I suppose you could say that Shakespeare was a classicist, whereas Shelley was a Romantic, wasn't he?" They conferred for a moment. Then, "Very interesting," agreed the Chairman. "We think you are admirably suited for a dramatic career." And I got the grant.'

'After I got into the Old Vic School, Mona Swann wrote a letter to Michel St Denis saying, "Are you sure that this girl has a future in theatre? She could do Cambridge entrance." I'm sure she meant well, but from then on I was labelled as an intellectual and it was used as a stick to beat me with during my training. Glen Byam Shaw said to me once, "To me, Prunella, you seem to tackle your acting like a piece of arithmetic." It wasn't until years later that Uta Hagen stopped me feeling guilty about the analytical approach.'

For the first term Prunella lived at home and travelled up to Waterloo every day. She was only just seventeen and her parents thought her too young to live in London on her own; anyway, there was no money to pay for digs. But living at home 'meant stomping off through the woods to the pub at Wotton Hatch where I would leave my gumboots, then change into day shoes and get on the bus to Dorking North Station. At night the process was reversed.'

At the end of her first term the school had to move. The Old Vic theatre was structurally unsafe and overrun by rats—the building was steeped in atmosphere, but the ceiling was full of holes and leaked, and students were not allowed to go into the circle in case they fell through the floor. Students and staff helped pack up at the end of the winter term and in early 1950 they moved into what had previously been a girls' school, at 70 Thurlow Park Road in Dulwich. There the teaching regime became even more intensive and very demanding. Prunella realized she needed to find somewhere to live near the school if she was to survive. Her Uncle Cuthbert had left her his stamp collection, which she now sold through the dealer Stanley Gibbons for £308. This gave her enough money to move to digs in London, and it also kept her in funds for the remaining years of her training. 'My son Sam has never forgiven me for the sale—he says Uncle Cus's collection would be worth

51

thousands now.'

Her mother was not in favour of the move, partly because she felt Prunella was still too young but also because, with her own interest in theatre, she got vicarious pleasure from discussing the training with her. In May 1950 Bim wrote from Bucks Mills, where she had gone for a few days' holiday, 'I think digs on your own might be lonely—but we'll work it out. I know it's been a strain going backwards and forwards—and we've all had to put up with things—and you've been very good. When I get fussed sometimes—just try to remember that it all comes of loving you, and just wanting everything to come right for you in the end—and forgive me. This adjustment business. Try not to cut things up too much—Old Vic v. Home. I know they are awfully different, like two separate lives and sets of people—but they are both in Life and part of it, as we all are, and the more people you understand, the greater actress you'll be.' After a certain amount of persuasive argument, Prunella had her own way and found digs in Alleyns Road in Dulwich, quite near the school. Not only did being close to the school make the time there less stressful, but the money from uncle Cuthbert's stamps also meant that she could concentrate on classes and not have to take a casual evening job. Her father was able to help by giving her £1 10s. a week.

There were about forty students at the school, and Prunella was probably one of the youngest; Joan Plowright was in the same year. George Hall, who went on to become Director of Acting at Central School, and now teaches at Yale and at the Royal Academy of Music, was another of her contemporaries. He says the school was determined to be classless, and made a deliberate point of recruiting from a wide cross-section of people, unlike some of the other more fashionable drama schools which sometimes seemed more like finishing schools.

Prunella has mixed memories of her time as a student. She got a scholarship because she had given a good audition, but then found it hard to cope with the constant critical appraisal of everything she did. Looking back, she is appalled how naïve she was. Straight out of a girls-only school, with her pigtails and thick glasses, she was small, just over five foot three. She had led a very sheltered life, was decidedly unworldly and, she thought, decidedly unsexy. Not obvious material to mould into a successful actress. She says that for a lot of her time there she was just terrified. 'Also my mother was not a very flamboyant person, and although I wanted to be an actress, I was very inhibited and thought it was wrong to show off. Again that parental thing, that one must think about other people. It takes quite a long time when you're a bit immature, or extremely immature—which I was—before you can sort out the *morality* of being an actor. Contrary to popular supposition, actors—the best actors—are not selfish people. They have to be extremely unselfish and extremely modest and un-self-centred I think. On the other hand you do have to have a certain instinct for performance and I found it very difficult to sort out in my head what the ethics of acting were.'

There were note sessions at the end of each term, during which the directors told each student what they thought of their work. These terrifying ordeals, which could go on for ten hours, took place in the large room where they did gymnastics, ballet, fighting and so on. The students would all sit in a row, opposite the tutors, and each student was told what was wrong with

53

them in front of the whole group. 'The notes were harsh,' says George Hall, 'and we all came out weeping. They were perhaps rather better at taking apart than putting together. You went ashen when it got to be your turn to be criticized and you got other people to write it down, because you only remembered the worst things.'

Prunella recalls one devastating occasion when she left the room in floods of tears and was found outside in the passage curled up on the floor, by two of the tutors, Litz Pisk and Jani Strasser. They scooped her up, wiped her eyes and tried to comfort her. Sylvia Short, a friend and fellow student who had been at the note session, wrote to her afterwards: 'What I wanted to say to you—and since it's 1.30 a.m. I don't suppose it will be very lucid—even at the risk of repulsing you by entering into parts of you which I know you wish to keep to yourself—is something like this: I don't know if there has ever been anyone in your life to whom you have broken yourself down completely, to whom you have sacrificed your own identity, self-control or personal pride. What I am trying to say is that self-control and unwillingness to burden other people with one's problems is a degree of maturity which I find most desirable and enviable. It seems to me that you have (whether it's superficial or not) this maturity and strength and it is one of those things about you which makes people like you so much. It gives you that directness, honesty and generosity which St Denis spoke of as the qualities you must bring to the stage and will bring to the stage.

'But at the moment this has a negative effect for you—*perhaps* because you have achieved this control too soon, without going through the stage of self-love and effusion which gradually forces one to find self-control because of the humiliation and suicidal effect of discovering, in many relationships with people, that this self-giving must give way to self-witholding if one is to go on living with ones-self. But if you skip the first stage and go right into the later stage, perhaps the later stage is superficial—tight and not relaxed. You must know, Pru, that I say this knowing that I may be wrong, and certainly knowing that I, myself am in no position to talk . . . With you then it seems, that perhaps you give (or rather gave) to Mr Shaw and others, too, perhaps, a feeling that you are closed and unapproachable—the negative side of this maturity I speak of . . . With you one senses (and this is not just me—it is also Litz and John and Suria and Jani and Michel) tremendous depths of sensitivity and appreciation and artistry which is now overbalanced by whatever fear it is in you that makes you close yourself into yourself, that makes your maturity for the moment a hindrance rather than a help to your expression. All this I know you know, and I hope you won't shoot me for talking about it—but the thing is I know that you are one of the most interesting and potentially great people and artists at the school—and the staff knows it too—as Litz told me last week—she sees through your shell to your core of sensitivity, as tonight's messy but ultimately successful discussion must have shown you. If nothing else, remember that Shaw is famed for not being able to express himself in words.

'If this is of any use to you—good; if not, no harm done. Have a good holiday. Much love, Sylvia.'

*   *   *

Litz Pisk taught movement, and Jani Strasser, who was

55

subsequently head of the music staff at Glyndebourne, was in charge of voice. They were brilliant teachers, and both voice and movement were classes Prunella really enjoyed. 'Litz talked about sculpture all the time. She taught us to be aware of our shape in the air . . . what the character's shape meant in architectural terms, and in terms of the period. There was a lot of work in period costume, and in each case Litz would talk to us about the philosophy, history and attitudes of that period. For example in medieval times women wore clothes which made them look pregnant, though many of them weren't, and hennins [head-dresses] which went upwards to match the gothic architecture, reaching up to God, emphasizing the connection between the physical and the spiritual. She was a wonderful teacher and had a profound effect on us all. We thought she was a genius.'

After the war, materials and goods were in short supply. George Hall recalls that for music and voice they wore what looked like black 1950s bathing suits with terrible knitted tops and old-fashioned swimming-trunks. 'They were prickly, ticklish and horrible, and would have made anybody in the world look hideous.' The girls also wore ingenious practice skirts with a million fasteners so that they could be very wide or very narrow, and the men wore trousers that had fasteners all the way down, so that they could be rolled up to become Elizabethan breeches or anything else the part demanded.

George Hall also told me the fifties was a time in theatre when the designers had a great deal of influence and actors were encouraged to use a lot of make-up. He began to think that make-up had to be used as an essential disguise, and if, when you came on stage, people recognized you, then you had failed in some way. To help with this, nose putty was used a great deal to alter the shape of the nose and face, and wigs were used for most character parts. Prunella still prefers to work in a wig, and uses prosthetics when she wants to alter her appearance for a part.

George Devine took them for character improvisation—'a fascinating class where you took something out of a pile of clothes, wigs, hats and so on, and used it to create a character and improvise a scene'. Prunella says she played a lot of old women quite successfully, but felt she was not so good at the young romantics. She remembers Michel St Denis saying to her one day: ' "Prunella, I don't understand your work. If you were a cabbage I should say, there is a good cabbage." This was one of the only encouraging comments I ever received from him. I do remember one other note given after a mask exercise, when, greatly daring, I chose a young mask instead of my usual middle-aged or character mask and did an improvisation of Daphne going down to the river to bathe, being surprised by Apollo, running away, and being turned into a laurel bush. At the end of it Michel said, "Very good, Prunella, you got right away from yourself, you were beautiful." ' She pauses, then adds, 'Sometimes it seems to me that the whole of my professional life has been a struggle to get away from the cabbage parts, and be allowed to play some of the beautiful ones.'

The teaching at the school, which included many classes now considered essential for an actor's training, was radical for that time, and had a widespread and very positive effect on many other theatre schools around the world—but it was tough. George Hall remembers that 'somewhere along the line the word encouragement slipped out of the vocabulary. I think what was difficult for Pru and others was that there was a huge discrepancy in age. She was still a schoolgirl; most of the men were ex-service. It could have been made much easier, but the directors were not encouraging. I don't think they were sadistic, but we were judged from such a lofty height. In terms of drama training in England at that time it was totally new. The Old Vic School was both wonderful and awful.'

Timothy West explains that it was a time of changing attitudes, 'when what was happening in the theatre was the emergence of new drama, which was not poetically or classically based, and therefore there was a lot of vernacular reality going on. Pru didn't fit into that very well, and she probably looked more like a schoolgirl than an actress, with her glasses and plaits. She was not a type they were used to, neither a sex bomb, nor a sort of drawn-out spotty person in a plastic raincoat. So it took her a bit of time to be appreciated there, and being someone who has a fairly low measure of self-confidence, she would automatically think she was not getting it right.' When asked now why she wanted to be an actress, Prunella says: 'The chief reason was because it would give me the chance to play people infinitely more interesting than I am, and say things infinitely more intelligent and entertaining than anything I could think of myself.'

During her traumatic two years Prunella fell deeply in love with fellow student Michael Vowden, and they provided much-needed moral support for each other. It was a romantic affair; they were inseparable, went out together all through their training, and corresponded for many years afterwards.

At the end of the course the students put on

58

showcase productions, to which an invited audience of celebrities, theatre directors, agents, critics and friends came. The pieces were chosen from a wide variety of plays. Prunella was in Programme A, which included an operetta by Offenbach, *Fortunio's Song*, in which she played Fanchon, a grisette, and Vanbrugh's *A Journey to London*, in which she was cast as Miss Betty, a Norfolk hoyden: Prunella remembers this as 'quite a flashy little part which got a lot of laughs' and indeed a few notices in the national press. The performances coincided with the public airing of some differences over funding, between the management of the theatre, the school officials and the Arts Council. The school was threatened with closure, and three of the school directors had resigned in protest. But one reviewer commented: 'Whatever its troubles at the top it [the Old Vic School] certainly deserves a proud and permanent place in the Old Vic's organization when it can nurture the kind of talent it offered last night, especially in Sir John Vanbrugh's *A Journey to London*. This unfinished and typically unfathomable frolic about country bumpkins on the spree and highborn ladies with low gambling habits introduced two certain stars in Maureen Quinney and Prunella Scales. They are both eighteen but they have an attack, a comedy sense, and a general technique far beyond their years. They shone out like beacons last night from a production which by student standards, was quite brilliant.'

4

'Not everybody can act, but everybody can get there'

'I had no agent to find work for me, so I borrowed twopence and phoned Denis Carey, the director of the Bristol Old Vic. I don't know what made me think of it but I knew he had seen the show. I said I wondered if by any chance I could possibly have a job. When I went and saw him he remembered me, and gave me work as an acting ASM (an assistant stage manager who plays small parts), and that was my first job. I was buying props, setting the furniture, giving the cues and occasionally prompting. I was a hopeless ASM because while I was on the book I was absolutely fascinated by what was going on on stage and didn't keep my eyes on the script. I remember Laurence Harvey, the leading man, shouting at me, "Darling, please will you give me the line." He had asked for a prompt and I was watching someone else on the stage and had lost the place. In fact I learnt a hell of a lot from that time, and as a director these experiences were very useful later.'

*　　　*　　　*

Prunella's very first professional part, in September 1951, was as an aged cook in Anouilh's *Traveller without Luggage*, and as she was just nineteen she played it as a young tweeny. The next play, at the end of September, was Miles Malleson's adaptation of Molière's *Le Bourgeois Gentilhomme*, translated as *The Prodigious Snob*. Miles Malleson played the lead and Prunella and John Neville, who'd played the valet in the Anouilh production, were the juveniles. 'My first entrance was a disaster. John Neville waved his arm at the wings and said, "Here she comes!" I took a step forward—there was a tearing sound—my train had become firmly caught on a nail and I couldn't get on to the stage. The ASM had to come and unhook it. The wardrobe mistress, who had no time for me, was terribly scornful, but she did teach me how to hook the train over my arm when walking downstairs so it didn't drag on the ground.'

The Bristol Old Vic did a four-month winter season of six plays, each of which ran for three weeks. Prunella, as acting ASM, was not in all of them, but in the fourth play, *Love's Labour's Lost*, she played Jaquenetta. She was now earning £5 10s. a week, and with the £1 her father still gave her, she could support herself. But her first professional job was short. After a four-month stint at Bristol, Denis Carey told her he didn't think he could renew her contract. 'He said, "Try and get some more experience. You were so good in the end of term show at the Old Vic; try and get some more parts like that." '

Prunella remembers being in a group at the Old Vic School when a student told Michel St Denis that she had got a job at the Bristol Old Vic and said, 'Isn't that great?' All Michel said was, 'Could not be better,' in tones of pained surprise. She was certain he wasn't expecting her to succeed, and she admits that when she left drama school she had little confidence in her abilities. 'I was very young for my age, and some of the

61

negative feedback from my training gave me a hang-up about both my looks and my ability. Many people think that I'm very confident, but I'm absolutely not.'

She spent Christmas 1951 at home with her parents, and then, on an impulse, rang the office of Al Parker, one of the leading theatrical agents, and spoke to Ronnie Waters. He had seen the graduation show at the Old Vic School, realized she had potential, and almost immediately found her an offer of work with a weekly rep company at the Connaught Theatre in Worthing, playing the juvenile lead in *The Romantic Young Lady*. In weekly rep the actors rehearsed next week's play during the day, while playing the current production every night, plus matinées. It was a rigorous training ground. Andrew Sachs was then working as assistant stage manager at Worthing. He says, 'She was about nineteen at the time and kind of special. I was the lowest of the low, I don't know why I should remember her, but something about her must have been exceptional.' Prunella stayed at Worthing for only one production, because through Ronnie Waters she was offered the part of Morag McLeod, a Highland schoolmistress, in a black and white film, *Laxdale Hall*. Made just after the very popular film *Whisky Galore*, based on the novel by Compton MacKenzie (whose stories in turn are the inspiration for the television series *Monarch of the Glen*), it, too, was set in the Highlands. 'I was sent on a sleeper to Aberdeen, the first time I'd ever travelled first class. I had a lovely time doing it and was reasonably good. I had to learn the Highland accent from a friend of my mother's. It was a fascinating film to work on and I met some wonderful actors, although it didn't have the success of its predecessor.' This was the first film Prunella was in, and there had been no film training at the Old Vic School: 'I think it was all right, but goodness, I could have done with some technical advice. It was a great experience.'

This was a time for a lot of firsts. In 1952 Ronnie Waters sent her along to audition for a BBC TV production of *Pride and Prejudice*, and she was cast in her first television part, as Lydia Bennet. Richard Johnson played Wickham, Peter Cushing, Darcy, and Daphne Slater, Elizabeth. 'Lockwood West played Mr Collins. He was very flamboyant and I knew he worked a great deal for H. M. Tennant, the somewhat gay-orientated West End management. I thought, this is what is known as "an old queen"; they are very powerful in the theatre, so I must be very respectful towards him. Little did I know that I would end up married to his son!'

This was the early days of television, and plays were transmitted directly to the public, with no way of recording them for future use. The cast rehearsed in a church hall in Hampstead, then moved to Alexandra Palace for the performance. 'Because it was broadcast live, you had to rush round behind the set for your costume changes. Broadcast first on a Sunday, there was a second transmission the following Thursday.' In live TV, once the cameras started to roll performances had to go on regardless of any mistakes. If you forgot your lines someone else had to cover for you. It was an adrenaline-inducing experience. This was the first time Jane Austen had been performed on television, and the production was generally very popular, although Prunella's friend Michael Vowden had reservations. He wrote to her from Stratford-upon-Avon: 'The real trouble, I think, is the medium—and particularly the restrictions it puts on the plotting of the moves—and that needs the freedom of a stage

63

without the dictation of a camera. So that I got the impression that a viewer who had never read P & P wouldn't know very much about it afterwards.'

Prunella and Michael had stayed together after they left the Old Vic School. They wrote long, long letters to each other and phoned frequently. Michael had got a job first with a small touring theatre in Somerset, then as an ASM and non-speaking waiter at the Arts Theatre in London, and after that with the Shakespeare Memorial Theatre in Stratford-upon-Avon. As Prunella became more successful, Michael began to have doubts about himself as an actor, and left Stratford to take a trainee job with Shell-Mex. This meant he had to live and work in Newcastle upon Tyne; he loathed the city and, even more, he hated being so far from Prunella, who was working almost constantly. By this time Michael was talking of marriage, and for a while they thought of becoming engaged. However, what had been a close and loving relationship between colleagues became distorted by distance, and in the autumn of 1954 Prunella told Michael she couldn't marry him. She had met someone else.

That spring Prunella and her mother had travelled to Paris to visit Henriette de Waligorski, the French teacher from Moira House, who had returned to her flat there after the war. She introduced Prunella to some Jewish friends of hers, Bernard Frank and his mother and brother. Bernard's father had died during the war in a German concentration camp. Later in the year he and Prunella started seeing more of each other: 'We were very much in love in a romantic way. I was in my early twenties, but completely immature sexually. He was very clever; his subject was tenth-century Japanese demonology. We were seriously

64

thinking of getting married, but it would have meant two years in Tokyo while he did his thesis, and the rest of my life in Paris—and no more acting. Two incidents decided me. The first was on a visit to Versailles, when we saw two men in eighteenth-century costumes. We thought they must be the famous ghosts. However, it became apparent that they were only extras on a film when they disappeared into the nearest loo. I just realized all of a sudden I couldn't give up acting.'

The second incident happened later that week, when Bernard took her to the top of one of the towers of Notre Dame. 'I heard a very English voice say: "Oh, mummy, it can't be much higher," and round the corner came the children of a neighbour of my mother's. I didn't know them well, or even like them much, but it suddenly hit me that I couldn't marry a Frenchman. I'm basically and needfully English, God forgive me. I thought, no, I can't spend the rest of my life in France.' However, the couple continued to write passionate letters for the next nineteen months, during much of which time Bernard was in Tokyo completing his thesis. After a while the letters tailed off, and in April 1956 Bernard wrote to her to tell her he was marrying a Japanese girl. They remained friends, and Prunella still speaks French fluently. 'Maybe it's something to do with wanting to be an actress. Speaking another language takes you into another place.'

Later in 1954 Prunella was asked to audition for the film *Hobson's Choice*, to be directed by the celebrated David Lean. He was very encouraging at the screen test and offered her the part of Vicky Hobson, the youngest daughter of the bullying patriarch, who was to be played by Charles Laughton. 'I adored him, and we got on terribly well, partly because we were both

65

Yorkshire.' Although Prunella has spent much of her life in Surrey, where she was born, she feels strongly affiliated to Yorkshire as part of her family background. She had to learn period Lancashire for the part, because 'I've always been picky about dialect and language and I did have to sort out the difference between that and Yorkshire.'

Robert Donat was to play the rags-to-riches role of the illiterate Willy Mossop, Hobson's skilled and much exploited bootmaker. 'When David Lean introduced us, Robert Donat said, "Any relation to Bim Scales?" I said, "Yes, daughter." He nearly fell over, and said, "That makes me feel very old." ' He had played Mossop at the Liverpool Playhouse when Prunella's mother was there, and she had told her how brilliant he was. Donat was present for the first week's rehearsal, when the cast had the unusual luxury of rehearsing on the set, but during the week he had an asthma attack. As a result of this the insurers refused to cover him, and he had to leave the film. He was deeply disappointed as, according to his son, while he was prone to asthma, he never had attacks during the actual shoot. David Lean brought John Mills back from holiday; he learnt the part, including the Lancashire accent, in a week, and gave a brilliant performance. All the cast enjoyed working with David Lean, who said to Prunella, 'The next one you do, do it in colour.'

Not only was she working in theatre, film, and television but she also managed to find work in radio. The poet Terence Tiller, a director in the features department at Broadcasting House, had been one of the judges at a speech festival which she had taken part in while still at school. Prunella wrote and asked if he could give her any work; he remembered her, and used her in poetry programmes for several years. 'I earned £8 per broadcast, and it absolutely kept the wolf from the door. I've always loved radio, it's a medium that sets you free.'

In 1953 Prunella joined Salisbury Rep, run by Guy Verney with Frank Hauser as his co-director. She was cast in a pantomime, *Babes in the Wood*, then as Desdemona in *Othello* and as Nora in the Ibsen classic *A Doll's House*—at that time Salisbury was doing a weekly rep. Six months later she played Nora in Huddersfield in a completely different translation. 'Learning was never a problem for me. For one production we had a guy who did find the learning very difficult and still didn't know it by the Wednesday. This was regarded as very peculiar. In rep it was quite essential to forget the week-before's play, as you galloped on to the next one. I used to wake up very early in the morning, learn an act, and then go back to sleep again. I always wake up early, and have to grab half-an-hour's kip before making up for a show in the evening. I can lie on the floor almost anywhere and sleep for ten or twenty minutes.' Her ability to fall asleep anywhere is illustrated by the following story. 'When I was playing Desdemona at Salisbury, Othello was a large actor who took a long time over the last scene, after he had killed me. We'd done a matinée and I was quite tired and I fell asleep, only to awake with a shriek when he killed himself and fell across me. As he'd already smothered me once, he had to do it again.'

Later that year she went to the old Theatre Royal in Huddersfield to play one of the Bennet daughters in a stage version of *Pride and Prejudice*, and stayed on to play Cinderella in the pantomime. Asked how she felt about playing such diverse parts, she has no

67

reservations about it; she would put as much effort into pantomime as she would into Jane Austen. Her son Joe says: 'One of her things is not to count the cost of any creativity and originality which she puts into any piece of work. If you have more complicated ideas, for example, than the part actually requires, that doesn't do any harm. The chances are that in some way it will reinforce your performance. Bravery comes into it—you have to be prepared to fall flat on your face.'

Prunella was rarely out of work, which meant frequent touring round regional theatres and living in a strange selection of theatrical digs. Looking for digs was always one of the priorities when arriving in a new town. In Huddersfield, Norman Rossington, also in the Theatre Royal company, told her to go to Mrs McCarthy at 13 Commercial Street, just opposite the theatre. 'I knocked on the door and Mrs McCarthy opened it. "Yes, love?" She was broad Yorkshire. Me: "Have you got a room? I'm working over at the Theatre Royal." She showed me a room with six beds and a fold-down sofa which she used to let out when the panto was on. She said, "I'll put down the put-you-up for you love, and then you can roam about a bit." So I had a double bed, but failed to find a companion for it.' This was not the only place where she stayed in unappealing digs. In early 1955, when she was playing at the Grand Theatre in Blackpool, she wrote to her mother that she was 'staying in a perfectly bloody hotel here with paper flowers stuck in all the wall tidies'.

In 1954 Prunella was in a London revue, *Reprise*, at the Watergate Theatre in Villiers Street—a compilation of sketches and numbers from the 1940s and 1950s. 'It was a small theatre so you didn't need a very strong voice. That was great fun—for the first time in my professional life I felt that I was doing myself some good. I love the immediacy of revue. You have to make a point, whatever that point may be, in a very short time. It puts you on your toes, it's up-front and stimulating.'

After several stints of touring Prunella's first major London show, in 1955, was the inaugural production of Thornton Wilder's *The Matchmaker*, directed by Tyrone Guthrie. Sent to audition for H.M. Tennant, she was given the part of the juvenile, Ermengarde, the niece of the Yonkers merchant Cornelius Vandergelder. Thornton Wilder attended some of the rehearsals, usually accompanied by his sister. Sometimes, having seen his first draft performed, he rewrote the parts where he thought it needed some improvement, so Guthrie and the cast had to rehearse it as a work in progress. *The Matchmaker* was an American play set in America; however, one of the reasons it opened in Britain was because as an expensive production with a large cast, funding was possible from the Edinburgh Festival if plays opened there. After Edinburgh, the play went on to Birmingham, then to the Haymarket Theatre in London. It was a successful and much acclaimed production.

During the London run Prunella rented a bed-sit in a house in Albert Bridge Road belonging to the actor Peter Gray and his wife, Daphne Newton, who played the cook in the play. 'It was my first West End show, which was lovely, and I was getting a better salary— about £20 a week.' The show was a hit and ran for nine months. 'The only note I can remember Tyrone Guthrie giving me was during the run after he had seen the show and had come round to talk to the cast.

I came down from my dressing-room on the top floor, running to catch my bus home to Battersea, and as I passed him outside Dressing-room One he said, "Do something about your make-up dear; looks like three raspberries on a plate." Which of course is still true, because when you have a round face like mine, you make as much as you can of the features so that they take up as much room as possible.'

On another, even more humbling, occasion she missed an entrance. 'I was actually doing a change of costume, not even a quick change. There was no tannoy; I was on the top floor and the elderly callboy used to climb the stairs and knock on the dressing-room door. One night I missed an entrance—I was "off" for the leading lady, Ruth Gordon. I went round to her dressing-room afterwards and said, "I'm terribly sorry, Miss Gordon, I can only tell you that I am going to do that change in the wings from now on so that it will never happen again." Ruth Gordon: "I'm glad to hear that. The first thing I am going to teach in my drama school is, not everybody can act, but everybody can get there." I was duly humiliated.'

*   *   *

After the London season *The Matchmaker* transferred to America. It was the first time twenty-three-year-old Prunella had crossed the Atlantic. 'The crossing was really great fun, although too long. I used to walk round the funnel ten times twice a day, and on one very rough but fine day I met the Captain up there who grunted approvingly, and took me on to the bridge.' She wrote to her parents on 9 October 1955 from Cunard's RMS *Media*: 'Sea voyages give one the most deliciously suspended irresponsible feeling. I

70

sleep, eat, sew, knit, write letters and purr.' She was reasonably impressed by her first encounter with a new continent. 'The first sight of the New York skyline against the stars as you come up the Hudson is one of the most beautiful man-made phenomena I've ever seen. The Statue of Liberty, however, is quite horrid, I think, even floodlit.' She was met by Louis Connick, the young Cadillac-driving American who had stayed with them at Kempslade one summer to help her mother with the garden. Louis waited with Prunella on the dock until after midnight when her luggage was finally unloaded from the hold, then swept her off in a taxi to his mother's home on Park Avenue where she was given a warm welcome. 'The apartment is Very, Very Nice, lots of double doors and brass filigree finger plates and veneer and madly good furniture.' The next day Louis took her sightseeing. 'Yesterday, which was a gorgeous day, dry and clear under an even blue sky fading to white over the horizon all round, we went on to the roof of a hotel called Beekman Towers and looked over the city. It's much *redder* than I expected, not white and staring at all, but incredibly clear and knife-edged in every shade of pink and brown and orange and cream.'

For the first two weeks after their arrival in the USA they rehearsed in New York. 'It has been a most exhausting week. Not a great deal has happened except intensive rehearsals. We're all a bit bored with the piece now and are longing to open. Off to Philadelphia on Tuesday, so ho! For a fortnight of brotherly love.' They opened in Philadelphia at the Locust Street Theatre, then after two weeks moved on to the Colonial Theatre, Boston, for a further two weeks, before the Broadway opening. Prunella visited all the Philadelphia sights including Independence

Hall, where 'a dear little man with a fat tummy bursting out of his uniform, and a bald head, taught me all the American History I'll ever know (and only when I asked him, which was refreshing!) There's lots more to see.' The show went quite well and got good notices, but 'it's a vile and horrid theatre and we need a lot of playing in. Guthrie came up after the rather terrifying first night and said with a beaming smile and no hesitation at all, "Well—that was a pisspot of an evening wasn't it—rehearsal call tomorrow at four o'clock." '

On 6 November she went to Washington by train for the day, and was impressed by the Lincoln Memorial. 'It is a VAST Greek temple in white marble with a magnificent white marble statue of the gentleman inside, sprawled in a chair, scowling at the world. Really splendid.' In Boston, where the play was 'a smash hit', she stayed at the Charlotte Cushman Club, founded by 'a lady of mysterious origin and obscurely theatrical connections, for actresses on tour. It has a gracious nineteenth-century interior and, praise God, the first wooden lavatory seats I've seen since we landed. It is supported by a committee of Boston ladies who all wear hats.' She also ventured to give herself a home perm. 'Alone I did it, after the show one night.' She explained to her mother, 'there's a rather alarming moment when your entire scalp and both towels and anything else within reach turn a livid purple, but with the application of MAGI-CURL, Richard Hudnut's exclusive secret formula (God knows what it's made of, sulphuric acid I expect), all this disappears, leaving, to everyone's intense surprise including, I suspect, Richard Hudnut's, your hair.'

'My goodness, WHAT a first night,' she wrote to her parents after the show opened at the Royale

Theatre on Broadway on 5 December 1955. 'They were a dream house—well, you can see by the notices. And the *flowers*. I got six boxes, and Ruth Gordon got over twenty. The Management (who have been absolute stinkers over one or two things during the rehearsal period and previews) sent us all pink double camellias, with SILVER FROSTED laurel leaves in cellophane oval boxes labelled "Affectionately". We had a party here afterwards for Tyrone Guthrie and his wife and one or two others, which was tremendous fun, in a nice quiet way. The done thing is to sit in a restaurant called Sardi's until midnight when they bring in the morning papers with the page turned back and the notice marked.'

During her time in New York, Prunella was offered a room in an apartment in Greenwich Village by Esmé Church, a well-known English actress in her sixties who ran the Bradford Civic Theatre and the school attached to it. She was playing an elderly character part in *The Matchmaker*. 'My half is self-contained, and the whole thing belongs to Margaret Webster (director) who is in England. It is a gorgeous flat on the third floor of a very old house with no elevator and ceilings that drip dust. The drawback is that Esmé has to come through my room to get to her bedroom. However, it is only for three months, it shouldn't kill either of us.' After the initial buzz and excitement of the first night, and with *The Matchmaker* an acknowledged success, they settled into a routine. But Prunella found that while playing eight shows a week, it was difficult to explore very far outside New York. The only night they had free was Sunday, when it was possible to go away for the day and stay overnight, but necessary to be back for the evening show on Monday. She began to find that playing Ermengarde, a relatively minor role, was becoming tedious, especially after nine months in London.

Sylvia Short, the supportive friend with whom she had trained at the Old Vic School, was now living in New York, married to the actor Fritz Weaver. They all had lunch one day and they asked how she was enjoying New York; she told them she was going out of her mind with boredom. Her days were free, but she had found nothing interesting to occupy her. Fritz and Sylvia told her she should go to class. Prunella was wary of this, as there was a slight distrust in England in those days of the Method classes run by Lee Strasberg. The perception was that Method actors did not have enough regard for text, style and character, but relied too much on their own psyche to interpret parts, which could make their performance too inward-looking. Fritz and Sylvia suggested a different idea. Prunella wrote to her parents in the middle of December that she had begun to go to classes 'run by an actress called Uta Hagen at a place called the Herbert Berghof Studio. They are for actors and we do exercises and work on scenes and so on. Uta is brilliant and it is quite fascinating (a) working with Americans on modern naturalistic scenes (which they all seem to play quite perfectly) and (b) watching them work on Shakespeare and Wilde which so far they haven't shown the smallest feeling for that I can see. But of course the students vary tremendously.'

The teaching at the Berghof Studio, which Uta had co-founded with her husband, Herbert Berghof, was in part based on the teaching of Konstantin Stanislavsky, from which the Method had evolved; but unlike the way she had been taught Stanislavsky at the Old Vic School, Prunella found the training, 'clear, helpful and systematic. I went along every Thursday for the rest of

74

my time in New York. The classes blew my mind. What one got with Uta and Herbert was that same respect for modern technique and psychological approach, without neglecting the necessary apprehensions of period and style and character.' The Thursday classes were from 11 a.m until 3 p.m. 'The first hour was devoted to physical exercises—lifting imaginary suitcases, balancing full cups of tea, etc. These became progressively more complicated— carrying an imaginary suitcase, with a headache, or in a hurry, and led to others, travelling in a bus, going up and down stairs. These were followed by exercises with real objects and achieving a purpose or overcoming some obstacle. Carrying a stolen suitcase, or wearing a new hat. I think the chief value of these exercises was that they helped one to observe more acutely behaviour in other people and in oneself, and to be accurate, economical, and interesting in carrying it out.'

The rest of the class was spent in working on scenes from plays. These they had to rehearse—so there was always something to do. 'It was a make-over as far as I was concerned because it reconciled me to Stanislavsky—who was a great teacher—in a very positive way; I had always been uneasy about it at the Old Vic School.' Prunella says that for one of the first times since she had left drama school, she felt confident and at home in the profession. One of Uta Hagen's precepts in her book *Respect for Acting* has been adhered to closely by Prunella. 'Self-glorification and narcissism block the spontaneous behaviour, the genuine give-and-take of any actor. Guard against it the way you would any other destructive disease.'

Just before Christmas the management put on a party for 'the casts of their two successes' on the stage of the Majestic Theatre next door. 'Champagne, spaghetti, prawns créole out of great big saucepans, and presents for everyone, actors, stage management, wardrobe, dressers, everyone. We all got PORTABLE RADIOS! And the cast of *Fanny* at the Majestic (who were already a success last Christmas and got their radios then) had cameras. Quite fantastic the whole thing. I heard one actor remark cynically, "I suppose they have to cut down the profits *somehow* to avoid super-tax!" '

The Matchmaker continued to attract full houses, and was so popular it was featured in Ed Sullivan's TV show in mid January, when excerpts from the play were broadcast live from the studio. 'It was an exhausting day.'

*   *   *

Prunella's romance with Bernard Frank had virtually finished, and the sometimes fraught relationship with Michael Vowden had dwindled to an intermittent correspondence. It seemed the time had come to end it; she enclosed a poem with her letter to him.

So be it. Let us live our lives upon a broader
    grander scale,
Which scorns the vulgar aerogramme, or cards
    dispatched by surface mail.
Oh we will gear our lives afresh to this new turn of
    fortune's wheel
And think in transatlantic terms more noble than
    we used to feel
And each to each communicate our monolithic
    hopes and fears
By international telegraph, at intervals of several

years.

Michael answered on 4 January 1956. 'My behaviour during the three months since you went away—never writing to you, not even for Christmas, not even to thank you for my Christmas present (let alone sending you one), and generally letting any link between us lie like some pathetic dereliction—has been rude and unkind and shameful. I am deeply ashamed of it, and humbly say that I am very, very sorry. I've been walking around with your last two letters, postmarked November 20th and December 8th, unopened in my pocket, taking them out time after time and looking at the envelopes in panic. I finally read them ten minutes ago.

'The letters were perfectly wonderful of course—and the second one (it is a very clever, sweetest-saddest poem incidentally), put me in such a fit of shame that I was jerked into writing this, on sight of it.

'I miss you continually and quite dreadfully. Can you understand now why I haven't written? . . . How you've put up with it for so long, I don't know. Nor would anyone else who heard about it. And I shall never be able to thank you for it.'

Not long after this Michael gave up his job with Shell-Mex, became an announcer for BBC World Service, and married very happily. He and Prunella remained friends until he died.

5

'I thought you were lovely'

'Some directors are more helpful than others. I like lots of direction. I'm begging for direction. Obviously you have to learn to use what you're offered; directors work in different ways, and you should be versatile and humble enough to use what you can. If something doesn't make sense, I just say, I'm sorry, I just don't understand.'

*   *   *

On the second night out on the voyage to America, Prunella had received a cable from her agent Ronnie Waters saying, 'Stratford deal set, happy trip.' On her arrival in New York, there had been a letter waiting for her, confirming that the Shakespeare Memorial Company had offered her a contract for their next Stratford-upon-Avon season, and asking her to find out if she could be released early from the play. She had told her mother, 'If it means breaking my contract, I'll probably have to pay my fare home, but IF the parts are good it may be worth it. Anyway, we'll see.' After thinking about it, she decided the Stratford deal was too good a chance to miss, the management agreed to release her and she paid her own passage back to England. By mid January she'd had enough of New York anyway. 'Only two more months now before I come home,' she wrote to her mother. 'Now that Christmas is over I feel almost on my way—half-time behind me, you know?' By mid February she was ready to depart. 'I've made some very good friends here, and shall be sad to leave in lots of ways, but knowing I was only here for a few months has forced a certain transience in my relationships! Still, in this business no departure is for ever, and the world gets smaller every day.'

She arrived home at the end of February in time to start rehearsing at the beginning of March. Margaret Webster, the owner of the flat where she had stayed in Greenwich Village, was directing *The Merchant of Venice*; when rehearsals started, Prunella found she was having trouble with the part of Nerissa and one day during a rehearsal Margaret asked her: 'Tell me, when you were in New York, did you ever go to Uta Hagen's classes?' 'I said, "Yes, I did," and she nodded. "Oh, that explains it then." ' Margaret Webster didn't like the way Uta Hagen worked, which must have made it much harder for Prunella, who says she didn't know quite what Margaret wanted. 'Her approach was absolutely different. I think she was deeply mistrustful of the Method, because sometimes when Method-trained actors come to Shakespeare they can't seize it stylistically, they can't get their heads around it. I was probably being much too inward-looking. I didn't make a very good Nerissa: it's quite a difficult part and I wasn't very happy with it. That can be miserable, but you have to go on every night and try and find something.'

Stratford Memorial Theatre was being run by Anthony Quayle, who had seen Prunella's performance as the flirtatious hoyden Miss Betty in the end-of-term show at the Old Vic School. Glen Byam Shaw, one of her tutors at the school, was a co-director. As well as playing Nerissa, Prunella was also Jaquenetta in *Love's Labour's Lost*, and Juliet in

Measure for Measure. The fourth play that season was *Othello*, in which she was part of the crowd—'the fourteenth Cypriot'. Geraldine McEwan, whom she was later to partner in *Mapp and Lucia*, played the Princess of France in *Love's Labour's Lost*, which was Peter Hall's first production at Stratford. Emlyn Williams played Shylock in *The Merchant of Venice*, and Harry Andrews the title role in *Othello*. In 1956 there were few black actors in mainstream theatre, so the part of the Moor was usually played by a white actor in make-up.

Prunella had digs with Zoe Ziedler, an Irishwoman who worked for a publisher and also let out rooms to actors. Prunella didn't find her Stratford experience very easy and wrote to her mother on 7 June, 'I am fairly adequately occupied though haven't enough to work on in the plays, and I'm NOT good as Nerissa, let's face it. Wish to God Glen had produced it . . . For the rest I sing, drive, punt and play tennis. Most demoralizing!'

There was, however, one occasion which helped restore her confidence. At an end-of-the-season cabaret party in November, to wind up the Stratford year, Prunella did a monologue, 'The Life of a Holiday Queen', from the revue *Reprise*, in which she wore high heels, a bathing costume, and a long blonde wig. Glen Byam Shaw came up to her afterwards, full of enthusiasm. 'That was wonderful, Prunella. You were funny, you were intelligible, you were cogent: I have never found you so sexually attractive as I have tonight.' She thought, 'Shit! Why didn't I know *that* when I was a student!'

*   *   *

It was a time of change in the theatre. May 1956 saw the première of *Look Back in Anger*, written by twenty-seven-year-old John Osborne. Many theatre critics were outraged, though Kenneth Tynan thought it 'presented post-war youth as it really is'. Timothy West explains what was happening. 'Until then the whole of the West End had been a mixture of stars in famous plays, or new plays written by people like Terence Rattigan. These were rather gentle plays and mostly about a particular sort of society to which if you did not naturally belong, you aspired to belong. Now, however, some of the more traditional actors began to be classified as old-fashioned.' Fortunately this did not apply to Prunella, who was young enough to be part of the new, less traditional way of working.

In October 1956 Frank Hauser was appointed as director of the newly reopened Oxford Playhouse Theatre. Three months later, in January 1957, after Prunella's not very happy season with the Shakespeare Memorial Company, Frank cast her as the Pupil in a new translation by Donald Watson of Ionesco's *The Lesson*—the first performance of the play in English. The second play of the evening was *Medea* by Jean Anouilh. Frank, who had worked with Prunella at Salisbury Rep two years earlier, wrote in his programme introduction, 'From Stratford comes Prunella Scales, who shares with Edgar Wreford and Monica Stewart the formidable difficulties of *The Lesson*. From Nerissa to Ionesco is a light step for an actress who had already played Ibsen, pantomime, and for two years in *The Matchmaker*.'

Robert Tanitch, then an undergraduate, was a great admirer of Prunella and her work, and thought the Frank Hauser production of *The Lesson* was the best thing he'd done at the Playhouse. Robert, who later became a playwright, author and theatre critic, took notes on shows he watched. 'Who would have thought that the professor would get so carried away with his own words that he would kill his pupil? But he does and more—though in accordance with the Lord Chamberlain's requirements, he rapes her symbolically. Edgar Wreford is very good as the professor and Prunella Scales is just right for the pupil who can't subtract and gets the toothache. She can multiply. She suddenly multiplies the most fantastic sum in her head, explaining to the astonished professor that she has memorized all the answers. "But they are infinite!" he cries. "But I managed it!" she replies coyly.'

Prunella stayed with the Oxford Playhouse for four and a half months. 'The ideal is to work with a company over a long time. Oxford was a bit like that. The trouble is that it is a sort of luxury to get a company where you have a sympathetic director and you're all working towards the same ends. It doesn't happen very often. When it does happen it is very rarely that anyone can afford to prolong it. We had that feeling working with Frank in Oxford, and I felt the same thing working in Nottingham with Richard Eyre some years later in 1972.'

In February, after *The Lesson*, she was in André Obey's *Frost at Midnight*, again in a first English translation, by Warren Tate. In March she was in Dudley Fitts's translation of *Lysistrata*, with Constance Cummings playing the lead. Frank Hauser wrote: 'With Prunella Scales, Pat Keen, George Selway, Ian Hendry and what seems like a cast of thousands, this is virtually the first nearly uncut version to be staged in England. With its music and dancing, its ribald comedy, and above all its profound antimilitarist

82

passion, it should prove a tremendous attraction.' It was such a success that they followed the two-week run with a four-week tour, returning to the Playhouse for an extra week at the end of April.

Prunella found working at the Oxford Playhouse stimulating: the coffee bar, which opened at 11 a.m., was full of undergraduates, and everyone met in a pub, the Gloucester Arms, after the show. According to her contemporaries, Prunella was popular and fun to be with, and she found the Playhouse a sociable and friendly place. 'That was really the first time that I began to feel I was in the right job. Frank stretched me, and gave me some fantastic parts, and I, on the whole, managed them and learnt a lot. He was very knowledgeable and intelligent; the sort of director who made you feel you could do it.'

It was three-weekly rep: two weeks in Oxford and the third week in Cambridge, which gave three weeks in which to rehearse the next play, while performing the current one at night—a treat for those brought up in weekly rep. But it also meant that they had to have digs in both Oxford and Cambridge. In Oxford she stayed at 12 Wellington Square, 'a dreary square', she wrote to her mother on 30 January 1957, 'but madly convenient. There are legions of undergraduates living here and we all have breakfast at a refectory table in the basement. My room is tiny, and I have to do all the washing (clothes, not me) at the theatre, but digs are so awful in Oxford (as far as I can make out every other building is a *brothel*), that I am very lucky.' She would like to have a flat in Blackwell's, the bookshop. 'Talking of flats, can you go on looking out? Really vital to get one on leaving here, I feel.' On 24 April 1957 she wrote to her mother from Cambridge, where *Lysistrata* was just finishing its run.

83

'Cambridge burgeons extravagantly—all the cherry trees and the tulips are out, and the lilac is in bloom in Grantchester. We—that is to say I—punted up the river there yesterday, 3¾ miles each way and I fell in once. However a kind lady in Grantchester hung my clothes on a line and I ate lunch in the Orchard wrapped in a cellular blanket under my coat. I have just sent out shameless postcards saying here I am, what about it? Our advance publicity is *so* bad here that otherwise one runs the risk of missing people altogether.'

In May 1957 Prunella was cast in *Change in the Wind*, a one-acter by George Neveux, translated by Pauline Bentley, which needed a companion curtain-raiser. For this Frank Hauser chose *A Prior Engagement*, which he described as 'a light-hearted one-acter by Robert Tanitch, an undergraduate at St Catherine's. This is the first play by Mr Tanitch to reach the professional stage. And the first time we have included the work of a local dramatist at the Playhouse.'

Robert, in his last year at Oxford, was a member of the Experimental Theatre Club. Past and present members, who included John Schlesinger, Ned Sherrin and Sandy Wilson, met to celebrate the club's twenty-first birthday in 1957. Prunella, still working at the Playhouse, was one of those invited to take part and performed the monologue 'The Life of a Holiday Queen', which had so impressed Glen Byam Shaw. Robert also wrote and performed his own monologues, and together with Prunella and Dudley Moore, then an organ scholar at Magdalen College, they put together a very successful cabaret for a May Ball. As a result, in July 1957 when Prunella had finished working with the Playhouse, they were invited to the Royal Court Theatre Club, a restaurant run by Clement Freud at the top of the theatre building in Sloane Square, where for a two-week season Robert, Dudley and Prunella did a midnight cabaret.

When two years later, in 1959, the Oxford Playhouse Company toured Europe to Copenhagen, Lisbon, Zurich and Verona, Prunella played Olivia in *Twelfth Night* and Hermia in a *Midsummer Night's Dream*.

*   *   *

Prunella had always been unhappy about the shape of her face, and now felt it was limiting the parts she was offered. In 1958 the Audrey Hepburn look was in, and everyone wanted to be thin and svelte with high cheekbones. Her self-esteem was not helped when an American film director came to see her in a popular Victorian melodrama, *The Silver King*, at the Players' Theatre, under the arches at Charing Cross. The production was by Maurice Browning and the cast, including John Bailey, Fred Stone, Prunella and Tony Sympson, encouraged the audience to boo, hiss and cheer with gusto. Afterwards the American was full of qualified praise. 'You are a wonderful actress—now what are we going to do about your face. Have you tried surgery?' She went on a drastic diet which was very popular at the time, and which she thought was safe because it had been endorsed by a Harley Street doctor. She did lose quite a lot of weight, but she also became ill—and the shape of her face didn't change. 'As a young woman I felt that I hadn't been given a useful enough face, particularly for films, to play some of the parts I'd like to have tried. People think, "Oh, you've got a round fat face and so you're a character

85

actress." On behalf of all actors, I can't bear people being put in boxes—in categories. I think it's deeply unfair. Things do get a bit easier as you get older.'

There was great variety in the parts Prunella was offered, and she played in many different venues. Her son Sam says she has a very strong work ethic, so she is always good to have in a company. 'She's extremely generous but she's also very hard-working in that way which says—when she's leading a company—"We are here to work, and you are coming with me." This is part of the job. She has always been very good at feeding lines to people. If you can phrase a feed line a comedian will hire you.' It must also be a good way of making sure that you are not out of work.

In 1960 she played Anna Bowers, a young mother, in *All Good Children* at Bromley Little Theatre, and later that year, aged twenty-eight, she played the seventy-year-old Mrs Savage in *The Curious Savage* in Dundee, where Nicol Williamson, Glenda Jackson and Edward Fox were all members of the very exciting Repertory Company directed by Anthony Page. 'Top marks must go to Prunella Scales for her interpretation of Mrs Savage,' wrote a reviewer.

Although she was away on tour much of the time, from 1957 onwards she had a permanent base in London at 30 Cheyne Court, an Edwardian block of flats at the bottom of Flood Street in Chelsea. The block was serviced by a porter, Frank, who, as Timothy West remembers, 'wore a smart blue uniform with gold trimmings, and seemed to appear from nowhere when you needed help'. Miranda Mackintosh, whose parents, the lessees, lived at number 37, was the original landlady of number 30 and shared the flat, on the top floor, with three other girls: Margaret Geddes, Prunella and Joan Dodsworth. Margaret Geddes, who answered the same advertisement as Prunella in October 1957, remembers that Prunella got the bigger room because she had to pace about while learning her lines. Others came and went over the years. The flat was large, with four rooms, each big enough to be used as a bed-sitting-room. As all the girls worked, this arrangement gave them both companionship and privacy. A bathroom and an ancient unmodernized kitchen, a small maid's bedroom at the end of a passage with a lavatory off it, a large sitting-room, and a small dining-room, made up the shared facilities. The dining-room could be booked for dinner parties, of which there were quite a number. For a pound a week each, paid into a kitty, a weekly grocery order was placed for general basics and communal needs, but each person was responsible for their own evening meal. Because they led such different lives they seldom cooked together, though they often met up in the evenings with their various visitors, around the kitchen table, for long discussions.

A cleaning lady, Mrs Cole, came in once a week but there was a rule that the bedrooms must be tidy on the cleaning day. If not, the room would be left untouched. Miranda remembers Prunella as a fun-loving and generous person who got on well with everyone. She says she was incredibly hard-working and ambitious, and was often up at 6.30 a.m., sitting in the kitchen translating French plays into English. Miranda's father, Hugh Mackintosh, who wrote poetry and ballades, was very fond of Prunella; on one occasion they made a recording of some of his poems. For a while in 1961 Prunella went out with Miranda's brother Julian. When Miranda left for Africa two years after Prunella had moved in, she took over the lease. It was in the leasing policy that each of the Cheyne Court flats must be rented to one approved family and ideally not to a group. An actress would certainly not have been acceptable. When Prunella went to see the landlord, she had to conceal her profession and prove her suitability. Wearing her most conventional clothes, and with Stephen Kaye, her respectable, titled cousin, in tow, as sponsor and guarantor, she passed the interview.

In 1959, while staying with Margaret Geddes at her home outside Edinburgh, Prunella met Bill Blackwood of the *Blackwood's Magazine* family. An interesting and wildly eccentric engineer, he lived in a large house not far from Margaret, where he had his own printing press in the conservatory. He had decided not to work in the family company, and had ambitious, and not very successful, schemes for building ski-lifts on the Cairngorms near Aviemore. In spite of their very different lifestyles and backgrounds, they fell in love and even discussed getting married. However, as Bill pointed out in one of his letters, this was a wildly impractical plan, as he had no money and needed to stay in Scotland to work, and she did not want to give up acting and needed to stay in London.

The ski-lifts were little more than a rope attached to a tractor to haul the skiers up the mountain. Bill owned three of these tractors, named in Prunella's honour as P.S.1, P.S.2 and P.S.3. So besotted was she that, on her mother's hand sewing-machine, she made a cover for P.S.2. Bill wrote to her in January 1960: 'If you can't get canvas let me know. Let me also know thickness, weight, wot-have-u etc. Presumably your sewing machine cannot handle heavy tarpaulin-type canvas. It's not necessary to have it frantically thick.' He wrote again on 1 March. 'From Cuvvahed tractor to Cuvvah-less Gal, Thank-u-thank-u-thank-u. She looks wonderful in flesh coloured robe. Contrasts beautifully with tangerine complexion. AND FITS! Yes truly; not just being polite. In spite of the fact that one of the side boxes for carrying stuff is still in situ. And it appears to be possible to tie her down fairly tight. P.S.1 and 3 will be mighty jealous and screaming "Want one too!" They'll just have to scream.'

Bill and Prunella remained together for two years, initially writing almost daily letters and meeting when they could. Prunella seriously looked into the possibility of finding work in Glasgow, but found it impractical. Bill's scheme for ski-lifts failed when his company was refused planning permission to build facilities on Cairngorm and he had try to find other work. Coincidentally, in early February Prunella found herself with no acting work for the first time in her life. Needing money to pay the rent, she took a temporary job with *Which?* magazine at the suggestion of one of her flatmates, Susie Balfour, who knew someone who worked there. Her task was to rewrap blocks of margarine in anonymous wrappers and deliver them to various people for testing. The difficulty she had in finding the delivery addresses has left her with a lasting rage about the inadequate labelling of streets and the invisibility, from a driver's seat, of most house names and numbers. Bill wrote: 'Ta for month-old pensive missive bemoaning miserable situation. Wot a come down to be working for "Which". Hope things have improved and that you are now back at real work again. Well if it's any consolation, things are much blacker up here in spite of all the white stuff lying around. We've been kicked off Cairngorm. So the future is black indeed.'

By 1961 they had drifted apart, though they always

remained friends.

*   *   *

Prunella met Timothy West in early July 1961, when they were both in a rather improbable BBC television play called *She Died Young*. The director, Campbell Logan, had also directed Prunella in the first TV production of *Pride and Prejudice*. This time she was cast as the Bishop of Lichfield's daughter, who was debauched by Boswell in a pub. Timothy had the small part of a Regency buck whose one line was, 'Can't say I blame him, sir. Damme, she's a morsel.' The cast were dismissive of the script, and Timothy and Prunella sat around a lot eating Polo mints and doing the *Times* crossword together. Prunella thought Timothy 'very charming. He wore a different waistcoat every day and a variety of decorative ties.' She discovered he was married, and lived with his wife and small daughter in Wimbledon.

On transmission day there was an electricians' strike and the show was cancelled. Prunella and Timothy escaped and went to the cinema together to see *The Grass is Greener*, with a starry cast—Deborah Kerr, Robert Mitchum, Cary Grant and Jean Simmons. The film is gently romantic: a story of upper-class infidelity between the lady of the manor and an American visitor who drops into the stately home as a day tripper. This being 1961, she does the right thing: renounces her passion, and returns to her home and family. But the theme of 'love versus duty' may have been prophetic.

The strike went on; the play had to be postponed, and the cast were dispersed. When it was eventually revived later in July, Timothy was otherwise engaged.

90

He had been offered the part of the elderly Colonel Grey-Balding in a touring production of *Simple Spymen*, in which Andrew Sachs had taken over the lead from Brian Rix. When Timothy's part in *She Died Young* was recast, Prunella sent him a large postcard with a picture of Piccadilly Circus: 'Shattered you're not with us—paralytic tedium of it all now totally unrelieved . . . Returning fresh to this script is to realize anew the unspeakable (in every sense) banality of EVERY SINGLE LINE. Tchah ever so and tush withal. Pru.'

This triggered a correspondence which became more intense after they met again in August, while both playing in Oxford, Prunella in *Whiteman* at the Oxford Playhouse, and Timothy in *Simple Spymen* at the New Theatre. Being in the same town gave them a chance to spend some time together, including a romantic day punting on the river Cherwell. 'Dear Mr West,' wrote Prunella afterwards in a disguised hand, 'I thought you were lovely in Oxford this week I saw you several times oh you were good. It made all the difference to my Life. Of course you have just the sort of caracter [sic] I like and you certainly do it well don't you. H. Green (Miss).'

Timothy's marriage to Jacqueline Boyer, an actress, had been rocky for some time, and by the time he met Prunella it was over in all but name. He and Jacqueline had been married when they were both very young, Timothy only twenty-one. His various engagements often took him away on tour, and although at the beginning they lived together in Salisbury in a dilapidated second-hand caravan, this wasn't so easy after their daughter Juliet was born in 1957. Jacqueline found the situation difficult to cope with, and it was not helped by her own ill-health. Her

91

behaviour was unpredictable; she suffered quite severely from emotional highs and lows. As a result she spent a lot of time living with her mother, and had to be hospitalized when her mood swings became too extreme.

Prunella accepted this unresolved situation philosophically. For a while she and Timothy put off the inevitable, though they realized that their friendship was rapidly becoming more serious. Touring in different plays and desperate to see each other, they met whenever their paths crossed, or could be made to cross. Prunella was offered a part in *The Marriage Game*, a comedy about six girls sharing a London flat, all with marriage firmly in mind. She wrote to Timothy, 'rehearsing this Monday, so I suppose lunch would be possible though wildly frustrating. Bless you for sweet letter . . . Refuse to apologize for my writing. God bless you too. Love, I think, P.'

The next day, Thursday, she wrote from the Oxford Playhouse. 'Darling, *Cheltenham*? How very unsuitable—also it's 100 miles from London, and I'll probably have a morning call for *The Marriage Game* on 11th. However, after half an hour's perusal of Michelin Touring Guide which is the only map to hand, I do see that Swindon is sole alternative and not an alluring one. Await further instructions.'

From the Playhouse, on Saturday at 11.00 a.m. 'London seems an awful sweat for you on 18th. But I'll meet any train you like to catch on Sat. night or Sunday morn and we can go to my flat.'

'7.40 p.m. Might see you Monday then. Hope so, though it'll be awful. Love, I'm afraid. P.'

Train timetables became an indispensable part of their luggage as they travelled the country on different theatre tour schedules, desperate to meet when they could.

'Teatime, Monday. Shall have to go to Woking on Thursday, but there's a train to Durham at 11.50 arriving 5.57 a.m. Could you bear it? . . . Glasgow does look a bit uncertain.'

'9.30 a.m. Tuesday. Middlesborough, huh? Will try and find a nocturnal train, as have promised to spend Thursday with Ma.'

They snatched every possible opportunity to be together, often travelling overnight, and sometimes meeting on trains or at inhospitable hours of the morning. When apart they wrote to each other every day; Prunella explained why she was now using the backs of her old radio scripts. 'I've just been going through the drawers of my desk—this means opening them one by one, taking a despairing look inside and shutting them again as quickly as possible. And the second long one down—no, darling, the *second* not counting the little ones—is crammed to the point of total inertia (I mean you can't open it and when you have it leans forward like a drunk over a wall and you can't heave it back again), with SCRIPTS. So I found that if I cut the bottoms off and use them for telephone messages (always the thrifty hussif) the result is exactly the same size as the extremely expensive King size Bourgeois Bond. So I'm going to use it. So there. I mean they charge 2/4d for the Double *Economy* Pack . . . [new page written on the back of a torn off script] I say, it's rather absorbent, isn't it, do you think what you save on paper you lose on ink?'

Prunella's daily letters to Timothy give a running commentary on her work as well as her feelings. 'Tuesday morning. Wish you were here, wish you were

93

here, wish you were here. It's a cold clear autumn day and everything smells marvellous and I miss you. The more I think about it the luckier I feel to have you and the more terrifying it is to know I haven't really. I am very, very SLOW about some things, and still can't always believe that this is actually IT.' The next morning she adds a postscript. 'I have just realized I wrote to Sir John G. last week asking to read for "Lucy" a part that doesn't exist—at least not in *The School for Scandal*. Have written frivolous letter admitting mistake, but don't suppose anyone's going to audition actress who doesn't know the difference between that and *The Rivals*. Darling, going to post this now, though shan't have yours till this p.m. in London.'

Wednesday evening from the flat: 'Oh, WOE. No letter from you today. *Determined* not to ring up.' Thursday: 'MUCH better. Two lovely letters this morning.'

Neither of them wanted to talk publicly about their growing relationship until Timothy had sorted out his life with Jacqueline. Prunella wrote, 'Still frightened of accepting responsibility for something I can't help regarding, in a way, as a major disaster, although of course it may be a wonderfully Good Thing all round. I am a COWARD. No, actually, it isn't entirely that, it's the feeling that perhaps in this case one might be behaving in a horribly selfish and inhuman way, grabbing what one wants for oneself without any regard for two people in a very much weaker position.'

Once *The Marriage Game* was on its pre-opening tour, Prunella wrote to Timothy from the Kings Theatre in Southsea to tell him about her new digs. 'Have comfortable ground floor bedroom, with only three kinds of wallpaper and four kinds of chintz, the

94

usual neo-Jacobean rocking wardrobe, dressing table, running h&c (Ascot), one of the most lurid linoleums in my entire experience of touring and, final luxury, a large modern gas stove in the corner in case the notices are bad. An army of men arrived at 6 a.m. and performed a dustbin routine just outside the window, but I think this is a once-weekly-only occurrence.' A few days later: 'Have bought a great deal of wool and am embarked on a mammoth sweater as occupational tat. Long to give it to you, but large hand-knitted sweaters are a bit difficult to explain away unless you've been to Dublin, aren't they?'

When *The Marriage Game* opened on 3 October 1961 in Liverpool, she wrote, 'It went well *again* last night and notices are again good. It can't last. Ugly rumours of extended tour. They can't exceed eight weeks under the contract but it will be interesting to see what further geographical west-by-scales permutations result. Aberdeen and Plymouth for example. Horrid press call with lots of nasty little men in loud suits and moustaches trying to find out which of the girls were unattached and co-operative, culminating in our being hauled into St John's Park to be photographed from below sitting on a wall with our legs crossed.'

By the time she reached Eastbourne, Prunella found herself writing, 'Oh darling, it occurs to me that I really do love you *properly*, and it's awful. No it's not awful, of course, it's marvellous, but oh *dear*.' She asks Timothy to send her some typed envelopes so she can use them for her letters, in the hope this might make them more anonymous. She can, she tells him, borrow a typewriter from the company manager, but 'he's never there, and anyway you must have noticed it's a rather wayward and recognizable one'. Sometimes, as a joke, she disguises her writing. Timothy went to Eastbourne to see a matinée of *The Marriage Game*, and Prunella actually wrote to him from backstage during the show. 'This is the first letter I've ever written to someone under the same roof—if you still are, that is. Well at least you are seeing it in the worst conditions audience-wise we've suffered so far. We're all quite hysterical, as must be only too painfully apparent. Poor love, I'm so sorry, it's much less agonizing with a really rousing house. Act II. Oh, no, *really*. The moment Rex kissed me, an old woman in the third row of the stalls shrieked, "That's right, get in." In *Eastbourne!* . . . Or was it perhaps "Get him?" Don't know, feel ghastly, so false and self-conscious and theatrical. Darling, THANK YOU for coming all the way and sorry it wasn't a better show for you. And thank you for nice lunch.'

The next venue was the Theatre Royal in Brighton. 'Good digs, nice landlady, cat, two boxers (one in twilight of gestation) and a parrot. Tend to fall violently in love with boxers (No, no, the DOGS you fool) and am sorely tempted to bespeak one of the puppies. My room has a vast double and two single beds. It does seem a waste.'

6

'Can I wear my ring now?'

'Audition very bizarre. Arrived at Garrick Theatre to find a girl waiting in the wings to sing "I'm Just a Girl Who Can't Say No" rather *carefully*, and her two dancing partners changing into tights. Came it slightly grand with the stage-manager and made it emphatically clear that I had understood that this was an INTERVIEW, and was not willing or prepared to give an audition. However, when eventually admitted to that terrifying blaze of lights with cavernous void out front, they flung about three extraordinarily unfunny scripts at me over the floats and I read them in three different voices, and then they said can you sing and I demurred becomingly and eventually belted out a few bars of (guess what) "I'm Just a Girl Who Can't Say No" rather aggressively in chest, and they said, "Yes, thank you very much, that's all we wanted to know, the part doesn't carry much singing anyway," and I left with obscure and quite unjustifiable feeling that it had all gone Rather Well.'

*　　　*　　　*

Prunella wrote almost daily letters to Timothy in 1961. She described another audition, for a gas company documentary: 'Don't yet know whether they want me. It would be to play young married ad-type girl in ill-planned kitchen. The producer was smooth and the

97

director obviously a drug-addict. They thought I overplayed it grossly, but were quite impressed. Don't think I'd have to take off any clothes, but they were very anxious that one should be able to cook. Fearfully respectable and Little Women as you can see.'

With the *Which?* period well behind her, Prunella's schedule was incredibly busy: not only had she been touring with *The Marriage Game*, but at the same time she'd been doing radio work with the BBC, including plays, poetry readings and some *Children's Hour* programmes. She wrote to Timothy: 'You might well ask what I am doing of chez British Broadcasting on Sunday. It's a Wednesday matinée called *Dear Miss Prior*, and the script arrived this morning. Scales is the Voice of nearly All again. I play Glavina O'Dowd (a young Irish girl), her mother (adjacent speeches all down one page) and Master Popham Lowel, "a hearty extrovert lad of 10". If nobody madly minds. Shall *require* to be picked up on Sunday I should think.'

*   *   *

Timothy, like his parents, who were both actors, had worked his way up through repertory companies—spending much longer in rep than Prunella had. He had had no formal training and thought it possible that he might stay as a middle-of-the-road useful younger character actor, who would eventually become a useful older character actor playing supporting parts. Prunella, however, with the benefit of the Old Vic training and the Uta Hagen classes in New York, had a very different outlook. 'It made me think about the business in a totally different way,' says Timothy. 'It was wonderful.' Prunella says they have very much the same approach to work, though they come at it from different angles. At that time, like most actors brought up in the repertory system, Timothy lived from job to job, and stayed with a rep company until either he or the company decided they had had enough of each other. 'You had an agent who just looked for what we called "special weeks". They would ask, "Would you like to go and play a detective superintendent in a new play at Worthing the week after next?" If you didn't want to play another detective superintendent the week after that, you would look for a crook. But you didn't think any further than your next engagement.'

In the 1960s, however, this way of life began to be threatened. Timothy thinks this was for two reasons: 'Television and the motor car. Television, because people saw plays where the scenery didn't wave about when you slammed the door—and the doctor wasn't the man you saw last week playing the wronged husband; and the car, because it meant that people were more mobile and didn't go so much to their local theatre. If they really enjoyed going to the theatre they felt there was no reason why they couldn't go to London.' And it wasn't only audience attitudes that were changing. Actors became reluctant to spend a whole year, or even just a whole season, with one company. They didn't want to get stuck in one place, because there was always the hope that they might be discovered—and offered something better in television, films or the West End.

At the end of 1961 Timothy was in Blackpool with *Simple Spymen*, and decided as New Year's Eve was on a Sunday he would have enough time to get down to London for the party at 30 Cheyne Court, then back to Blackpool in time for the Monday night show. Prunella was delighted. 'Thursday. Will meet any train

99

you like to catch. Sitting-room bed will be free for thee. Sweater finished. Not *actually* made for two, though you might think so.' Again, on Friday: 'Wish I could tell you what a difference you've made to life. Too superstitious to trust it yet, but even so I'm a changed girl, and many people have noticed it.'

The New Year's Eve party was a great success, and Timothy went for the 9.10 train from Euston the next morning, which should have given him plenty of time to get back. But during the night there had been a major snowfall; the lines were blocked, the trains delayed, and he was stuck in a taxi in a snowdrift when he should have been on stage. Unaware of the drama, Prunella wrote happily the next morning: 'January 1st 1962. Darling heart, Thank you from all of us for coming and for all your help and hard work, and thank you from me for the record, washing up this morning and coming at all. Here is your collar. Found in Mary's room by a FASCINATED Mrs Cole. She found Jean-Marie's waistcoat in Nicky's room too. Can't decide whether this will shock her into giving notice or give her such a vicarious thrill that she'll decide to stay after all.'

Timothy telephoned that evening to tell her of his disastrous misadventure. To miss an entrance, let alone a whole performance, was an almost unforgivable crime. Prunella was devastated. 'I am so sorry about you being off. Felt I should have rung on Saturday night and said don't come. But can't help being glad you did . . . Oh, and you must be so COLD and HUNGRY, oh DEAR.' Next day she had a further thought. 'Joan said why couldn't you come and live here? I suppose if Nicky goes abroad you could, come to that. Still can't get over your success chez les girls. No, sorry, that sounds insulting. Are you Well

Known Lady Killer?'

*   *   *

Prunella had had a small part as a council worker in the film *Room at the Top*, and in January 1962 was cast in two very early episodes of *Coronation Street* as Eileen Hughes, a bus conductress. 'The character had a slight flirtation with Harry Hewitt, and I hoped I might become a household name, but it was not to be.' Later in January she wrote to Timothy, who was on tour, to describe an audition for a revue, *Not to Worry*. Two days later she heard that she had got the part.

'Guess what, they want me. Rehearse next week, open Brighton, then Cambridge, then possibly in [at the Garrick Theatre], they hope. *Dreading* it. It was written by the producer, and was done in Edinburgh last year . . . I bet it'll be one of those awful *Marriage Game* type of shows where you have to work like stink to make anything of it at all. Promise you'll help me, thank God you'll be back before it opens. Must dash to post. In flap. Yr. ever-loving P.'

Next day, Friday: 'Acquisition of job has thrown me, paradoxically enough, into turmoil of *insecurity*. First thought, after normal sequence of surprise, delight, relief, apprehension, etc., (and even before some of these) was, oh dear, shall be rehearsing when Tim comes home and not have time to look after him. Still, that's Theatahland for you and I supposes one must (one day) learn to cope. Find that, almost without realizing it, had been looking forward terribly to you being back, and it seems too CRUEL to have to go off again myself. Only Brighton and Cambridge, though, with any luck, and perhaps you could stay here while I'm away if you wanted to.'

101

Not to Worry, with Alec McCowen, Lynnette Rae, Prunella and five others, opened with previews at the Theatre Royal, Brighton, on 6 February 1962. Prunella wrote to Timothy, who was going to visit her: 'Rehearsed till 2.00 a.m. last night—NOT going to be a smooth show . . . Haven't yet made up my mind about it, longing for you to see it and tell me what you think. The digs are hysterical. Eric is a Glasgow engineer who makes miniature engine boilers as a hobby. Jean his wife, plays the piano accordion at a club in the evenings. They have a dog, Patch, a cat, Smudge, and a son, Buster (had considerable difficulty allotting these names at first). It's all chaotic and a bit dirty and VERY nice. Miss you terribly. Any hope of staying till Saturday?'

After Brighton, on 12 February the show went on to a second preview week at the Arts Theatre in Cambridge. On the 14th Prunella writes: 'Well, we got it on. Nightmare for the stage management with new trucks, etc. Nice young male house, though not full. Haven't seen any notices yet. Can't remember much about it, a sort of nightmare dash from change to change, seemed to spend most of the evening in the passage under the stage. Didn't find "Once upon a Telly" went as well as usual, though first half was fun. How one misses tracking spots having once had them—salutary influence of revue on one's ideals. Longing to get back and be domestic with you. P.' Changes were made to the running order of *Not to Worry*, and numbers were cut or restaged. 'If only they'd leave us ALONE for a couple of nights. Stan [author and director] is having a rough time with the management and the company is tired. But enthusiastic and discerning houses so far.'

On 22 February the revue went in to the Garrick in

102

London but did not do as well as they had all hoped. The hardworking cast could not transform the somewhat patchy collection of sketches into a hit. Robert Tanitch, who had become friends with Prunella after they'd done the cabaret together, commented, 'Miss Scales works like a Trojan (nineteen changes!), for no reward.'

At this time Prunella was earning better money than Timothy, but they pooled their resources, which meant that they could sometimes make more daring choices. In 1961 the Shakespeare Memorial Company had become the Royal Shakespeare Company, and at the beginning of 1962 it staged an experimental season of modern plays at the Arts Theatre in London while using Stratford for Shakespearean productions. Prunella was in Gorky's *The Lower Depths* at the Arts, and Timothy was offered three small parts in one play and then the larger part of a homicidal fruit-picker in the very successful, *Afore Night Come*. He went on to join the BBC Radio Drama Repertory Company for a year, where Andrew Sachs was already employed. Actors employed by the BBC Drama Rep. were unable to take other work, so in his free time Timothy repainted parts of the girls' flat, including the lavatory—and a row of flowerpots.

Later in 1962 Prunella played Estella Fitzjohn in the film *The Waltz of the Toreadors*, with Peter Sellers in the lead. The film was being made in Brighton, close enough to London to go down by train every day, but she says she had, regretfully, to refuse an invitation from Peter to have dinner with him because she needed to get home. Over a series of Sunday nights in May 1963 she played Mabel, and Timothy played a 'pathetic over-age boy scout', in *The Trigon*, directed by Charles Marowitz, at the British Drama

103

League in Fitzroy Square. The play was a reasonable success and liked by the critics, though Robert Tanitch thought the basic fault was that 'one does not know what is going on'.

*   *   *

While Timothy was away on tour, he would try to go home to Wimbledon for his daughter Juliet's sake whenever he played near London. He and Jacqueline had now discussed getting a divorce and had agreed, amicably, to go their separate ways. Timothy decided that when the time came he would take on the role of the guilty party to make things easier for her. But Prunella was still afraid that in their happiness they were being selfish, and although she adored Timothy, she was worried by his decision. 'Being a terribly unsure person in lots of ways, I nearly always require to feel RIGHT. In the sight of others, I mean. Want to have the approval of absolutely everyone . . . So I don't quite understand your attitude about requiring to be completely wrong over the whole thing in everybody's eyes. Where have you found the strength to withstand such censure? I admire it very much.'

The deciding moment came when Timothy, arriving home at the end of a tour, found a strange man staying in the house. He turned up on Prunella's doorstep one morning with some of his belongings, saying, 'Jackie's turned me out. She's having an affair, with the lodger.' He found himself temporary accommodation in Turnham Green at first, but soon moved into a room in a flat just around the corner from Prunella, owned by a mutual friend, Dougie Dryburgh. Timothy was now considered an honorary member of the Cheyne Court community, and joined the ranks of the flatmates' male friends, collectively known as the Cheyne Courtiers. When a new girl, Enid Pound, wanted to move into the flat in 1962 she was interviewed by Prunella, as the landlady, after which Timothy came in to the room and offered her a glass of sherry. Enid thought he was probably the back-up interviewer and always felt that the glass of sherry was a litmus test. If you accepted it—you were in.

This was the beginning of the swinging sixties, but already many of the old rules were out. There was a big shift in social behaviour, which gave the young more sexual freedom than their parents had ever experienced. Enid said they always covered for each other if one of their mothers telephoned early on Saturday morning asking to speak to her daughter. The standard excuse for the daughter's absence was that she had got up early to go shopping. There was an unspoken rule in the flat that boyfriends were not allowed to appear at breakfast, though trays could be taken into the bedroom. Timothy, however, was different and was accepted by them all as part of the family. Enid felt she was sharing a flat with someone who was very happily in love and who wanted to share the joy.

Timothy and Jacqueline agreed to a divorce in 1963. As Timothy had chosen to take responsibility for this, he and Prunella (to be referred to as Miss X) had to be discovered together in a hotel room in order to provide the necessary evidence of his adultery. But there were logistical problems. Timothy was directing *Simple Spymen* in Cheltenham, so they agreed to be 'discovered' there. But as Miss X was filming in London she had to leave early, and the London enquiry agent who was to be the witness was unwilling to catch a train to Cheltenham that arrived early enough to discover them together. Apparently that presented no problems: twin dents on the pillows and a provocative nightgown draped on the bed were deemed sufficient. It was all very civilized, if slightly farcical, and the evidence was accepted.

While waiting for the divorce Timothy and Prunella had already chosen a sapphire and diamond engagement ring in an antique shop in the Lanes in Brighton. The ring they really wanted was an emerald, but at £15 they agreed it was too expensive; so they bought their second choice, for £8.10s. They became officially engaged when, returning to London from a visit to Timothy's parents in Brighton, they were caught in an unromantic traffic jam. Timothy had received his *decree nisi* that morning. Prunella remembers: 'We stopped at a red traffic light, and I said, "So, can I wear my ring now?" Tim said, "Oh, of course, of course! Sorry—will you marry me?"— popped the ring on my finger and leaned over to kiss me, whereupon the lights changed to green and we had to drive on.'

Once married, the couple would need a place of their own to live, and in July they found a top-floor flat in Albert Palace Mansions, Lurline Gardens, just south of Battersea Park. The flat was up five flights of stairs and in very poor condition, but they could buy the lease and it was cheap. Because they had very little money and couldn't afford a removal van, they transferred their bits and pieces of furniture to the new flat themselves, carrying them from Chelsea, across Albert Bridge, down to Battersea, and Prunella moved in, on her own, while Timothy took over her room at Cheyne Court. It was important to preserve the proprieties even in 1963. Prunella told one reporter: 'I used to think people calling to see me were breathless at the sight of me—then I realized the haul up the stairs is quite a tidy one. I could tuck myself away up there and get down to hours and hours of script learning.' Prunella and Timothy set about repainting the flat to make it more habitable, helped by Enid Pound, who was between boyfriends at the time. Enid remembers lots and lots of laughs. 'They were in love, and young, and silly. It was fun to be with them.' Prunella recalls a minor problem with the pigeons that used to nest under the bath. 'They must have got in through a ventilation hole. It was all right, except that we felt guilty about disturbing them at odd hours.'

*   *   *

Prunella became a household name when she was cast in her first major TV sit-com as Richard Briers's young wife in *Marriage Lines*. She had been playing a cockney barmaid in an earlier show during which she had a scene with Richard. He thought they worked well together and asked her if she was interested in doing a sit-com with him. A pilot episode with Prunella, shot in May 1961, was successful and now the BBC wanted to turn it into a series. Although both Richard and Prunella had some reservations about the dangers of being type-cast in a sit-com, the prospect of being able to work in London with a regular income was attractive; and they liked the script.

The series was about a newly married couple, George and Kate Starling, played by Richard and Prunella, learning to cope with the ups and downs of married life. Kate, the daffy and somewhat simple young wife, was terribly keen to do everything right but managed to do most things wrong. Tom

Hutchinson in the *Guardian* described her as 'a flustered young innocent believing that a bun in the oven was a teatime edible'. Like many young brides she was learning on the job. She burnt the dinner, forgot to clean the house, and got into trouble for not ironing her husband's shirts properly. Her plaintive and frequent pleas of 'George . . .' when things went wrong were infuriating enough to drive any young husband to take refuge in the nearest pub.

'It took *Marriage Lines* and the fluffy, slightly high pitched but charming-as-Christmas Kate Starling to bring her [Prunella] well and truly into the limelight,' wrote Merrill Ferguson. 'This, from where we sit, is something like poetic justice in reverse. For Kate, whom we adore unstintingly, has always appeared to us as something of a twit, and Prunella is anything but.'

Prunella herself thought Kate Starling 'a much more efficient housewife than I am. But I don't really approve of her. I feel she is quite a nice girl, terribly sweet, but narrow.' Directed by Graeme Muir, the show was very much a lightweight reflection of contemporary life. Richard Briers played a bumbling, highly-strung husband, who dropped the words 'Sorry, darling' like confetti throughout each episode. Shirking the responsibilities that came with marriage, he was terrified when his wife had a baby, and got into trouble for being led astray by Miles, his somewhat louche friend, played by Edward de Souza. Timothy West made a passing appearance in one episode, with his character very firmly sent off to South Africa at the end of it. Richard Briers thinks the writer, Richard Waring, liked to keep tight control over his cast, and imbued the script with his own, somewhat chauvinistic, attitudes. When the sit-com was sold to Australia the local censors, fearing their viewers might be shocked by any faint suggestion of sex, insisted that the married couple were seen to be sleeping in single beds.

Rehearsals for each weekly episode were Tuesday to Friday from 10 a.m. until 1 p.m., then it was home to learn next day's part. For those performing in live theatre at night it was a chance to have a break. Saturday morning was a technical run-through. Sunday was a twelve-hour day on the set, with a slow, plotting stop-and-start until about 5 or 6, then a run-through, followed by a live performance in front of an invited audience in the evening, from 8 to 9.30. This would be taped and shown about a week later. Monday was a day off, to recover, and to give them time to begin learning the next week's episode.

Richard Briers found Sunday a very long, stressful and terrifying day. He said one of the worst things was that the audience would queue up outside the dressing-room windows, where the actors could hear their comments while they were waiting to be let in to the studio. It could be very off-putting. He didn't like the artificiality of the frenetic pre-show warm-up of the audience by the joke-telling compère, and he hated the loud jangling music that went with the show. 'The secret of good comedy is that you have to care about the people in it.'

Marriage Lines proved so popular that it eventually ran for forty-four episodes in five separate series over a period of five years. The first episode of the first series was shown on 16 August 1963, the tenth on 18 October. Eight days later Timothy and Prunella were married.

*   *   *

On her wedding day Prunella got up and walked north across Albert Bridge to wake up Timothy in Chelsea. The *Evening News* reported: 'Prunella Scales today stepped out of one marriage and into another. Only a few days after completing her part as the wife in the TV series *Marriage Lines*, she married Mr Timothy West at Chelsea Register Office.'

They decided to keep the wedding fairly low key. In 1963 there were still certain reservations about a divorced man remarrying, especially if the new bride had been thrust in to the public eye as an innocent young wife in a TV series. Timothy also felt that as his divorce was quite recent, it would be inappropriate to invite all their friends to a riotous celebration of a new marriage. Only Prunella's cousin, Stephen Kaye, and his friend Betty Turner were at the Chelsea Register Office as witnesses. Prunella's diary simply reads: 'Saturday 26th October, 12.00 wedding.'

Betty was a photographer whom Prunella had known and loved for many years and whose portraits she used professionally. She had introduced her to her cousin Stephen while he was still acting, and they had got on so well that they had moved into adjacent flats in Chelsea, not far from Cheyne Court. For the wedding Prunella wore a pink Jaeger dress with a checked coat, and a black fur hat borrowed from Melody Sachs, Andrew's wife. Afterwards Aunt Freda gave them a lunch at Prunier's, attended by the bride and groom, both sets of parents and the two witnesses.

Timothy was rehearsing in Robert Bolt's *Gentle Jack*, and Prunella was also working, so they could only manage a two-day honeymoon. Prunella collected Timothy after his rehearsal, and they drove to the Compleat Angler at Marlow because it was close and had a good restaurant. 'What we didn't know about it was that at that time it was a famous dirty weekend place, and it was the first *clean* weekend we had ever spent together.' No one in the hotel ever referred to Prunella as Mrs West. 'The "lady" is waiting for you in the lounge, sir.' Or, 'I think the "lady" has just gone upstairs, sir. Would you like to join her, or would you like a nightcap before you go up?' Prunella, respectable at last, was somewhat miffed.

7

'Why—do you want him here?'

'Tim was a dog person; I've always been a cat person, and soon after we married I said I wanted a cat. Tim, although in two minds about this, allowed me to acquire a cat from a farm belonging to friends of my parents, a ginger cat we called Lion. We took the cat with us to our cottage in Stratford when Tim was with the RSC and I was working in Birmingham, and as the cat was clearly unhappy about moving to Warwickshire, and seemed to adapt very poorly to touring, we were very nervous that he would try and walk back to London. One morning I was at the wash basin, Tim was in the bath, and a towel slipped off the rail behind his head into the water. Tim leapt out of the bath and said "Christ!" I asked him what was the matter. He looked round. "Oh, thank God. I thought it was the kitten committing suicide." I realized then that Tim had become a cat convert.'

*   *   *

With both of them working, Prunella and Tim decided they could afford somewhere larger than the flat in Lurline Gardens and found a small three-up-and-two-down terrace house in Barnes, at 18 Lillian Road, just south of Hammersmith Bridge. It was well situated and an easy walk across the bridge to the underground station. The house, fronting on to the road, was pretty, with a kitchen, a tiny garden and the use of a garage at the back. By knocking through an interior wall, they were able to make the two very small downstairs rooms into one larger one. They took out a mortgage, but Prunella's parents, who had lost so much money on the house they had bought with a loan in 1940, were very worried. 'All that debt hanging over you.' When in 1965, after working with the Royal Shakespeare Company in London, Timothy was invited to go with the company to Stratford for a season, Prunella got a job not too far away at the Birmingham Rep, playing Hermione in *The Winter's Tale*, and went too. 'We let the Barnes house, we couldn't afford not to, and found a cottage in a village called Tredington.'

At the end of 1965, to their great joy, Prunella became pregnant with Sam, who made his first stage appearance *in utero* in a Feydeau farce, *The Birdwatcher*, at the Hampstead Theatre Club. The director, Richard Cotterell, remembers this well because it was the first play he directed. Before rehearsals started he had carefully plotted all the moves. When, quite early on the first day of rehearsal, he asked Prunella to get up from her seat and move to the window, he was somewhat taken aback when she asked, 'Why?' Realizing an answer was imperative, Richard thought rapidly and suggested she was doing some tapestry and needed a better light to thread her needle. The motivation was accepted, but Richard said that when he went home after that first day, he sat up for the rest of the evening and into the night, justifying all the moves he had planned.

At the beginning of 1965, when the third series of *Marriage Lines*, in which Kate Starling had become pregnant, had been made, Prunella had worn padding

113

which expanded by the week. But now, in February 1966, when she was actually pregnant, the fifth series required that a second birth be written into the script. 'To my horror I found that Richard Waring had written an episode where Kate had had the baby and gone home. I said, "I'm not having a baby on television for anybody, and ours isn't due for another three or four weeks." ' Eventually the episode was rewritten so that the screen birth happened (off camera) before Prunella's due date. The last episode showed her coming home from hospital with the baby, but this posed a problem—the show was recorded live every week in front of an audience, and she was very obviously still pregnant. The author thought he had solved this by rewriting the episode to show Kate at home, sitting up in bed with her new baby in a cot beside her. When they rehearsed it, however, Prunella's large bump was still very evident, so they scooped a hole out of the mattress large enough for her to sink into, so that when filmed she looked flat. This, the last episode, went out live on 3 June 1966. Samuel Alexander Joseph was born at Queen Charlotte's Hospital on 19 June.

It was unusual at that time for fathers to be present during childbirth, but Timothy was determined, and was in fact one of the first fathers at Queen Charlotte's allowed to witness the birth of his child. It was a long labour. 'Tim was brilliant; he was reading to me, doing the *Times* crossword and talking.' After about twenty-nine hours, apparently with no birth imminent, Timothy decided he must go and get something to eat. No sooner had he left the building than Prunella went into full labour.

'Where's my husband?'

The nurse sounded surprised. "Why—do you want

114

him here?"

'Yes, that's the whole point.'

They rang the house in Barnes, where her parents were waiting for news. No Timothy. They rang his agent and a couple of other possible numbers. Still no Timothy. Then Prunella remembered that Richard Briers, her TV husband, lived only about 150 yards from the hospital, and as he was sometimes a drop-in refuge for expectant fathers, she suggested they ring him. Sure enough Timothy was there, listening to Al Jolson records and knocking back a few whiskies with Richard and his wife, and having one of those 'How dreadful it is what women have to go through' conversations. Prunella spoke to him herself. 'Get over here quick, it's happening!' Timothy raced across the road, was gowned up, and arrived in the labour ward just in time. As Sam popped out, Timothy said: 'Very good! No retakes.' Which, Prunella says, made her laugh so much she had to have stitches.

*   *   *

Prunella went back to work quite soon after Sam's birth, in a revue at the Yvonne Arnaud Theatre in Guildford called *Night is for Delight*. Given the uncertain nature of an actor's working life, both she and Timothy felt they had to take jobs when they became available; so childcare was essential, and they decided they must stretch their budget to cover the costs of an au pair. Rosie, the first of many, came from Aberdeen and had been recommended to Prunella by her own childhood nanny, Nan Patterson. When Prunella was working away from home, Rosie travelled with her and looked after Sam during rehearsals and performances. Because Prunella and

Timothy's work took them all over the country and sometimes overseas—and because neither of them liked the telephone—they again kept in touch by writing letters. Prunella wrote from Guildford to Timothy, who was at the Arts Theatre in Cambridge: 'Took Rosie to the show last night. I think she was dazed: everyone was sweet to her and sent up her accent and told her what lovely hair she had and she hardly stopped giggling all evening.'

Luckily for their finances, television commercials were well paid, although there was at that time a certain snobbery about 'real actors' making commercials. The *Daily Mirror* of March 1967 confided to its interested readers that there were an increasing number of 'legitimate' actors being used in advertisements. 'TV advertising, in fact, has become respectable. Among actors it has also started a whole new working concept. Now actors have realized that it can provide them with a reasonable bank balance allowing them to do the work they like, but which they could never ordinarily afford to do.' Prunella and Richard Briers, because of their *Marriage Lines* fame, were asked to star in a commercial for Mace supermarkets. The *Mirror* also noted, however, that Prunella would be 'taking a sabbatical into what the trade calls "the real theatre" '.

This was because towards the end of 1967 she was cast in 'real theatre' as the young flapper Jackie Coryton, in Noël Coward's *Hay Fever*. The cast was headed by Celia Johnson, Richard Vernon and Roland Culver, but as the play came in only a few years after Noël Coward's own production for the National Theatre, comparisons that were not always flattering were made. Noël Coward himself went along to see a run-through while they were rehearsing,

116

and 'when he shook hands with us afterwards I said that Lynn [Lynn Redgrave, who had played Jackie in his production] was a very hard act to follow. "Oh yes," he agreed as he passed on down the line, "*wasn't she good.*" ' However, Prunella received good notices for her performance, 'as the frightened rabbit of a shy, hunched-shoulder flapper'. The play did a pre-London tour, Prunella taking Sam and Rosie along with her. Before the opening in Brighton, she wrote to Timothy to say that because of some unexpected visitors who had stayed the night, 'I had to sleep with Sam, who wakes at six and sings and makes plughole noises for an hour, and Rosie, who snores very gently all through it, and what with that and a really appalling hangover, didn't think I'd be able to open at all. But caught up just in time, and it was OK I think, though will be better and haven't seen any notices yet.'

'Friday. I must cook pap and two veg. for Rosie and Sam. We're living a very "Look Back in Anger" existence with the clotheshorse the salient feature of the room, and in a way thank God you missed it. But Sam is being pretty ravishing and has settled down v. well. He sings rather loudly from 7 a.m. on, which is not very engaging, and I swear has woken me up every morning by sheer hypnotism through the bars of his cot.'

Prunella drove up to Edinburgh with Rosie and Sam for the next date, in such a strong headwind that she thought the car had broken down because it went so slowly. They were staying in Edinburgh with her ex-boyfriend Bill Blackwood and his family, and she told Timothy: 'It's like the next Pinter play—Mrs B bedridden upstairs, Nurse on the ground floor, Bill in the garage and Kate the cook in the basement, and

117

nobody speaks to anyone except to complain about the others. The only thing that really works is a Dolland aneroid barometer in the hall c.1870.'

In Glasgow she encountered 'full houses here and sycophantic notices. Sam and Rosie went off safely yesterday [to Rosie's family in Aberdeen]. Sam distressingly jovial, I was nearly in tears . . . Spent yesterday in bed mostly asleep and felt alarmingly fresh and energetic and *normal* for the show, makes one realize how "sub" one is generally: is this to continue until Sam is grown up? Will I never be able to bring full energy and concentration to a part? Perhaps marriage/babies are incompatible with work, am I giving less than full value, I seem to have felt tired for months, it's all so *unfair.*'

Prunella, playing a triple role of wife, mother and actress, was exhausted. In the 1960s mothers were still generally expected to stay at home, and when challenged about this, she admitted that in an ideal world women should stay with their children for the first five years of their life. 'But you can't if you're working. What should women do?' What she did do, very successfully, was engage a series of au pairs, such as Rosie, all through the time the children were growing up, so that even when she was working they always had the security of being with someone they knew. But when Sam was very young she insisted on taking him with her whenever possible. So when in January 1968 the management took *Hay Fever* to Canada for two weeks, one-and-a-half-year-old Sam went along too, together with the new German au pair, Jutta. The long flight was an ordeal for them all.

'Oh goodness dearie me. Well we were *eight hours* on that plane and I hardly stopped being frightened for one minute. In fact a very good flight and a beautiful landing—but we took off at two and lunch didn't arrive till HALF PAST THREE, by which time Sam, who had remained remarkably cheerful and winsome, was so crazed with hunger that he couldn't eat and had to be forcibly fed between screams. The prescribed teaspoonful of sedative failed to have any effect at all but eventually Sam slept for about 3/4 hour. Otherwise constant yell. Everyone very nice about it. Even Roland Culver only said, "This aeroplane is more like a school bus." When we arrived Sam was a good deal photographed perched on piles of luggage scowling at Celia Johnson, so I hope he's sold a few seats.' At the end of the first week Prunella told Timothy, 'Sam is being angelic and has learnt a lot of new words, one of which I am afraid is "elevator".'

Two days later she wrote again: 'Weather has been very dramatic. The first Sunday it was so cold the cars were all wrapped in frozen rain like polythene—when you opened a door it shattered like the toffee on a toffee-apple. Then the Monday it snowed very heavily in the morning and stopped magically for the dress rehearsal, leaving all the little cherry trees on the sidewalks encrusted with ice, and looking incredibly valuable. Fantastically efficient clearance of the main streets, and now you'd hardly know, and it's not much colder than at home.'

Prunella tells a story of one of the times when both she and Timothy were at home together. 'It was then,' she says, 'we learnt to close the curtains of our front room. When Sam was a baby we usually never bothered. One evening Timothy was trying on his costume for a play in which he had to dress as a woman; so there was Timothy in drag being advised by me how to put on his make-up, and me stripped to the

119

waist feeding Sam. We got some very strange looks from the neighbours.'

*   *   *

In the summer of 1968 Prunella was at the Chichester Festival, playing the title role in Peter Ustinov's *The Unknown Soldier and his Wife*. Timothy was working in London in the play *The Italian Girl*, but spent most of his days in Chichester, where Prunella, Sam and the mother's help were staying in a small rented cottage. 'One evening Peter Ustinov came to dinner. The cottage ceilings were very low and Peter was quite tall, so when he stood in the middle of the small front room, the red lampshade covered his head like a fez. When I came in from the kitchen with the vegetables he announced in a thick accent, "I wish to apply for the Turkish Rights." '

Just before they opened there was a photo-call on stage. When the photographer asked Prunella to come to the edge of a rostrum for a shot, 'I refused as I felt a bit giddy, and suddenly realized I was pregnant again.' Knowing that their house in Barnes would not be big enough for four of them and an au pair, she and Timothy began to look for something larger. One day while driving home from a friend's house in Wandsworth, Prunella saw a tall, thin, four-storey Victorian house on the South Circular Road. She and Timothy thought it looked very promising. The house, which was divided into four flats, was owned by a retiring grocer who told them it had been in his family for two generations. Prunella was worried that it was far too big, but Timothy decided it was what they needed. They sold the Barnes house at a profit, and with that, a mortgage, and a loan from cousin Stephen,

120

they were able to buy the house in Wandsworth. It needed a lot of work to restore it, and while the work was being done Prunella and Timothy camped in the basement, Sam and the au pair lived on the top floor, and the workmen took over all the spaces in between. The essential work lasted about six months, but it took much longer than that to finish it all. Prunella says it took them thirty-one years to pay off the mortgage.

Timothy and Prunella's second son, Joseph, was born on 1 January 1969 at King's College Hospital in Denmark Hill. This time the birth was much quicker, lasting only eight hours. On reflection Prunella doesn't recommend having a baby on New Year's Day: 'The staff are likely to be off with a hangover, and forever after you have to have this ghastly New Year's Day tea party with a hangover yourself.' She remembers there was a marked contrast in the way the births of the two boys were registered. 'Following Sam's birth at Queen Charlotte's Hospital a very elegant man in striped trousers and dark jacket knocked and came in. "Good morning Mrs, er . . ." he looked at his list, "West." Many congratulations on the birth of your, um, son. When you and your husband have decided on a name would you mind coming down to the office and registering him?" So this we duly did, and got a very posh birth certificate from Queen Charlotte's hospital. By the time I was pregnant with Joe, our gynaecologist, Richard, had moved south to King's College Hospital in Denmark Hill, a large and very busy hospital in, at that time, quite a rough area. I was in a very big ward, and it was a less rarefied atmosphere than Queen Charlotte's. After Joe's birth a typed slip was sent to me at home saying, "Please register your child without fail by such and such a date." So I tottered down to Denmark Hill between feeds, and went into the Nissen hut beside the hospital, into an office full of tables where I stood in a queue. I sat down at the next available table and the Registrar asked: "When was baby born?"

' "New Year's Day." I said proudly.

' "Oh yes," she said. "That would be January the . . . ?"

'I said "First."

'Her next question. "Are you married to baby's father?"

' "Yes."

' "What are you going to call baby?"

' "Joseph John Lancaster."

' "How are you spelling that?"

'I dictated all the names.

' "And it's a little . . . ?"

' "Boy."

'At which point, I'm afraid, I collapsed in giggles.'

*   *   *

Two weeks after the baby was born Prunella wrote to Timothy, who was on tour: 'Joseph is coming along splendidly as far as one can tell. I'm doing the night feed as well now, he doesn't seem to fancy bottles. Sam is very jealous, as expected, but very sweet with him.' She had asked Sam if he would like to hold Joseph and Sam had said yes: 'For 30 seconds it was all magic—then Sam got bored and said "Here-you-are" and *threw* him back. He says "Joseph will go away very soon" quite often; also "When is he going back inside your tummy?" But it is all so manifest that I think it should settle eventually.'

With two children her life became even more hectic. It was not so easy to take them both with her when she was on tour, and Sam, who had been used to going everywhere with her, remembers this as unsettling. 'I had two and a half years on my own, by the time Joe came along Ma and I had established a working pattern.' It did to a certain extent limit the work Prunella was able to do, because she felt very strongly that she should be there as much as possible while the children were small. 'Being an actress and being a mother is a strain, especially if you think that being a mother is as important as I do. It was all right with one baby, but with two, that was when the guilt started. If you're in a play you have to hold something back of yourself for that play. It's like carrying a baby; it takes some of your strength; you have to give to *it* as well as to your family. Of course you could say that you shouldn't take on a play like that, but if it's offered, and is good enough, you have to do it.'

Timothy's parents, Harry and Olla, both actors, were unable to help with childcare; not only was their house too small, but they were both still working. Prunella's parents were too frail to cope with the children on their own, and she was becoming concerned about them. Her mother had had a heart attack in 1965, and although she had recovered it had made her very much less mobile and she found it difficult to get up and down stairs. Her father was also not well, and had had to retire; their pensions were small and it was hard for them to make ends meet. However, her parents loved having the children to stay, and were able to cope for short periods as long as the au pair was with them. Sam says there seemed to be a lot of au pairs. 'There were a lot of people coming in and out of my life. I was quite a handful and very active. We had some madly good and some madly strange ones. One only lasted one day. Joe and I tried to get together to try *not* to get rid of them. It was an unfortunate necessity, but it is quite strange, that sort of relationship. It didn't make for much continuity.'

Joe also remembers the various au pairs very well and says they never blended together. 'You learn different people, like learning different languages. You don't mix them up.' Joe has very fond memories of growing up in the house in Wandsworth. He remembers sounds from his childhood: the clicking noise of the drawer handles on Prunella's dressing-table while she was putting on make-up, and the sounds of different doors closing. He can also remember the smell of Timothy's cigar smoke, even though Timothy hasn't smoked for over fifteen years.

*   *   *

For much of the time when the children were very small, Timothy was away touring with the thirty-strong Prospect Theatre Company. In 1969 they were doing Shakespeare's *Richard II* and Marlowe's *Edward II*, and later they took *Richard II* to Vienna and then to Bratislava. It was difficult for Prunella. While they were apart she and Timothy wrote to each other at least once a week. Prunella's letters contain family news; how the boys are doing, how she is coping at home, and occasionally, if she had been able to get to see a performance, encouragement and advice for Timothy. At the end of February 1969, when Joe was barely two months old and Sam two-and-three-quarters, she wrote: 'Thank you for the v. generous cheques, it is churlish of me to bind about being overdrawn when you are helping so much.' With two children, an au pair, and an old house to refurbish, there were clearly pressing financial reasons to go

124

back to work. In the same letter she told Timothy she had been sent 'the Willis Hall script again [*Children's Day*], offering re-written lead, so I'm looking at it. Starting, guess when, end of April.'

She took the part in *Children's Day*, and in March wrote to Timothy to give him their touring schedule. 'Very glad to hear the "Richard" went well, shall try and ring tonight or tomorrow to hear more. Is the company nice? The boys are blooming, Joseph likes standing up best. Hates sitting, but stands propped against people or furniture for hours on end.' On 22 April she wrote again: 'Herewith gas bill, which though not as much as you thought is still pretty shattering: I promise the next one won't be as bad, I've got everything off most of the time now. BUT—I'm afraid I can't pay it, nor Harvey's, which I also enclose. Don't know *what* we're going to do for money. Have heard nothing about Tetleys.'

Luckily the Tetley commercial came through. As part of the agreement a very large box of complimentary tea bags arrived in Wandsworth. Timothy, who was at home, undid the large box, then all the smaller boxes within the large box, and so on and so on, like dismantling a Russian doll, until he got down to the individual tea bags. These he proceeded to hide around the house in drawers, cupboards and among Prunella's clothes, so that for quite a while every time she opened anything another tea bag fell out.

Even though Prunella was almost constantly in work, which must have been exhausting with two small children, money remained a worry. As well as everyday living costs there were other expenses: she was giving her parents £5 a week towards their rent and paying her au pair £9 a week. She told her accountant in June: 'I can't get anyone for less, and if I have nobody, it means that I can never accept any work again. As you can see I am going through a bad patch, and things are pretty desperate. Unless I can get something good in late September we shall probably have to sell the car. But of course that would curtail our lives considerably, both professionally and domestically, and we hope it won't come to that.' In two months' time, she told him, she would be rehearsing a new play for four weeks, for which she would be paid £7 a week rehearsal money, and £30 to £40 a week when it opened in September. Temporarily out of work when she wrote, she had an overdraft, though she was hoping for two broadcasts in July for £31. 10s. each. In August she wrote to Timothy: 'Boys are well—Joseph eats a good deal of eggshells, like a terrible old hen, I suppose it's calcium deficiency.' She was still concerned about money. 'Would welcome suggestions about cutting down. Shall stay in digs in Cheltenham, not buy any more plants for the garden, etc. etc., but short of sacking Jane [the current au pair] and selling the children I don't know what else I can do. I feel a frightful failure . . . very depressed about it all. It seems so easy to get into debt, and so cripplingly hard to climb out of it.'

By September she was much more cheerful, as the cheque for a commercial had come through and she was busy paying bills. With neither of them earning a regular income, financial anxiety seems to have dogged their early married life. Juliet, Timothy's daughter by his first marriage, was now nine and living with her mother in a flat in her grandmother's house in Putney. She would sometimes come to stay with them in Wandsworth, especially when her mother was ill, and Prunella welcomed her with open arms. She loved having another female in the house, and Juliet looked on her as an extra mother. When she was old enough Juliet was sent to Mayfield Comprehensive School in Wandsworth, but it was large and impersonal and she wasn't very happy there. Her grandmother thought it would be a good idea for her to have the benefit and security of boarding-school during term-time, and Juliet herself decided that she wanted to go to Moira House. Although Prunella thought it might be hard for her to go to a school where both her stepmother and stepgrandmother had been, Juliet was determined. To Moira House she went, and loved it. The school was still small, with only 150 pupils, ninety of whom were boarders, and Juliet says it was a friendly, caring place. Like Prunella before her, she loved the feeling it gave her of belonging somewhere.

When her mother married again and went to live in Wales, Juliet was fourteen. After some discussion between both families, it was agreed that Juliet would come and live with Timothy and Prunella in Wandsworth in the school holidays. She was quite independent and much older than the boys—eleven years older than Joe and nine years older than Sam— and although she got on well with them, she also enjoyed the company of the au pairs, who were nearer to her age. She says she always found Prunella a wonderful listener if she, or any of her friends, needed advice.

*   *   *

Wherever possible Prunella and Timothy tried to be together. In January 1971, when Timothy was filming in Madrid and earning much better money, Prunella was able to take the boys to join him for a holiday. ' 'Spect you'll still be shooting, but we'll talk about that. If by any chance you get this in reasonable time, have you thought of somewhere to dry sheets, pyjamas, etc. in the apartment. Will bring disposable nappies for Jo-jo, but some sort of radiator (or reasonably adjacent laundrette) would be helpful.' If it wasn't school-time they always tried to take the boys and, if she was free, Juliet, with them when they went away, especially in the summer holidays. If it was term-time the boys would stay with the current au pair, and Juliet at her boarding-school. Sam remembers, 'There were quite long periods at primary school when I didn't see Ma, when she was touring.'

In 1972 Prunella and Timothy went to Australia together, with the Prospect Theatre Company's productions of *King Lear* and *Love's Labour's Lost*, in which Prunella played the Princess of France. They took with them Sam, seven, Joseph, five, and Kelly, the au pair. They opened at the Adelaide Festival, then went on to Sydney and Melbourne. It was the first time Prunella had been to Australia and she loved it—not to mention working with Timothy and having the family all together. There was no need now for letters.

Another time, when Timothy was filming in Luxembourg, Prunella took the boys out to join him and then brought them back via France. Joe remembers it well. 'For one half term she took us to Paris, Strasbourg and Luxembourg and we stayed in fairly cheap, dusty, elegant European hotels. I really liked travelling, it was very interesting. We went to Jordan, Egypt, and the US and Australia twice.'

The boys were at an age when they argued relentlessly and loudly. Eventually Prunella found a way to dampen it down: 'One morning when they were fighting I said quite matter-of-factly, "Listen, Daddy has got to go to work, so I'm going to shut the door on you and you can sort it out. If you hurt each other I'll take you to hospital, but I am very very *bored* with this going on, and Daddy and I want to have our breakfast." So I left them, shut the door, and went into the kitchen. There was barely a sound after that, just a few squeals, and after a while they came in and sat down quietly and had their breakfast, and it was much, *much* better after that. I may have read this in a book, but I gathered that half their rows were for attention, so if you let them realize that you are not interested then they don't do it any more.'

Although they were increasingly in the public eye they always tried to keep the children away from publicity. When Sam was about eight he asked Prunella at breakfast one day if he had to be an actor. 'No, of course not, of course you don't. What would you like to do?' 'I really want to be a professor of chemistry.' He later changed his mind.

Prunella's father died in 1978 following a stroke, but her mother, who could still manage on her own, had stayed on in their rented Surrey cottage. When she, too, had a stroke in 1980 it left her paralysed on her right side. Sadly, for one who so loved words, the stroke affected her speech, though being very determined, she taught herself to write with her left hand. Prunella had to put up with insensitive comments from some of the neighbours in the village, wondering why she didn't go home to look after her mother. 'They had no idea what it was like not to have money. I was the only reason my parents could pay their rent. If I'd stopped working and come home to be with them, they couldn't have afforded anywhere to

129

live.' When her mother had a further stroke in 1981, and was no longer able to cope at home, Prunella and her brother Timmo found a local care home where her friends could continue to visit her. Prunella went down there as often as she could.

In 1982 she wrote to her school friend Veronica Conyers (Goldschmidt) to tell her that Bim had died. 'Our darling Ma died on November 5th after a final stroke ten days earlier—one couldn't hope for her to carry on, she was helpless and almost blind. She'd coped with a wheelchair for almost two years, and been in a nursing home for twelve months . . . One mustn't be too sad, but we shall miss her dreadfully.'

8

'There's more than a streak of exhibitionist in me, I find'

'There may be times, of course, when you're doing a job and don't necessarily respect the writing, or you don't agree with the director about something, or you are badly cast, so you can't identify with it as closely as you would like, or the costume isn't right, or the audience on that night are unsympathetic to the play—all these things can conspire against you. But you have to rise above this situation; whether you are acting or directing, you're there to deliver the writer's work to the people who have paid to see it.'

*　　　*　　　*

Though Prunella was not entirely happy with *Children's Day*, it did well enough to go in to the Mermaid theatre in London in 1969. The critics were impressed by the energy, if not by the script. One critic wrote: 'In this furiously paced farce, four of the seven characters are so busy being wittily turned on—that I couldn't believe in them as people who had married, had kids and were now on the verge of divorce.' Robert Tanitch thought the play had faults and was being played too much for laughs. 'As it stands now the best thing is Prunella Scales listing the silly things very young children do, which is both funny and true.' Since in many ways the play reflected her own situation, this was perhaps unsurprising.

Reading through her CV it seems to me almost impossible to analyse the numerous play, film and television parts Prunella has played throughout her life. She seems to be able to switch effortlessly between generations, between different social backgrounds, and from classical roles to comedy and farce. I ask Sam what makes her acting different. He suggests one good reason. 'It is hard to categorize her—which normally doesn't make for success. It's not always a good idea as an actor to be good at a number of things, particularly nowadays. But her own taste has been very helpful because she's never wanted to be pinned down. I think one of the things she does is not commenting on characters, but always playing them from their own point of view.'

A part she played in 1970 confronted difficulties in marriage, but of a very divisive nature. In *It's a Two Foot Six Inches Above the Ground World*, by Kevin Laffan, she played a long-suffering Catholic wife, Esther Goonahan. Almost constantly pregnant since her marriage, she has had five miscarriages and three surviving children. In desperation, she has been to a family planning clinic and gone on the pill. The resulting conflict when her husband—and the priest—discover what she has been driven to do is the moral core of the play. 'Kevin Laffan has something serious to say about Catholics and the Pill and I should have preferred it to be much more serious, much more Irish, much more Catholic, much more working class, much more Lawrentian,' wrote Robert Tanitch. 'The ignorance, the naïveté, and the interference of the Church and the dilemma of a practising Catholic would then have had a dramatic impact . . . It seems to me that Prunella Scales is acting in the play one would have liked *It's a Two Foot Six Inches Above the Ground*

World to be, but that everybody else is acting in the play that the management has decided that it is going to be.'

Because of the central, and somewhat contentious, argument for birth control, this brave play created a lot of controversy. Prunella wrote to Timothy: 'Very depressed tonight, not a good house, doing my best but not getting much back, probably overdoing it, but how can one tell when the director hasn't been near us.' She added a note at 10.15: 'They improved and enjoyed Act II. Feel better.'

While playing the guilt-ridden Catholic wife in the evenings, she was also playing a scatty, come-dancing wife, in a lunchtime production of Tom Stoppard's *After Magritte*, which must have provided some welcome light relief. She wrote to Timothy in April 1970 after a photo-shoot: '*Paris Match* was great fun, they had me (photographed) full length on the table in my black knickers (and corsage I hasten to add)—there's more than a streak of exhibitionist in me, I find.'

*   *   *

When the Prospect Theatre Company, with which Timothy was much involved, grew larger and finally ended up at the Old Vic, a smaller company, the Cambridge Theatre Company was formed as a spin-off in 1970 with Richard Cotterell as the director. Prunella was to work there later that year—based in Cambridge, it also provided medium-scale touring to other regional centres. In October 1971 she was cast as Natasha in the *Three Sisters* and as Avonia Bunn in *Trelawny of the Wells*; she wrote to Timothy: 'Three Sisters unimaginably difficult, specially my part, but I think we're all feeling that. I'm suffering a refined form of the "Spear-in-the-upstage-hand-Jeremy-darling" torture: because Natasha's a boring provincial insensitive neo-comic character, I feel like a boring provincial insensitive neo-comic actress who's being left to get on with it, and really has no bearing on the vital emotional and intellectual Soul of The Play. Sheer paranoia. Richard is being as helpful as ever but Christ it's difficult.' Richard Cottrell said, 'She was perfect as Natasha. The best Natasha I have ever seen. She wasn't nasty, she was just unrelentingly practical, which came across as very nasty. Of course she sweeps into that play taking over people's lives and it is logical because they are not looking after their own lives anyway, and they are ripe for take-over, poor things.'

Sometimes the set designer could make things very much harder. Prunella wrote to Timothy in October, 'Yes, well—we rehearsed for a month and a lot of creative work was done and it was all I suspect rather GOOD, and then we get in last Monday and there was the North Face of Mont Blanc built in tongue-and-groove on the stage of the Ashcroft Theatre in Croydon. You need crampons to stand up on it, let alone walk, and all the ghastly furniture keeps falling over, and the cutlery and glasses slide into the auditorium with a monotonous tinkle in the finest Tchekovian tradition. Richard, I know, shocked and furious, but didn't *say so to the company*, who, after behaving with Alpine heroism and sangfroid throughout the opening, are now beginning to murmur and disintegrate.' After Croydon they played Birmingham, Southampton, Norwich and Cambridge, but luckily as the tour went on the rake was modified and things improved for the cast.

Not only was the stage too steep for comfort, it was

134

very noisy. 'Every move on it sends Bongo-like reverberations throughout the home counties, and it's awfully difficult for the cast to hear each other.' Kelly, Prunella's current au pair, had gastroenteritis, which added to the problems. 'I've lost hours of sleep, up at 4.00 for days on end and the show at night and both plays to rehearse, it's ridiculous. Generally get 1½ hours kip before the performance which helps. Must stop and go to a Trelawny rehearsal.' Ten days later *Three Sisters* is going better. I feel confused by Natasha rather, but everyone continues to be delighted so perhaps I'll expand into it. I'm loathing Trelawny.'

Trelawny was one of the first plays in which six-year-old Sam ever saw his mother acting, and he was impressed. He came round to her dressing-room afterwards: 'Mummy, you're very good in *Trelawny of the Wells*—are you good in *Three Sisters* as well?' The critics agreed with Sam. In Cambridge Michael Grosvenor-Myer wrote: 'The performance of the evening comes from Prunella Scales. Her superb timing and sensitive delivery make of the vulgar but good-hearted Avonia Bunn a woman of moving warmth and affection.'

In September 1972 Prunella joined Richard Eyre's company for a season of plays at the Nottingham Playhouse. She played Katherine in *The Taming of the Shrew*, which rehearsed for three weeks followed by a three-week run, and later in the season directed *Major Barbara*, with John Phillips as Undershaft and Tom Wilkinson as Adolphus. This was one of the first plays she had been asked to direct. She says, humbly, that the result was OK, although because she cares more about the play than about making her mark, she may not make a very sensational director. She enjoys directing very much. 'You can have an input into lots of parts for which you're completely unsuitable; like very young parts if you're much older, or parts played by men. You can say things about the play which, as a woman, you couldn't possibly say or embody. You can feed into the production your perceptions of life which you couldn't use in your own performances. I think I can direct quite well because the Stanislavskian training I have undergone helps me to help actors. I'm concerned about the inner life of the actors and inner life of the play, rather than about "production values".'

Another play Prunella directed was *Lady Windermere's Fan* at the Palace Theatre, Watford, in September 1985, and in November 1986 she played the seasoned actress Madame Arkadina in *The Seagull* at the same theatre, in a new translation of the play by Michael Frayn. The *Times* critic, Irving Wardle, had nothing but praise for her performance. 'One mainstay throughout the production is Miss Scales's Arkadina, a brusque business-like presence, every inch the star performer on holiday. The finale may be a disappointment; but not the last sight of Miss Scales cheerfully whistling a French tune at the Lotto table while Trigorin delays the moment of breaking the news of her son's death.' John Peter in the *Sunday Times* called the production 'jewel-like'. He described the setting 'as a world full of painfully ordinary people. Prunella Scales's Arkadina is not a theatrical *grand dame* but merely a conceited and quietly insufferable woman. Her plea to Trigorin is not so much a sentimental performance as a coolly conducted attack: the continuation of bullying by other means.' Another reviewer, Peter Kemp, was also impressed by the production. 'Prunella Scales turns her [Arkadina] into a convincing prodigy of artificial verve. Her voice audibly relishing its own virtuosity—with little tricks of emphasis and intonation—is that of the seasoned professional. Her repertoire of physical resourcefulness, constantly attracting attention to herself by elegant fidgetings, is that of the practised actress. But behind it all, you are never allowed to forget, lies insecurity.'

Prunella's versatility was shown when, shortly after the making of *Fawlty Towers* in 1976, she played six separate women in one play. *Anatol* was adapted by Frank Marcus from six original sketches by Arthur Schnitzler, chronicling the main character's hypocritical attempts to seduce six women during a series of intimate dinners. Derek Godfrey played Anatol, and Prunella played Cora, Gabrielle, Bianca, Annie, Elsa and Ilona. Robert Cushman wrote of her performance: 'She distinguishes them magnificently, the brisk *ingénue*, from the fastidious *bourgeoise*, the masterful, breathily enchanting circus-rider, from the delicately emotional wife, trying to focus and hold on to some finer feeling. Only once does she resort to caricature in an effort to find a new character; but the variables in the performance are ultimately less important than its common factor, which is vitality. The actress is continually alight.'

At the beginning of 1977 a new play by Terence Frisby, *It's All Right If I Do It*, took an outspoken look at the problems of staying married. A couple, played by Prunella and John Stride, accuse each other of various sexual infidelities during their fifteen-year marriage. An 'adults only' play, it had mixed reviews. Some critics found it distasteful that Prunella, whom they associated with *Marriage Lines* and *Fawlty Towers*, used 'the language of the bar room to describe her last sex exploit'. Others found it sad, honest and extremely sophisticated, but, Prunella says, 'my mother found it deeply shocking'. She is not at all worried about doing unsavoury parts; she says 'it all depends on what the author is trying to say. I would have a go at anything, but it is nice to be able to bit a bit more selective. I'm always longing for a controversial play to come up, and it doesn't matter how sympathetic or unsympathetic the part is if the play is worthwhile. It is all to do with the play, and if you think you could play the part for the good of the play, hooray.'

When, two years later, the Old Vic Company put on a production of *What the Butler Saw*, the black comedy by Joe Orton, Jack Tinker noted in the *Daily Mail*: 'The cast acquit themselves splendidly. Prunella Scales, as the psychiatrist's nymphomaniac wife, manages Orton's dangerous blend of fecund allure and feminine authority to a dazzling perfection.'

Prunella was in 'a rather edgy comedy', *Make and Break*, in April 1980, written by Michael Frayn and directed by Michael Blakemore. Leonard Rossiter played the lead, as a frenetic and ruthless entrepreneur who cannot take his mind off his work; Prunella his much put-upon secretary, Mrs Rogers, who for the first half sits impassively behind her desk at the Trade Fair. Prunella says, 'Leonard Rossiter led the company brilliantly—never let his own performance deteriorate and was rigorous with everybody else. If you slackened pace he had a quite salutary habit of coming in regardless, so if you weren't careful you lost the last line of your speech.' B.A. Young, in the *Financial Times*, wrote: 'I wondered why Prunella Scales was cast in such a static part; but when she comes out of her slot to dine and dally with her boss, for whom she has a secret liking, all is made plain. Her blend of simplicity, efficiency and affection adds up to a lovely performance.'

*   *   *

In December 1980, Prunella wrote to Veronica in America, 'We shall be in Australia in March. I'm in a success at the Haymarket for only the 2nd time in my life, but we close on Jan 24th and I fly to Hong Kong on Jan 25th to join Tim for *The Merchant of Venice*. He's playing Shylock, and I'm taking over Portia— positively my last fling as a juvenile. Can't help looking forward to it though.' From Hong Kong they took *The Merchant of Venice* to Australia, where they opened at the Perth Festival, followed by a ten-week tour. Sam and Joe went with them, plus the *au pair*. 'We took the boys with us whenever we could, and spent most of our income that way.'

Prunella had now been to Australia several times and loved it. She had worked there first with the Prospect Theatre Company in 1972, and again with the whole family in 1982, when Timothy was director-in-residence for one term at the University of Western Australia and she directed him in *Uncle Vanya* at the Playhouse, for the National Theatre of Western Australia. 'We were lucky to have been able to afford to take the kids with us on these tours, nowadays young actors can't possibly afford it and everything suffers: work, partnerships, as well as the children. At Edinburgh in 1971 we were actually staying in the student hostel adjoining the theatre, and the kids were able to watch Tim in *King Lear* from the gallery, standing up in their pyjamas.'

On 30 July 1981 she apologised to Veronica for not writing sooner. 'I've just opened in a new Simon Gray

139

play at the Queen's Theatre. It is directed by Harold Pinter, who is a SLAVE–DRIVER, though wonderful, and I have got behind with everything. Just surfacing now, the notices have been splendid and we hope to run for a bit, though of course you never know now, people are very careful with their money.' The play, *Quartermaine's Terms*, was indeed a success. Douglas Orgil in the *Daily Express*: 'Language is supposed to be the means by which we communicate. In this splendid play, Simon Gray demonstrates how language can cloud issues and separate people . . . In a fine cast Prunella Scales conveys the quiet desperation of her spinsterhood.' Jack Tinker added in the *Daily Mail*: 'Prunella Scales has several wonderful moments along the related path of her mother's slow, vengeful journey to the grave.' Robert Tanitch summarized her character as a 'spinster who cannot cope with her malevolent invalid mother and pushes her down the stairs to her death, then turns to religion and drink'. Prunella says 'it was a very happy job'.

In late November 1983, while working at the Midlands Arts Centre in Birmingham, she wrote to Timothy from 'one of those only *fairly* naff hotels full of broadcasting personnel having b&b, where once you've adjusted to the strip lighting and the smell of floral contract carpet, you find that they *do* have room service as long as you're only on the first floor and make the waitress a cup of tea before she starts off down again'. She had a bad cold which precipitated 'the most cataclysmic professional mishap of my career'. A bottle of Benylin cough mixture broke inside her make-up case when it fell off the shelf in her dressing-room. 'Time between rehearsal and show spent trying to clean shower-cap, powder puff, make up brushes and plastic bags full of cotton wool and kleenex. Benylin infested false eyelashes defy description, also it managed to get inside both lipsticks, don't want to write about that either.'

The following September she and Timothy were in a farce by Bamber Gascoigne, *Big in Brazil*, at the Old Vic, in which Prunella played a small-time Huddersfield actress, Daisy Wray, pretending to be the famous actress Mrs Patrick Campbell. The play had somewhat mixed reviews.

*   *   *

In December 1984, Prunella wrote to Veronica, 'I'm off to Australia for four weeks of *Queen Victoria* [the recital programme with Ian Partridge and Richard Burnett] in January, then home for five more episodes of *Mapp and Lucia*—the first five start going out in January. Not going to send you a photo of myself in the role of Mapp, I have perfectly globular padding and look revolting. Do you know the books? Published first in 1935, E.F. Benson. V. English. I'm playing it like a combination of Mona and Knotty, with bits of E.T. thrown in [these were some of Prunella and Veronica's teachers at Moira House].'

The first series of *Mapp and Lucia* was recorded for television in 1984. Prunella played Miss Mapp, with Geraldine McEwan as Lucia, and Nigel Hawthorne as Georgie. Geraldine McEwan says it was a wonderful cast to work with. 'We quickly developed a relationship with the characters we were playing and a good working relationship with each other. There were lots of laughs.' Her character, Lucia, is quite unjustifiably proud of her skill on the piano, which she plays indifferently. Geraldine, however, doesn't play the piano at all, so she and Nigel Hawthorne, who had

141

to play duets together, had tutoring to give them the necessary basics. To help her look as though she was playing the right notes, she put numbers on the piano keys, and she and Nigel would try to outwit each other in rehearsals.

The novels, set in England in the 1920s, depict a small-town society, largely made up of self-obsessed, gossipy and competitive middle-aged women, their ineffectual husbands and strange friends. Mapp and Lucia, each determined to control the small society in which they live, play a fierce game of one-upmanship. The author of the novels, E.F. Benson, said: 'Miss Mapp looks forty and takes advantage of that fact by being just a few years older.' Prunella described Mapp as a traditional country lady. 'She paints little landscapes, holds jumble sales, makes jam and bottles fruit. She patronizes everybody and would like Lucia for a friend—if she could still be top dog. She is extraordinarily large and her face is like a relief map—it's not very flattering really, is it? I had to wear lots of padding for the part—very uncomfortable when you're filming in midsummer.' She also found that when encumbered by this unfamiliar bulk it was quite hard to get through some of the very narrow doorways in Rye, where parts of the series were filmed.

She remembers it as a happy show. 'I weighed myself after the eighteen months of filming in the padding, and because I hadn't had to bother I'd put on about two stone, and had to go on a diet.' Timothy particularly enjoyed visiting her during the filming. 'You couldn't actually be sure about the people walking about in the street—if they were in the show, or if they were just residents of Rye—because they hadn't changed all that much.' He thinks the people in Rye tended to walk in a particular way because of the cobbled streets. 'They dug the outside of their shoes into the cobbles which gave them an appearance of bow-leggedness.' Prunella herself told an interviewer: 'I went into a shop the other day fully dressed as Miss Mapp to buy some crochet cotton and no one took a blind bit of notice. I was just like one of the inhabitants.'

The town of Tilling, where Mapp and Lucia live, is modelled on Rye, where E.F. Benson had once been Mayor. Outside shots were filmed there, interiors in the London Weekend Television studios in London. The first five episodes went out early in 1985 and were so successful that a second series was commissioned.

The white wisteria which drapes the front of the Wests' house in Wandsworth originated from Rye. While they were filming, Prunella saw it growing on one of the houses and told the owner how much she liked it. In between shots, the lady rushed out and pressed the name of the garden supplier into her hand.

The *Daily Mail* called the show 'The most delicate, delightful double act on television . . . the pure, small town British bitchery of Mapp and Lucia. The story is about the small enclosed world of a genteel middle-class town where everyone has some pretensions and is determined to catch the other person out. Mapp is the reigning queen, head of the pecking order—until the more stylish Lucia rents her home for a holiday, and stays on to grab all her status too.' The books and television series considerably exaggerated the bitchiness and self-obsession of the inhabitants, so that they became funny, but it seems there remained a good deal of truth in Benson's observations of the town. There is an active Tilling Society in Rye, some of whose members are extremely protective of

E.F. Benson and his characters. One day, at the start of filming, when they were just setting up the shots in the street for Geraldine and Prunella, a front door suddenly opened; one of the members of the Tilling Society put her head out and said to them fiercely, 'I hope you are going to get it *right*. We were rather hoping that Penelope Keith and Maggie Smith were going to play the parts—but I expect that you will be quite good really.' She then shut the door firmly and went back to peer at them through her front window.

Mapp and Lucia was enormously popular in America, especially among the gay population. Geraldine says that for a while after the release of the series, it became very fashionable in some sections of New York society to give English tea parties based on those given by Mapp and Lucia—'à la Riseholme'— then after tea and gossip the guests would settle down to watch some of the episodes on video. American *Vogue* wrote: 'Prunella Scales plays Miss Mapp and she is perfect. Blowsy, pulled forward, it seems, with the weight of her enormous wildly insincere smile, Scales gives Miss Mapp overwhelming energy and drive—she is unflagging, a loyal foot soldier in her own drive for social pre-eminence.' And the *New York Times*: 'The cast is outstanding. Lucia, slender, angular and wickedly pointed, is played by Geraldine McEwan, while Mapp, plumpish, round and insinuating, is brought to blazing hypocritical perfection by Prunella Scales.'

Geraldine describes Prunella as 'both modest and generous. She has an enquiring mind, enthusiasm, and an incredible and wonderful commitment and keen interest in everything she does.' Her son Sam sees her as 'an amazing mixture of someone whose instincts are collaborative—because she is an actress who has been working in the theatre all her life, and that is how theatre is made—but who has enormous knowledge of, respect for, and ability to profit from, social strata. She has a very well-developed sense of social difference in her parts. She has always been good at tickling the audiences' ears, which is a peculiar skill of people who need to be funny. From a technical point of view as an actor, I think she is very fast, light and energetic and front-footed in all things that make for dancing relationships on stage—and comedy is well served by that.'

9

'I know, I know, oh, I know'

'John Howard Davies sent me along to meet John Cleese, who was in bed with flu in his rather posh flat, in Hyde Park Gardens. John asked: "Did you like the scripts?"

'I said: "I think they're brilliant."

'John: "Any questions?"

'Me: "Why did they get married?"

'John: "Oh God, I knew you'd ask that."

'We chatted and I got the part, I don't know why. I don't know how they had seen Sybil, but I think it was my idea that she was a cut below him socially—not very well educated, but very careful about her speech. What she had fallen for was Basil's poshness, and he had fallen for her because she was attractive in a blowsy kind of way. I think he and Connie were a bit shocked by the characterization. They had thought of Sybil as someone more in his bracket—but it seemed to work.'

John Cleese agrees. 'I wrote Sybil slightly differently from the way Pru did it. Connie and I both had a slightly different concept, and we were a little dubious after the first day's rehearsal—it wasn't what we were expecting. We wondered if it was working. By the second day we realized that the choices Pru was making were very good and probably worked better than what we had in mind. I can't remember now what we *did* have in mind.'

*   *   *

John Howard Davies had directed the first four *Monty Python* shows, so John Cleese knew him very well. He thinks Howard Davies is a remarkable director, extraordinarily good on both acting notes and on casting—it was he who suggested that Prunella would be right for the part of Sybil Fawlty in the comedy drama which he would direct and in which John Cleese was to star. Although at that stage John had not met Prunella, he had seen her in *Marriage Lines* and was aware that she was very good. *Fawlty Towers* is probably the most widely-seen production Prunella has done.

*   *   *

The idea for the series came from a hotel in Torquay, the Gleneagles—now a popular detour for sightseeing buses—where John Cleese and members of the cast had stayed in 1971 during the filming of *Monty Python*. The hotel proprietor, Commander John Sinclair, was so intolerant, rude and eccentric that most of the cast rapidly moved to more friendly lodgings, but John Cleese and his wife, Connie Booth, seeing the potential for a sit-com, stayed on and made notes. Many of the scenes in *Fawlty Towers*, written two years later, were based on actual incidents which took place in the hotel. Commander Sinclair was a short, rather fiery man for whom everything to do with 'service' to guests was just too much trouble. His wife, Betty, apparently tried to keep him in order but without much success. One of the guests, Richard Saunders, recalls how on one occasion when he went to the bar to order drinks, Sinclair slammed down the service grill, said the bar was closed and refused to serve him. To Sinclair's fury, Mr Saunders declared that he would go to another hotel nearby, whereupon Sinclair threatened that he would not re-admit him if he was late. When he returned at 11 p.m. he found all the doors locked, and had to batter on the door to get Sinclair out of bed to let him in.

There are other stories, often repeated—of Sinclair leaving Eric Idle's briefcase on the far side of the garden wall because he could hear an alarm clock inside it ticking and thought it might contain a bomb, and of berating Terry Gilliam, who was American, for his bad manners in cutting up his meat first and then eating with his fork only—as well-mannered Americans do. Apparently one foreign waiter who worked briefly for Sinclair was so traumatized that he called a taxi and made his escape to London. Sinclair died in 1981, but some of his family, his employees and even former guests have confirmed that John Cleese's portrayal of him was very true.

Even after thirty years, *Fawlty Towers* is still considered one of the top five British situation comedies ever produced—an astonishing thought, considering that only twelve episodes were made. It has such universal appeal that it has been sold to more than sixty countries (although when Spanish television bought the series and dubbed it, the nationality of Manuel from Barcelona was changed to Italian).

When the idea for the series was presented to the BBC in 1974, an unnamed commissioning editor was dismissive: 'This is a very boring situation. The script has nothing but very clichéd characters and I cannot see anything but disaster if we go ahead with this.' However, his opinion was overruled and the first six episodes of *Fawlty Towers* went on air at 8 p.m. on

Prunella. A portrait taken in 1950 when she was just
eighteen and still training at the Old Vic School

Above left: Edith Scales, Prunella's maternal grandmother, who, it was alleged, wore 'very tight boots'. When she became ill—until her death in 1925—she was looked after by her youngest daughter, Catherine (Bim), Prunella's mother

Above right: Bim Scales as a schoolgirl with her sister, Freda, thirteen years her senior

Above left: Bim and John Illingworth after their wedding at St Philip's Church, Birchencliffe, Huddersfield, 5 September 1930. Bim had her leg in plaster following a car accident

Left: The Forge, Sutton Abinger, where Prunella Illingworth was born on 22 June 1932, in an upstairs bedroom, while her father waited downstairs

John Illingworth, Prunella's father, taken at Bucks Mills in the 1940s while he was on leave

Bim Scales, Prunella's mother, taken in about 1929, during her time at the Liverpool Playhouse

Prunella in the garden of the Forge, aged about one year

Prunella's brother Timmo, with his despised curls. He was twenty months younger than she was

Left: Timmo and Prunella on a beach at Climping on the south coast, where the family would go for picnics

Middle left: Portrait of young Prunella

Middle right: Prunella, aged nine, as Princess Caraway in *Fat King Melon and Princess Caraway.* The play, by A. P. Herbert, was directed by Bim Illingworth at Bucks Mills in 1941 to raise funds in aid of children in bombed areas

Left: Glad Tidings, a Moira House production. Prunella is the angel in the centre and her friend Veronica Goldschmidt is the angel sitting on her right

Above: Polyphoto strip of Prunella aged about fifteen

Right: Prunella as Miss Betty in the Old Vic School graduation play, *A Journey to London*, in the summer of 1951

Below: Some of the cast of *A Journey to London*, with Prunella in the centre and Michael Vowden on the extreme right. The Old Vic School graduation in 1951

Left: Prunella as Nora in *A Doll's House* at Huddersfield Theatre Royal, 1953. Six months earlier she had played Nora at Salisbury Playhouse in a different translation of the same play

Left: Cinderella in the pantomime *Cinderella* at Huddersfield Theatre Royal, 1953

Below: In the film of *Hobson's Choice* made in 1954, Prunella as Vicky Hobson, the youngest daughter of the shoe-shop owner, with Daphne Anderson as her elder sister

Right: Prunella played a season with the Shakespeare Memorial Theatre Company at Stratford-upon-Avon in 1956. In *Love's Labour's Lost* she was Jaquenetta with Harry Andrews as Don Armado

Left: Playing Myrrhine in *Lysistrata*, with Gary Raymond, at the Oxford Playhouse, 1957

Left: As Marita in *Whiteman*, with Michael Picardie, at the Oxford Playhouse, 1961. It was during the run of this play that Prunella and Timothy West spent a romantic day punting on the river in Oxford

Left: Eileen Hughes, a bus conductress, in *Coronation Street*, 1962. Prunella was in two very early episodes of the series

Below: As the naive Kate Starling in the very popular TV series *Marriage Lines*, with Richard Briers as her husband, George. The series, about the tribulations of a young married couple, ran for five years from 1961 until 1965

Left: Prunella Scales marries Timothy West on 26 October 1963. Witnesses at the Chelsea Registry Office were her friend Betty Turner, a photographer, and her cousin Stephen Kaye

Left: Prunella decorating the top-floor flat at Lurline Gardens—the first home she and Timothy shared—in 1963

Above: Prunella in the garden
with Sam, just after he was born

Right: Sam with Timothy's
daughter, Juliet, in the
garden at Lillian Road in
1968

Above: Timothy and one-year-old
Sam in the summer of 1967

Left: Sam, Timothy,
Prunella and Joe, taken
at Wandsworth in 1974

Above: Sybil confronting Basil in *Fawlty Towers*: Prunella and John Cleese, 1979

Below: Alan Bennett, Prunella, Judi Dench and Timothy West in a fundraising evening for the Cambridge Arts Theatre, November 1982

Above: Prunella: 'I don't think Sybil was a dragon—she was an intelligent and funny woman, rather sexy in all those chic 1960s and 1970s clothes'

Prunella as Miss Elizabeth Mapp in *Mapp and Lucia*, 1985. Miss Mapp's wedding, with Georgie, the Major, Miss Mapp and Lucia. Fellow actors are Nigel Hawthorne, Denis Lill and Geraldine McEwan

Prunella doing crochet while waiting for her call during *Mapp and Lucia*

Prunella and Timothy's narrowboat, built in 1978

Left: The 1992 television production of *A Question of Attribution*, with Prunella as Her Majesty the Queen

Below: Prunella meets the Queen

Above: As Aunt Juley in
Howards End, 1992:
Prunella with her son
Sam. They were both in
the film but not in a scene
together

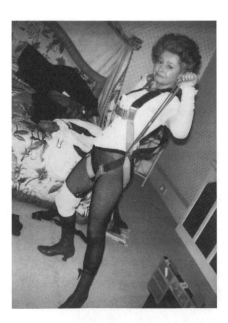

Right: Aunt Agnes in the
film *Stiff Upper Lips*, 1996:
Prunella in her safety
harness before her ladder
climb

Above: Stiff Upper Lips: Prunella in
bed with Peter Ustinov

Below: As Miss Bates in the television production of *Emma*,
with Samantha Bond, Meridian TV, 1997

Left: Prunella as Clarissa Rayment, the woman who spent fifty years abandoned and forgotten in a county mental home before being rescued: *Too Far to Walk*, at the King's Head Theatre, 2002

Below: Dottie Turnbull, the customer from hell: Tesco advert

Left: Prunella with statue of Queen Victoria, Brisbane, Australia, 1987

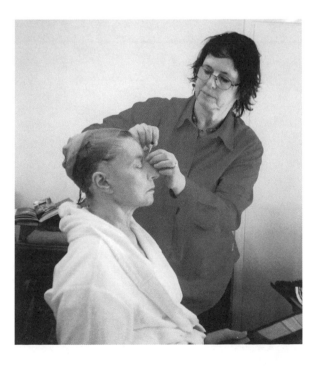

Right: Looking for Victoria: Prunella being made-up as Queen Victoria—Pauline Cox fixing the prosthetic nose, BBC, 2003

Right: Looking for Victoria: Prunella (as Victoria) sits at her desk, BBC, 2003

Above: Looking for Victoria: resting in between filming—Prunella taking a nap on the yellow sofa in the Speaker's flat at Parliament House, 2003

Left: Prunella, with Timothy, outside Buckingham Palace in 1992, after she had been awarded the CBE

Below: Prunella and Timothy in October 2003 cutting the cake at a party on board SS *Waverley* to celebrate their fortieth wedding anniversary. The only working seagoing paddle steamer in the world, *Waverley* made the round trip from Tower Bridge to the Thames Barrier for the occasion

Sunday, from mid-September 1975 until the end of October. When it was first shown the viewers were not quite sure what to make of it. The show was not an instant success, probably because it presented such a new approach to the situation comedy; slapstick farce on television was something out of a new mould. Unlike situation comedy, farce, with its element of danger, can be cruel, and is usually written about normal events which become more and more exaggerated until everything winds up to a frantic climax. 'It hits you as a totally new mixed bag of techniques available to television comedy.' But the show seemed to grow on viewers—the audiences built slowly, and it has now assumed iconic status with constant repeats. The second series was made in 1979.

Basil Fawlty, together with his wife, Sybil, run a small hotel in Torquay, Fawlty Towers. They are helped by Manuel, a waiter from Barcelona who speaks very little English, and a waitress, Polly, an art student, who is the most efficient person there. John Cleese plays Basil, a snobbish, manic hotelier who thinks of himself, erroneously, as a cut above most of his guests. He is terrified of his wife, an efficient, bossy, dominating woman, who sees right through his faux gentility and pretensions and brings him to heel when his behaviour gets out of hand. Prunella had a clear history of Sybil in her head. 'Her parents have been in catering and so she knows about running a boarding house, South Coast, Eastbourne, type of thing. Sybil's trouble is that she has married out of her class. She has been fooled by Fawlty's flannel, and too late, she realizes she is landed with an upper-class twit. Whereupon the rot sets in because he has all these posh and potty ideas about how to run a hotel, and she has a great deal more practical experience and know-how. But behind all her apparent disenchantment with Basil, there is some real affection for him.'

Sam West suggests that Basil's relationship is not entirely based on fear, it is more complex. 'What Prunella does is look at this dragon, Sybil, and say— OK, why are they still married? She's obviously an attractive woman, she obviously keeps him on his toes. Class-wise he helps her to aspire, and they probably had a very good sex life at the beginning. These are the sort of things which make this relationship work so that it is not just a comedic one. It is true.'

John doesn't remember any particular conversations Prunella had with him about the part. 'Although she probably did—there are conversations all the time. I do remember her reading on the first day. The great problem with the programme was we were always under tremendous time pressure to get the damn thing learned and rehearsed so that we could do it properly on the studio day. There was so little time for everything that the conversations were not leisurely, they were very focused and to the point, because I always had my eye on the watch. It was a terrific pressure.' Prunella says whatever role she plays she uses much the same approach. She always works out the person's background for every part she does. Who is this person? Where do they come from? Who are their parents? And so on. The accent is crucial. 'I've found that if you get the accent right and the speech patterns, you very often find things underneath the surface.'

One reviewer, Peter Fiddick, initially thought the success was mainly due to John Cleese, 'but over the weeks it has turned out to be a far richer mix than that. There is Prunella Scales, a smashing actress at any time, having a ball as Mrs Fawlty, adopting a refined whine somewhere between Henry Cooper and Twiggy and attacking Cleese at the level she finds him, which is usually just below the nipples.' Another reviewer described Sybil as the 'toxic dwarf and beloved piranha fish wife of Basil Fawlty'.

Prunella loved working with John Cleese and says that in spite of the apparent chaos he is a highly organized and efficient person. 'He's got an enormous amount of energy, it's quite frightening. It's like working with a live machine-gun; you try and keep it pointing away from you. It was absolute heaven, but very hard work. He's extremely rigorous: I don't know anyone in the business who works harder on the script, on his own performance, or on others' performances. We had a week to work on each episode and John went home to a basement and worked for two hours solid. I tried to work at home, but we didn't have a basement and with two sons it was sometimes distracting. In *extremis* I once moved into a quiet hotel for a few days and plunged into the reading; waking up every two or three hours through the night to learn the lines.' They had to be word-perfect by the Wednesday.

The scripts for *Fawlty Towers* were written by John Cleese and Connie Booth, who worked out the plot in great detail before writing the episodes, each of which contained one key idea interwoven with sub-plots. Initially John concentrated on the dialogue for Basil and Manuel, and Connie on that of Sybil and Polly, but as they became more familiar with the characters and the actors they became less specific and began to both write all the dialogue.

Most scripts for a half-hour sit-com are about sixty pages long; the scripts for *Fawlty Towers* contained so much detail they ran to about 135 pages, and the finished film often overran the allotted thirty minutes. John Cleese says each series took thirty-six weeks to write, about six weeks per episode. Each episode took one week to film. Most half-hour sit-coms had about 200 camera cuts, *Fawlty Towers* had 400. John says timing was one of the keys to the success of the series, and because they had such a short time in the studio, there was extensive editing to get the timing right.

John says the inspiration for Manuel's character was the realization in the early seventies that so many foreigners whose first language was not English were being employed in London restaurants that it was almost impossible to get what you ordered. So he made Manuel Spanish. Andrew Sachs had worked with John making management training films, mainly about customer relations, and when John suggested he might like to play the Spanish waiter, Andrew said yes, but he wasn't sure if he could manage the Spanish accent. Would John let him play the part with a German accent, as German was his first language and therefore one with which he was more familiar? John said no—Manuel had to be inefficient and incompetent, so he could hardly be German. Manuel from Barcelona it was. The moustache was Andrew's idea—he thought it not only right for the character, but also useful as a disguise to prevent him being so recognizable away from the set.

Andrew believes *Fawlty Towers* is a tragic story. Basil is on the point of a nervous breakdown, and both he and Sybil are needing deep psychological help. Both are incompetent. Sybil seems to be running the hotel, but it is a very dysfunctional management. Andrew firmly believes that Manuel is the only happy person at the hotel. 'He likes his job. He knows he is loved. He knows this because they keep hitting him,

173

which means they are taking notice of him. That was exactly what happened when he was a young lad in Barcelona.' I ask him if he ever got hurt during filming. He says that although it looks violent it isn't. 'I was quite light on my feet and could, and still can, fall fairly easily without damaging myself. It was carefully rehearsed and John is immensely strong. When he lifts me up, as he did, he just did it. There were a couple of times when I got hurt, but only when he deviated from rehearsal.'

John Cleese is amazingly flexible, and very tall. Sometimes, as Basil, he seems to the viewer to be almost physically out of control, which adds to the sense of danger. The scenes were all carefully rehearsed, including the violence, but occasionally things went wrong during the live performance and the cast had to carry on regardless. On one occasion, when the script required Basil to whack Manuel on the head with a heavy frying pan, John grabbed an ordinary pan by mistake, instead of the carefully padded prop one, and gave Andrew such a mighty blow that he nearly knocked him out. On another occasion, when there was a fire in the kitchen, Manuel had to come back into the restaurant with his jacket smoking. The fire itself was managed with no mishaps, but the blend of chemicals Props used to create the jacket-smoking effect was too strong. It soaked through the jacket and caused painful skin burns on Andrew's back and arms which lasted for several days.

*　　　*　　　*

The series was set in Torquay, though the external shots were actually filmed at the Wooburn Grange Country Club, near Bourne End in Buckinghamshire.

Unfortunately the Country Club was destroyed in a fire several years ago—it had been empty for three years after an unsuccessful attempt to run it as an hotel trading on the *Fawlty Towers* association. The interior shots were filmed in a studio. The budget for the show was small, another reason that the schedule for each series was very tight, despite the complexity of the script. John Cleese says, 'When everything was pretty much polished to our satisfaction, we would go off for five days and film all the outside bits for the entire series. This required a lot of pre-planning and organization, because one day it might be at the restaurant trying to get the duck, then the next day a completely different episode with the ladder at the side of the hotel, then the next day the guests departing, for another episode. So it was pretty tough, as we only had five days to get all that done. Then there would be a little time after the filming for people to catch their breath and then we would start the studio work for the next six weeks.'

Each episode was rehearsed for just under a week in the BBC rehearsal rooms at Acton. In conventional style, they worked in a rehearsal room with the floor marked up to indicate the set, and using substitute props. John says, 'The first day we would read it and start to block it; the second day we would finish blocking and start rehearsing it and the third day—a tremendous day trying to get the stuff on its feet—we were just slogging away, doing it again and again and again, trying to figure out if the blocking was right, and trying to learn it and get off the script, and trying to see where the weak points were. Then we probably had a day off, possibly Thursday or Friday, then one more day's rehearsal, a tech, probably on Saturday. Sunday was the day it was recorded.'

The technical rehearsal on Friday or Saturday was when the cameramen, lighting people and designers came in and took notes while the cast did a run-through. They only got into the actual studio at the BBC TV Centre in Wood Lane for a full day on Sunday. Andrew Sachs told me, 'It was always a bit of a shock getting into the set with the real props and costumes and so on.' The cast would do a slow stagger through with the cameras in the morning, which could be very boring and tedious. Then they would do a dress rehearsal in the afternoon, and in the evening the audience would be brought in and they would do the show. The outside broadcasts which had been pre-filmed were cut in at the right place, so the audience saw them as part of the show. John says, 'By the time we finished in the studio on Sunday we were pretty tired. We got home late, and then of course we were back there the next morning by ten o'clock for a new show. How I found the energy and how Pru found the energy I don't know, but we were younger.'

Andrew, too, was pretty exhausted. In 1975 he was playing the lead in the frantic West End production of the farce *No Sex Please, We're British*, every evening after a full day's rehearsal in the studio. Sunday, his day off, was the day they filmed *Fawlty Towers*. He finds he still gets asked, 'Are you Spanish?' and 'Have you always been a waiter?' He says he does try to avoid Spanish parts now. One day he was stopped in Oxford Street by an American tourist who recognized him as Manuel. The American was surprised to learn that there were only twelve episodes, and that the series had been made nearly thirty years ago. He asked Andrew with deep concern, 'How have you managed since then?'

All the leading cast members have had the

experience of being identified with their characters. Andrew says, 'When you take into account all of our involvement as the performers in the twelve episodes of *Fawlty Towers*, it amounts to about three months' work out of fifty years or so of experience. It is nothing—it is the blink of an eye, and yet it is the one thing that people remember.' John agrees. 'This is what happens with any success. I'm mainly a comedian, Pru isn't, she can do anything, but there is no question that any kind of big success is double-edged. What happens in this business is that at a certain stage, well-knownness becomes artistically damaging because you bring to the part so much luggage that is nothing to do with the part, or the way you are doing it. Whatever I do is always described as John Cleese doing a Basil Fawlty, and I assume that is the same for Pru.' He's right. It seems that to many people Prunella is still identified with Sybil—only one of the widely different characters she has played in her life, and which she played for far fewer episodes, and years, than her part as Kate Starling in *Marriage Lines* or later as Sarah France in *After Henry*.

Because of Sybil, many people think of Prunella primarily as a comic actress, but this is far too narrow a description—she is a skilled classical actress. She says you can't differentiate between comedy and drama—each has elements of the other. 'All comedy is based on pain, from pratfalls on in. And if you don't get the laughs in *Macbeth* and what are generally considered "straight" plays like Beckett's, you are failing the author.' She believes the perception of female comics varies from one country to the next. 'In French comedy you can be female, intelligent, attractive and young. In American comedy, as a female, you can be pretty and dumb and funny—or

177

intelligent and ugly and funny. But in English comedy you are not allowed to be female and funny unless you are post-menopausal, or so eccentric as not to be a sexual threat.' She adds that it is a gross generalization, but 'on the whole nowadays, and partly because of *Fawlty Towers*, I'm not offered women who are very attractive or very intelligent'.

Timothy West agrees that Prunella's identification with Sybil Fawlty may possibly have limited some people's perception of her. 'Clearly to give a successful performance in a hugely successful and popularly watched TV series gives you enormous presence. But we all know in this business that if you are really very good at one thing, the immediate reaction from the profession is that you are probably not very good at anything else! And then you have to prove that, and that is sometimes very hard, and often means deliberately turning down things which you feel might belong in the same category. So that you go right off and do something very, very different, which probably won't have anything like the same public appeal.'

John Cleese has a great admiration for both Timothy and Prunella. 'They have done absolutely top-quality work. They have done very little rubbish, and so many of the classics, and often not for very good money. It's almost more in the tradition of the great European actors, who just do fine work for the sake of the work. They have a massive artistic education that they have crafted. Now people get so much of their identity from work, but in their case it's not just an identity, it's a real love, a deep, deep interest in what they do.'

Even now, thirty years after the series was made, questions about Sybil come into almost every interview Prunella gives, and she has a well-practised reply. 'I am extremely grateful to Sybil. The repeat fees help subsidize our work in live theatre—which doesn't pay well at all, I'm afraid. Most people seem to remember Sybil as this hideous gorgon of a woman. Then when people meet me in the street they say "Oh, aren't you nice!" in tones of pained surprise. I don't think Sybil was a dragon. In fact when you look at the old shows, she was an intelligent and funny woman— and rather sexy in all those chic 1960s and 70s clothes. I consider her a heroine.'

Fawlty Towers is one of the most widely seen of all the shows Prunella has done, and while I was watching her make a Tesco's ad I learnt just how far this fame has spread. An assistant director from the team, Kate Martin, had spent her honeymoon in Java. She told me that soon after they got there, while trekking in some remote part of the mountains with a guide, her mobile phone rang. It was Prunella, not realizing Kate wasn't in England and wanting to know if she knew where something was—they had recently finished making one of the ads. The call ended, Kate put the phone away and said to her husband, 'That was Prunella Scales.' The guide turned round with a huge smile. 'Ah, Mrs Fawlty.'

10

'Nice to be working and all that though'

'I think people are rather confused by who the hell I am. My normal speaking voice is rather "RP" [received pronunciation] but because I've got a good ear, and have played a lot of character parts, and don't have a classically beautiful face, I've been lumbered with the "character-actress" label. This means you don't play heroines and you don't play the protagonist. There are lots of parts I'd have loved to play as a young woman but never did because of not looking conventional enough.'

*   *   *

An interviewer, Julie Cockcroft, once wrote: 'Prunella Scales is probably best known as "The Terror of Torquay", the shrill harridan who made Basil Fawlty's life such a misery in the classic comedy *Fawlty Towers*. With this image firmly in mind it is a shock to meet her in real life. Not only does she have a petite figure and youthful face, she is softly spoken and charming. A greater contrast to the forceful and vitriolic Sybil would be hard to imagine.' Sometimes, according to the press, it seems as though Prunella has never played any high-profile character other than Sybil Fawlty. She says she is very fond of Sybil and feels nothing but affection for *Fawlty Towers*, of which she is very proud, but to be constantly identified in the media with a part played only briefly some decades earlier can be frustrating.

From a regal Queen Victoria to the flamboyant Madame Arkadina in *The Seagull*, from fluffy Kate Starling in *Marriage Lines* to a down-trodden wife driven to murder in *Home Cooking*, the list of characters Prunella has played is amazing. Formidable mothers, put-upon daughters, wives of every sort—all are grist to the mill. Because of her versatility, it is very difficult to categorize Prunella's work. When I ask her if there is any pattern to the parts she plays, her reply is, 'Absolutely not.'

'If you think intelligently about technique, which she does,' says her son Joe—the onc family member who consciously decided not to act—'it can help you fix, analyse, remember, and know how to manipulate timing, register accent, say words very quickly and so on. She's prepared to analyse things objectively, to step back from the situation, to say, "Maybe that's good for me, but it may not be so good for the audience if I steal a laugh at that point." She's a very generous actress.'

*   *   *

In November 1986 a television drama called *Home Cooking* opened a season of one-hour plays under the title of *Unnatural Causes*, focusing on relationships which have gone radically and fatally wrong. Prunella played Judith, the mousy wife of a boorish hotel-keeper whom she suspected of a series of local rapes and murders. She spent much of the action in the hotel kitchen, cooking and scheming, before she took her revenge and killed her husband by locking him in the sauna and turning up the heat. 'Miss Scales was able to convey a time-bomb of mouthing resentment as she pummelled pastry and sliced through heads of

181

cabbages and cuts of lamb,' was one reviewer's response. The play included a raunchy bedroom scene where she was seduced by one of the visiting commercial travellers. He too met a grisly end. While admiring Prunella's acting, some critics were unsure about her playing a nude sex scene. The *Daily Record* screeched, 'Sybil Fawlty appears on the box tonight . . . NUDE! Who knows what Basil will say, but this isn't Prunella Scales in *Fawlty Towers*.' It seemed many of the critics still had trouble separating Prunella from her previous roles. '*Home Cooking* proved yet again the acting versatility of Prunella Scales. The role of Judith was a far cry from Miss Mapp in *Mapp and Lucia*—although the scheming was still the same.' In the *Sunday Telegraph*: 'To encounter the unflappable superwoman Sybil pawing incontinently at a lover couldn't avoid being a great culture shock.'

The play also upset some of her most loyal fans. A shocked clergyman wrote to her on behalf of his wife and himself, saying that when the play reached its climax with the bold and revealing incident of the bedroom scene 'we were frankly so offended and nauseated that we immediately turned off our set'. He felt that she had allowed herself to be cheapened. 'We hope that you will take serious thought before you accept any further roles which involve similar scenes, as we believe these are not only letting yourself and your image down, but also provide the kind of so-called entertainment which is offensive to those who still maintain standards of decency and propriety.'

Prunella replied that 'it was curious that while he had apparently no objection to her killing her husband in the sauna, he was objecting to scenes of romantic love. The nude scene wasn't gratuitous, it was necessary to the play.' When asked how she felt about the part, she said she was delighted to play Judith. 'A complete change from all the voluble characters I usually play. Judith is repressed and complicated. Sex to her is something dirty, quite unconnected with love. In her mind all men are dirty.'

A few years later, in *Mother Tongue* at the Greenwich Theatre, Prunella played Dorothy, an intrusive and exasperating sixty-two-year-old mother-figure, recently widowed, who, after her house burns down, finds she has to find a home with her daughter. The reviewer Margaret Burgess wrote: 'It is a tribute to the skill of Prunella Scales that I found myself admiring at the same time as abhorring her Dorothy. A lifetime of hiding her emotions and concealing unpleasant facts has left her with an upper lip which remains stiff even when her world is collapsing.'

Another complete change of character came in 1987 with the television play *The Index Has Gone Fishing* on Carlton TV, in which Prunella played Valerie Wells, a repressed librarian in the thrall of her demanding old mother, whose world is regimented by time. When her mother dies, Valerie's world loses its narrow focus and becomes so frightening that she throws every clock, watch and calendar out of the house. The change in her personality comes when she meets local bohemian bookseller Johnny Rowden, played by Paul Freeman, who is chaotic and fun. The *Daily Mirror* called her Val 'brillo bright, and punctual, the sort who wakes before the alarm. Freed from her domestic prison, she had a funny phase, then nervously sampled sex with the man who had been taking liberties at the library—with books—for years. It proved that Prunella Scales is in the genius class. Her round, open face tells all.' Prunella says she did a lot of research into the duties of a librarian, which 'is a

183

fiendishly complex business'.

From homicidal wife, to bossy mother, to repressed librarian, Prunella's range seems endless. In every part the characters she plays are so different that it is sometimes hard to recognize her straight away. Sarah France, in the long-running radio and television show *After Henry*, was perhaps one of the few exceptions because Prunella says Sarah was a character very close to herself, 'whoever myself is'. If she had her own way she would never appear as herself. 'However, it's no good acting your knickers off if no one knows that you are there. In an ideal world I would like to be known for the performance I'm giving, not as the actress who's giving it.'

After Henry, written by Simon Brett, began on BBC Radio 4 as a popular radio serial involving three women from different generations who share a three-storey house. The recently widowed Sarah, played by Prunella, finds herself in difficulties when the unexpected death of her husband leaves her with responsibility for her overbearing mother, Eleanor, played by Joan Sanderson, who lives in the basement flat, and her adolescent daughter, Clare, played by Janine Wood, who lives on the top floor. She manages to find some independence by getting a job in a second-hand bookshop. Much of the comedy comes from the fierce, though unacknowledged, competition among the three women to remain in charge of their own lives, while living together. All three resent the interference of the others. Sarah France was one of Prunella's favourite parts. 'It's quite sharp, it's quite painful in its quiet way, and I liked playing a part that for a change wasn't wildly eccentric. Sarah was an absolutely dead ordinary person.' The story struck a chord with its audience too, and was so popular that the brave decision was made to rewrite *After Henry* as an ITV sit-com. The gentle and perceptive television series was a hit when it was first shown in January 1988 and ran until 1992.

In September 1988 Prunella was in a Yorkshire TV comedy called *Natural Causes* with George Cole, who played a salesman from Exodus, the organization for bumping people off. As part of his sales patter he declares, 'We rely a lot on word of mouth, which is a bit of a problem because most of our clients aren't talking.' Prunella played Celia Bryce, the wealthy, neurotic wife of Walter, who wanted to get rid of her so that he could run away with his secretary. He hired the man from Exodus to do the job—drinks were poured out, but after much confusion and exchanging of wine-glasses, it was the man from Exodus who mistakenly chose the poisoned one.

December 1988 saw a complete change when Prunella was in two new Alan Bennett plays, *An Englishman Abroad*, directed by Alan Bennett, and *A Question of Attribution*, directed by Simon Callow, performed together at the National Theatre under the combined title of *Single Spies. An Englishman Abroad* is the dramatization of an actual meeting in Moscow between the spy Guy Burgess, played by Simon Callow, and the actress Coral Browne. Burgess, lonely and homesick, and kept under constant surveillance by the Russians, invites Miss Browne, played by Prunella, to his apartment. Desperate for news from England, he also has a special request. Will she take his measurements and order some new clothes for him from his tailor in London? Under the banter and trivialities, the loneliness of the man is disturbingly apparent.

The second play, *A Question of Attribution*, records

185

an imaginary encounter between Her Majesty Queen Elizabeth II, played by Prunella, and Sir Anthony Blunt, the Keeper of the Queen's Pictures, played by Alan Bennett. It was the first time a reigning monarch had been portrayed on the British stage. The Queen, whose afternoon engagement has been cancelled, wanders into the Long Gallery at Buckingham Palace where Anthony Blunt is examining Titian's *Allegory of Prudence*, a painting of two men which, when X-rayed, unmasks the possibility of a third, fourth and even fifth man. Is it a forgery? Blunt is up a ladder examining the picture and doesn't see who it is when he asks the Queen to pass him a magnifying glass.

Mortified when he discovers his *faux pas*, he gets into a conversation with the Queen about how to spot a fake from the real thing. Ostensibly about paintings, there are many layers of meaning: at the time when the play was set, Blunt was already under suspicion of being one of the Cambridge spies. Prunella went into minute detail to capture the look and persona of the Queen. She reproduced her vowels and her walk, and from one of the ladies-in-waiting was able to get advice as to what sort of stockings the Queen wore. She says: 'Research is absolutely crucial. I'm fascinated by the way people behave and it's a great pleasure, as well as, I suppose, one's moral and artistic duty, to get as near to the character as possible. It's more interesting, more fun—and more entertaining for the audience.' She works like this with every character she plays, exploring their mannerisms, style of speech and physical demeanour. 'I myself don't care a bit how people behave, but as an actor it's a major concern for every part you play, and you have to find out as much as you possibly can. It's like learning a language or learning a dialect.'

186

Jack Kroll, in *Newsweek*, said, 'Scales is superb, creating a queen who, behind the ceremonial triviality of her duties, carries a mind charged with awareness and insight.' Prunella found it easier to research the Queen than she did Coral Browne, 'because there are so many recordings of the Queen, whereas all the recordings of Coral Browne are of her acting'. There was also a physical dissimilarity. But John Russell Taylor wrote in *Plays International*: 'Prunella Scales, who looks not one bit like Coral Browne (she is five and a half inches too short for one thing), plays her wondrously, so that you really feel that you are seeing and hearing Miss Browne, though all your normal faculties tell you otherwise; and at the same time you can stand back a little and see how well the character is recreated, by writer as well as actress.' He also much admired the second play, especially the performances of Bennett and Simon Callow; 'and most miraculously of all, the Queen played by Prunella Scales in a way that goes far beyond imitation (immaculate though that is) to give us a feeling that we may really be seeing the person within the monarch. If the Queen is not really like this, then the less Queen she.' And Milton Shulman in the *Evening Standard* noted: 'In her prim blue suit, carrying the inevitable handbag, Prunella Scales has that tight, half-smile look and curt, but courteous manner with which the Queen treats her subjects in casual conversation. She emerges in Miss Scales's endearing portrayal as a sly, knowledgeable woman with a keen sense of both curiosity and humour.'

The Queen herself didn't come to the theatre, 'though she may have seen a recording of the television version'. Certainly Princess Margaret saw the play, as did many of the Queen's Household—

including one of her security men, who was so taken in when Prunella walked on stage that he had to stop himself standing up. Clement Freud wrote in the *Times* Diary on 18 January 1989: 'It must be very trying for the monarch to know that nightly, within trotting distance of Buckingham Palace, there is this brilliant half hour scene of herself with Sir Anthony Blunt to which, because of one thing and another, she is unable to go. She misses an outstanding performance by her stand-in.' Michael Billington in *Country Life* was delighted that Prunella went 'neither for exact mimicry nor for revue-sketch caricature, but somehow catches the essence while preserving the enigma'. Elsewhere he praised the way in which she radiated 'sharp-witted benevolence and possessive pride as she potters about the gallery muttering, "This rosebowl was a wedding present from Jersey." '

In a rare crossover of her public and private life, Prunella's royal impersonation came in useful on one occasion, albeit unwittingly. The actor Frederick Treves told a friend, 'I was giving Pru a lift when I was pulled over for speeding. The policeman was writing me a ticket when he froze, then waved me away. He had looked beyond me at my passenger, who was staring straight ahead. Then the penny dropped: Pru had played Elizabeth II on TV. The traffic cop must have thought, "My God! I've stopped the Queen." '

News of the London production captivated American theatre enthusiasts. The *New York Times*'s Frank Rich said, 'Rarely does a single scene in a one-act play become the talk of the town, but such is the phenomenon created by *Single Spies*. Without ever indulging in caricature, the extraordinary Miss Scales makes a completely persuasive Queen: shrewd without being intellectual, convivial without being intimate, charming without being warm. The mixture of the regal and the human is so successful that the rapt audience applauds the actor's mid-scene exit—a rarity in London—as if the actual Queen were leaving the theater.' Another US commentator noted that 'midway through "A Question of Attribution", a sudden hush falls over the audience. The unthinkable, it seems, has happened: Queen Elizabeth II has walked on to the stage. In fact, Her Majesty is actress Prunella Scales. But given the public awe in which the Queen is held, turning her into a stage character is a daring ploy, unprecedented in mainstream British theater.'

In February 1989 Prunella wrote to Veronica, still living in America: 'Haven't been sent to the Tower yet. Notices for *Single Spies* are extraordinary, and we *may* come to New York, but who knows when: we have to go for 6 months to the Queen's Theatre first, shame really, I loved being at the National and would have liked to stay longer. Just about to embark on 7 episodes of TV series *After Henry*—not sure whether you'll get it. So absolutely in purdah for 7 weeks. I may die of exhaustion, what with playing in the evenings, 8 perfs. per week and recording the TV on Sundays. Nice to be working and all that though.'

Following the extended season of *Single Spies* at the Queen's Theatre, Prunella played Mrs Candour in the National Theatre's production of Sheridan's *School for Scandal*. Anthony Curtis in the *Financial Times* found that the opening scenes ignited rather slowly. 'Things perk up, though, with the appearance of Prunella Scales as Mrs Candour who sends her lines whizzing to the back of the stalls.' Paul Taylor thought that as a member of this Restoration scandal school 'Prunella Scales is funniest. Posing as the soul of

189

discretion, her dumpy, bonneted Mrs Candour scarcely pauses for breath once launched on those cadenzas of regretful character assassination which she disguises as staunch solicitude.' The show ran at the Olivier Theatre throughout the spring of 1990.

In 1991 *A Question of Attribution* was produced as a TV play by the BBC. This time James Fox played Blunt. Prunella says her chief joy in the television production was having real corgis in the scene. 'Real dogs in the theatre are much too expensive.'

Prunella did eventually meet the Queen when she was awarded a CBE in December 1992 and went to Buckingham Palace to receive it. 'I went up and curtsied and she shook hands and said very quietly, "I suppose you think you should be doing this." '

*   *   *

Not only was Prunella performing at night and rehearsing for *After Henry* during the day, she was also in a film directed by Michael Winner. Alan Ayckbourn's *A Chorus of Disapproval* was shot in Scarborough in May 1988, with an outstanding cast including Anthony Hopkins, Jeremy Irons, Jenny Seagrove and Richard Briers. Set against the background of an amateur dramatic society rehearsing *The Beggar's Opera*, the characters are all dreadful performers who carry their own fears and ambitions into the rehearsals. Jeremy Irons plays the diffident Guy Jones, a young widower posted to his firm's Scarborough branch, who becomes involved with the drama society. All the women want to bed him, and the men to make him a party to local corruption. Prunella movingly plays the repressed Hannah Ap Llewellyn, the neglected, lonely wife of Anthony

190

Hopkins's dictatorial director of the show. She, too, falls in love with Guy, agonizingly conscious that her age and looks are against her, and is cruelly abandoned when Guy gets posted to Blackpool. The film was released in 1989, to muted reviews.

One day I asked her if she felt she had to change the size of her playing when switching between film and theatre. From the speed of her response it was obviously not the first time she had heard that question.

'No! I think that is a frightful myth. Of course technically you have to use more voice in a theatre than for TV, but it upsets me dreadfully that casting directors don't nowadays like using people who've been trained in the theatre. In my own days at drama school, we didn't have camera or filming facilities; when I first worked in film, I had to learn about it. It was harder for my generation, because you weren't invited to see rushes unless you were the star. You didn't see your own performance until the première, and only then could give yourself a few notes about not blinking and so on. Nowadays not only do you see the rushes, they also have video during the shooting. The director will say, "Come over here and look at this." They run the shot they've just done, and you can see exactly what he is talking about, and ask to do it again. It makes all the difference.'

11

Now We Are Married

'I think we both have very much the same approach to the work; although we've come to it from different angles so we may use different terminology. We do talk about the parts we play and hear each other's lines. When we see each other's work we take notes, and so do the children—they always have—they have been giving us notes ever since they could write. We don't really make a habit of acting together. We enjoy it from time to time, but we like to keep individual work going as well.'

*　　　*　　　*

Prunella and Timothy, who both learnt to act when repertory theatre was flourishing and actors had to be versatile, are worried by the narrow perceptions of some producers. 'Producers are often very patronizing in their assumption that actors can't adapt to the different media. They will cast untrained people who come along to audition for parts in serials, who may look completely right, be good in that part and have a great success. Later when they're snapped up for a film or a play, they may not be able to cope. There's a sort of inverted snobbery on the part of casting directors, a belief that an actor's training doesn't equip them to deal with the different media, and different characters. A well-trained actor should be able to cope with all media.'

192

Joe says of his parents: 'One of the late lessons I've learnt about their professional life is that they have this renewing every time. They come into a situation afresh, assess it, bring in their expertise, and move on to the next thing. Input, process, and output. What they're interested in is the process. You assume the quality of the process would assure the quality of the output, however, you are not aware of it and you don't count the cost. They could do any part standing on their heads, but they wouldn't attempt it without a great deal of research. There is a huge generosity about them.'

As the boys grew older, there were signs that Sam, at any rate, might be following them into the family business. Prunella wrote to Veronica for Christmas 1985 to tell her that Sam was reading English at Oxford but also acting with OUDS. 'We are only alarmed in case no work gets done. Younger son, Joe, is doing A levels, mostly music it seems, bassoon, etc . . . Isn't it horrid when they leave home, I mean, it's lovely being able to put something down on a chair—Blu-Tack, Scotch tape, nail scissors, etc.—and three days later it is still there, undamaged; but we miss them being around.' She also tells Veronica that she and Timothy are working together in a revival of J.B. Priestley's comedy *When We Are Married*, at the Whitehall Theatre, to be directed by Ronald Eyre. In its heyday the theatre had been the home of Whitehall farce with Brian Rix. Since then it had had a mixed history; the production of *When We Are Married* was part of an effort to launch the refurbished theatre as a West End playhouse.

A period comedy about three nouveau riche, middle-aged Yorkshire couples, set in the early 1900s, the play reveals the consternation and confusion which ensues when the validity of their joint marriage ceremony of twenty-five years earlier is questioned. It opened to rapturous notices and became one of the most popular shows in the West End. An American reviewer wrote: 'The veteran company imbue *When We Are Married* with a priceless, bygone English authenticity that no other cast on either side of the Atlantic is ever likely to re-create.'

Timothy and Prunella shared a dressing-room. 'I remember there were exactly sixty-two stairs to our dressing-room which we had to climb four times a day, up and down—six times on matinée days. It was a bit wearing but it kept us fit.' A TV production was made three years later for the BBC series 'Theatre Night'.

*   *   *

In January 1986 Prunella and Timothy were invited to take part in a fund-raising event in Cambridge in aid of the Cambridge Arts Theatre. George (Dadie) Rylands, a Fellow of King's College, and then eighty-three, had been director, actor and author during his distinguished career, and in 1946 on the death of Maynard Keynes had taken the chairmanship of the theatre. He had retired in 1982, at the age of eighty. Prunella had played a variety of parts for Dadie in 1961, when he had directed the whole Shakespeare canon on a fifty-five-record set of LPs for the Marlowe Society. He wrote to her: 'I was very pleased with your Rosalind. I hope there are some more parts I can offer you . . . So grateful you can undertake the Anne Boleyn scenes—hurrah! I suggest you might like to try and bring off the Lady Anne in Richard III. A set piece in the style of the early 1590s. What one has to give is a Wimbledon display rather than character.

194

They both go up to the net at line 192. Speed, variety and tempo, always a hot pace, strong service, backhand drive. It is the meeting of two fires.'

Director of the Marlowe Society for many years, George Rylands had a positive influence on many young actors, and his protégés included famous theatre names who willingly agreed to be part of the special evening. For this he had written and compiled a commemorative piece, *Strange Eventful History*, to be performed for one night only. The distinguished cast invited to Cambridge in 1986 included Dame Peggy Ashcroft, Eleanor Bron, Judi Dench, Sir John Gielgud, Sir Peter Hall, Derek Jacobi, Daniel Massey, Ian McKellen, Trevor Nunn, Michael Pennington, Prunella and Timothy, Michael Williams and Irene Worth. Most of them had worked with George Rylands when at Cambridge, all were his friends. Twenty actors would perform forty-five items— without a rehearsal, though they had been sent their scripts in advance. It resulted in a hilarious and often energetic gallop through a selective history of Cambridge, based on memoirs of people who had either loved or hated the place when they were there, interspersed with scenes or pieces from Shakespeare. The evening was reported as a triumph.

*   *   *

Prunella told Veronica Conyers in her Christmas letter that when she returned from Australia in 1991, 'We start rehearsing *together* for *Long Day's Journey into Night*, a co-production between the Bristol Old Vic and the National Theatre. Very exciting, though Timothy calls it Long Day's Journey to Professional Suicide.' Sometimes there was an unfounded assumption that they might have chosen a particular play as a vehicle for them both, but as Timothy commented, 'it is journalists who use the labels "show business couple" or "husband and wife team" '. He said they had come to this O'Neill masterpiece as two separate, individual actors, 'and that's the way we like to be treated professionally—as individuals, not as a married couple. The fact that we are married is entirely irrelevant.' Prunella added, 'What's more, any advantages in appearing together are counterbalanced by an equal number of disadvantages. On the plus side, generally speaking, we agree with each other on professional questions, and can discuss things without either of us taking offence. On the other hand this particular play is a very large and demanding work, and living together we can never really get away from it. During the rehearsal period it was very difficult to put the play to one side and actually relax.' She said there was another reason why they don't often work together: 'When I see people playing opposite each other who I know to be married it can take the *danger* out of a performance.' Timothy found it really rather strange to be working together: 'Normally, if one of us is in a play and the other is doing something else, should things go badly for one, then the other can offer advice and consolation. But when you are both in it together every sort of feeling you have is doubled. So if it is all going wonderfully, you feel doubly delighted. However, if it's not, you end up with double the misery.'

The play, by Eugene O'Neill, is largely autobiographical. James Tyrone, played by Timothy, is a classical actor who has given up a prestigious career for a commercial success and as a result despises himself. The family, continually at war and consumed

196

by guilt, failure and drunkenness, can neither forget nor forgive, and James and Mary Tyrone blame each other, after thirty-five years of marriage, for what they have become. Prunella did considerable research for her part as the morphine-addicted Mary Tyrone, by talking to doctors, psychiatrists, and ex-addicts in Wandsworth Prison. The play opened in February 1991 at the Bristol Old Vic and, after a regional tour, went in to the National Theatre in London in late May.

John Peter in the *Sunday Times* appreciated Prunella's performance. 'She shows you precisely that Mary Tyrone's fragile warmth both supports and conceals a character full of genteel self-righteousness and an almost insufferable decency: with her waiting for you at home, the temptation to stay in bars and green-rooms would have been irresistible. The victim as vampire.' Robert Tanitch saw other details. 'Mary Tyrone has lived out her life in terrible loneliness, waiting for her husband to come home drunk after the show. Prunella Scales, rigid in stance, blank in her looks, constantly patting her hair, constantly looking at her gnarled hands, creates an invisible wall behind which she retreats, out of reach of her family. The performance is deeply moving. Timothy West has tremendous authority.'

During their working lives Timothy and Prunella have written, compiled and presented many recital programmes—there are currently about 120 of them. These are usually performed on Sunday evenings, often for charitable causes. One such is an anthology of readings entitled *Parson's Pleasure*, exposing the idiosyncrasies of sundry churches, cathedrals, clergy and various well-known literary curates, which they first performed in October 1990. Another in their

197

repertoire, *The Battle of the Sexes*, I saw performed at the Greenwich Theatre in the summer of 2003. The small theatre was packed, mainly with older people. It was a very hot night; many of the audience were clutching bottles of water and energetically fanning their faces in a vain attempt to cool down. The couple next to me on one side complained because there was no programme; the woman on the other side was telling her companion rather loudly how she had a friend who had a friend who *knew* Prunella. The recital was in two halves—a skilful melding of classical and modern, funny and serious. When Prunella, who is tiny, first came on stage there was a murmur of surprise, probably because the audience, many of whom were used to seeing her on television, expected her to be larger. Possibly a few of the audience were expecting to see Sybil Fawlty.

Prunella is constantly trying to change the audience's perception of her. When our conversation returned, inevitably, to the Sybil Fawlty tag, I asked if this affected her work. 'The billing can be used to promote a play to get people in, but once they come in I want them to be surprised at what they are offered—if the author gives you that chance. If I was offered a play that I respected very much, but with a part like Sybil Fawlty or Dottie in the Tesco ad, then however much I respected the play, I might think very carefully before accepting that part, because it would reinforce a perception of me. The media tend to create expectations of different actors, which can limit the pleasure of the public as well as the work of the actor.'

*   *   *

Carole Hayman and Lou Wakefield wrote *Ladies of*

Letters in the 1990s, and Prunella and Gwen Taylor had read some of 'the collected correspondence of Irene Spencer and Vera Small' to an appreciative audience at a dinner in Soho one night. The 'ladies' went on to become a regular feature on radio, with Patricia Routledge as Vera and Prunella as Irene. The correspondence, between two middle-aged northern widows, gives a revealing, and very funny, glimpse into the sometimes hair-raising world of bring-and-buy sales, tennis club flirtations, gay sons, wayward daughters and their partners, and demanding grandchildren. Overtly genteel and covertly bitchy, they have a deeply competitive love-hate relationship in which each fights to have the last word. In September 2000 the letters were released on tape as an audio book, and they have now been issued on CD. In one of the more recent series on BBC radio the ladies took to emailing each other.

Prunella's own letters provide a useful insight to her and Timothy's working life. She wrote to Veronica in later 1992: 'Timothy and I are devoting ourselves to Regional Theatre at the moment. He as King Lear in Dublin followed by *Salesman* in Wales. I'm going to be buried up to my waist in Yorkshire—in Beckett's *Happy Days*!'

The Beckett play opened in the West Yorkshire Playhouse on 23 February 1993, and ran for a four-week season. Virtually a monologue, Winnie, played by Prunella, philosophizes and chats while she is progressively buried in a mound of scorched earth until only her head shows. Prunella told one interviewer: 'It was the most challenging thing I have ever done in my life. I probably started working on it as much as six months beforehand because there was such a lot to take in. It's incredible what a stressful play it is. It's written like music so you work on the text to play the notes and then to justify them in acting terms.' Jeffrey Wainwright, in the *Independent*, comments: 'The sheer technique required to play Winnie must boggle any spectator. The great intellectual effort has to be embodied in a complex series of modulations and expressions, each sounded out between actor and director. Prunella Scales, under Jude Kelly's direction, makes it all excellently spellbinding and comprehensible.'

Phil Penfold, in *Yorkshire on Sunday*, identified something central to many of Prunella's performances: 'What is absolutely certain in this mesmerizing production is that Prunella Scales is an actress whose extraordinary skills are paradoxically demonstrated to their most expansive breadth when she is almost totally confined in movement . . . By a mere flick of the eyebrow, or wrinkling the forehead, Ms Scales gives us fortitude, submission, hope, resignation and all other manifestations of the psyche. The lines bounce around like beads released from a broken necklace, some destined for obscure corners where they will do no harm, others lying treacherously underfoot. It is a performance that is both rare and to be treasured.'

Later in the year Prunella would play the lead, Dolly Levi, in *The Matchmaker* at Chichester, thirty-eight years after she had played the young ingénue, Ermengarde, in Tyrone Guthrie's production in London and New York. Set in New York in the late 1880s, the play involves a mixture of cultures, nationalities and religions. Prunella sees it as 'a play about money and the distribution of money but it's also a play about learning to live together'. Some audiences, expecting to see the Broadway musical

Hello Dolly!, may have found her performance unexpectedly muted, as one reviewer acknowledged. 'You might expect the shadow of Ethel Merman or Barbara Streisand or even Sybil Fawlty to hang over Prunella Scales as she assumes the role of marriage-arranger Dolly Levi. But anyone who saw her at the Lyceum in *Long Day's Journey into Night* will know what a versatile and imposing actress she is.' Another called her 'the most underrated actress in British Theatre. Her intelligent, unforced delivery is lively and engaging while seeming sometimes to get as close to natural speech as a person speaking lines of dialogue can get.'

*   *   *

In 1993 Prunella made several films for both television and the cinema. Following the lead in a four-part TV series, *The Rector's Wife*, she played Margery in the film *Second Best* with William Hurt, and then spent four days in Hollywood playing Maude in *Wolf*, a modern werewolf movie, with Jack Nicholson and Michelle Pfeiffer.

When in America once more in June 1994 to film part of BBC's *Signs and Wonders*, she wrote to Timothy from her hotel. 'When you come, don't attempt to put anything into a glass until you've checked for cling-film over the top. Makes a fearful mess even with water and I'd have been really cross if it had been whisky. Next door is potty American widow who *lives* here. She lies on the sofa with her door open and the television on and may move in before you get here, so hurry.'

Signs and Wonders is a four-part drama in which Prunella played a mother whose daughter, on a visit to

America, has been brainwashed by a religious sect, the Mercy World Mission. The emotionally distraught mother, trying to cope with the loss of her child and her useless husband, an alcoholic Anglican vicar, goes to California to try and rescue her daughter. Jodhi May played the daughter.

Prunella's letters home outline some of the high and low points of the job. 'June 15th. 4.30 a.m. Can't sleep, still jet lagged. My first day's shooting yesterday. Picked up at 2 p.m. got on the location set about 5.30. Jodhi May has to hit me a lot. The stunt man produced a sort of armour-plated flak jacket in rigid silver plastic which came up somewhere around my ears. I said it might look a little strange under a cardigan and had he anything else. So he came up with a garment that looked quite sexy until covered with a Viyella blouse. Also we did about ten takes and Jodhi doesn't pull her punches. After take seven I asked for some shoulder-pads because she was finding an unprotected bit with unerring accuracy every time, so in the last three shots I look like an American footballer. Cried quite a lot, which was gratifying, except that Vicki Make-up mopped up after every take. Leave it, Vicki, I said, I'm *supposed* to be crying. Yes love, but your mascara's running she said. Oh God, isn't it waterproof, I sobbed—well *I* didn't put any on you she said, I left what you had on when you came in, wasn't that waterproof? There was such a lot I thought it was better to leave it . . . MUST NOT let war develop with Vicki, she's nice really, and lent me lots of arnica cream when we wrapped. Should be O.K. by the time you get out, bit mottled this a.m.

'Was reading in bed round about midnight and the hotel shook, I rang reception.

' "Yes, ma'am?" said the desk clerk.

202

' "What was all that?" I asked.

' "All what ma'am?"

' "That—that noise just now."

' "Oh—that, ma'am, was a very *small* earthquake."

'Think I'd better post this one way and another.

'I just *hate* being away, thank God for the embroidery is all I can say.'

*   *   *

Trying to find any sort of consistency in the parts Prunella accepts is impossible—other than the challenge of playing such disparate and sometimes difficult characters. Later in 1994 she played Peggy, a 'treasure' of a secretary, in Meredith Oakes's *The Editing Process* at the Royal Court. The play, a comedy, takes a savage, satirical look at the reality of the corporate takeover of a small, specialist publishing house, snapped up by larger, brasher rival. Prunella plays a loyal secretary who has put up with her cruel boss for many years. Jack Tinker saw her as 'A figure of dowdy heroism, who represents the last vestige of loyalty and decency in their beleaguered little world. And she is its first victim.' Charles Spencer admired the way 'her bright twittering manner gives way to glimpses of domestic desolation, and her mad mirthless giggles at the end, when she realizes she's had a "cheap, vain, man-made substitute for life", is the one moment that goes to the heart'.

Prunella went from victim to saviour when she was cast as Mrs Tilston, a weird therapist in Carla Lane's sit-com series *Searching*, made by Carlton TV. Prunella, almost unrecognizable in a wild, untamed wig, is a matronly figure, obsessively tidy, who dresses in sweatshirts with religious inscriptions emblazoned on them. She has turned her large family home into a sanctuary for five women with severe emotional problems that prevent them from leading ordinary lives. A religious eccentric, Mrs Tilston is a qualified nursing sister with a degree in philosophy and very unorthodox therapy methods. Billed as a barrel of laughs, Prunella told one interviewer that 'All the best comedies are based on pain, from pratfalls on in.' Hurt underscores humour. '*Searching* is funny and touching, but I think that a new name will have to be invented to describe it. I call it a "drama-doc-sit-trag", rather than a sit-com.'

In early 1995 Prunella directed Timothy in Alan Bennett's play *Getting On* at the West Yorkshire Playhouse, a play about a Labour leader who is sidetracked by his hatred of where the world is going. While they were still in rehearsal, *The Winter Guest*, directed by Alan Rickman, had its première. Set in a seaside town, it concerns the lives of four couples trapped when they are cut off by blizzards. This turned into daunting reality when the audience tried to go home after the first night. Heavy snow had closed most of the roads round Leeds, and everyone in the theatre, with the addition of some stranded motorists, was forced to spend the night there. Playhouse staff, with the help of the actors, including Prunella, served soup and tea, much to the delight of the audience, after which the actors entertained them until the early hours of the morning with songs and sketches.

The very successful West Yorkshire Playhouse was burdened by an earlier building debt of £2.4 million and in 1996 came under serious threat. Timothy and Prunella are patrons of the theatre and were vehement in their pleas for support. 'The Playhouse is different from other theatres: it is shared by the people who use

204

it whether they are actors, directors, designers, audiences, schoolchildren at lessons or older people painting. Everybody mixes and mingles.' She has worked there frequently, both as director and actor, and has great admiration and respect for the way Jude Kelly ran it. 'All actors, given the choice, would like at least one production a year at a regional theatre like the Playhouse. A West End play, if it runs at all, can mean being tied up for six months or more. At Stratford you might be looking at twenty months. But at a regional theatre you play to successive intelligent audiences for four weeks and it really does give you a chance to learn quickly.' One other, compelling, argument she gave for regional theatre was that all tastes were accommodated at an affordable price and so large audiences were attracted. This in turn feeds a network of local public transport and surrounding restaurants. The West Yorkshire Playhouse was to her not just a theatre, but an important contribution to the social life of the region.

*   *   *

Prunella's next series of plays and films, set in India, were the very antithesis of Yorkshire snowdrifts. It seemed as though no sooner had she returned from India after making a film called *Stiff Upper Lips* in the spring of 1996 than she appeared in Jude Kelly's production of *A Perfect Ganesh*, written by Terence McNally, in which she and Eleanor Bron played two American tourists who travel to India for the first time, searching for spiritual comfort. The Hindu god Ganesh, the god of acceptance—a remover of obstacles and bringer of wisdom—helps them in their journey and acts as a chorus for the play. The more romantic Katharine, played by Eleanor Bron, is balanced by prosaic Margaret, played by Prunella, and they were praised for their playing 'with enough wit, tact and understatement to carry the play'.

The following year, in *Staying On*, Prunella and Richard Johnson played Lucy and Tusker Smalley, a British couple who decide to stay on in India after Independence. The play is based on the Paul Scott novel that is really an epilogue to the Raj Quartet, filmed for television as *The Jewel in the Crown*. Prunella played the wife, Lucy, left completely isolated a continent away from 'home' after her husband of forty years dies from a heart attack. The play opened in Cardiff in March 1997, and toured before going into the West End in May. One reviewer called Prunella 'wonderful as the blue-rinsed Lucy who has few friends and who yearns for change, but sticks by Tusker whose health is failing'. Prunella elaborated: 'It's not just about two people who stayed on in India but about the nature of loneliness, ageing and marriage over the years.' She also admitted, 'This play has frightened me. I've begun to think a great deal about what would happen if one of us died. The thought of either of us being left is horrifying. I hope I'd carry on working. Work would be the thing that saves one, the solace. I hope I'd cope.'

This fear of being alone becomes more acute as she gets older. She is terrified that Timothy will die before she does, leaving her to manage life on her own. Joe says, 'She does need other people all the time. It is a kind of dependence. After we had all left home the mother's help job turned into the employment of a sort of personal assistant/housekeeper, a hard job to do. Ma has this strange dichotomy of someone who is so talented, efficient, and capable in any acting

206

situation, and yet so emotionally dependent at home.'

In July 1997 Prunella was invited to become President of the Campaign to Protect Rural England, an environmental charity. The CPRE campaigns for cheaper and more efficient public transport, more environmentally sensitive road building, open spaces in towns, protection of green-field sites, promotion of the use of more brown-field sites, energy conservation, tightened green-belt restrictions, more controls on out-of-town shopping centres and open-cast mines, protection of wildlife, forests, ponds, dry-stone walls and so forth. They're strictly non-aligned on hunting with dogs, and firmly apolitical. Not to be confused with the Countryside Association, the CPRE, with a membership of about 45,000, is a much gentler, possibly more *noblesse oblige* group whose committee, as one reporter noted, is replete with double-barrelled names and titles and whose members are mainly middle-aged and middle-class. They are a useful and active pressure group which campaigns, agitates and advocates. Prunella, as an actress living in London, didn't quite fit some members' expectations because, apart from her country childhood, she had no obvious connection with the countryside. Nevertheless she was a tireless and persuasive campaigner and gave the CPRE a much needed public face.

When *Staying On* finished, Prunella joined the Peter Hall Company in a new Simon Gray play, *Just the Three of Us*, opening at the Yvonne Arnaud Theatre in Guildford. Dinsdale Landen played the local vicar; Prunella played Enid, a former English teacher, now a lush who, much to her shame, writes erotic pulp fiction to keep her husband Fred's publishing firm solvent; and Carli Norris played Fred's secretary. Enid, who has to drink herself into near oblivion to be able to begin a new book, descends into madness, developing needs which the others help her gratify. Set in a studio converted from a lighthouse, with a heavy chain hanging menacingly from the high beamed ceilings, it is an unsettling psychological drama.

Prunella combined her new duties as CPRE president with playing in *Just the Three of Us*. While rehearsing and touring she was able to visit some of the local branches and talk to members. She wrote often to Timothy:

'4 Oct. 1997. Play BETTER. We ran through on the Vic stage this morning. Peter had told Din that he should be in Chekhov, not Ben Travers, and me that I should be in Noël Coward not Chekhov—worked rather well. Peter being splendid, though the geography of the set doesn't help.'

'Sunday 19 October 1997. First day I've spent alone for years. Going to spend it learning the new bit (3 pages to go in tonight), and doing the house plants, haven't put any make-up on, saved hours. Also avoiding cold which hovers, got it from Carli—incidentally, what did you think about the kiss? Din hates it. I don't know—do you? Have taken to coming home in odd earrings, one show and one private, or, at worst, no show and one private, rather worrying when concentration doesn't extend to two ears.'

'21 October 1997. Off to Windsor for a CPRE rally, oh, the excitement, followed by yet another rehearsal with P. Hall. We're all longing for him to go to Australia so we can start playing it in. It's a lovely cold blue October day when my favourite things happened like you getting born and us getting married.'

'24 October 1997. Gosh. I do miss you: DREADING this tour—no real chums in the (very charming) company.'

'28 October. Tuesday. Lovely to talk to you this a.m. Last night *infinitely* better for the play, light dawning. Nice to be back in Brighton. All the staff send love and greetings. Did a CPRE Sussex Branch tea yesterday. FIVE media interviews on lorries, coming up this week, it's getting ridiculous.'

'1 November 1997. Just done your sock drawer. About eight weddings and four funerals. Took about 40 minutes, dead therapeutic I suppose, except it could never be said to be a FINITE task. Started a new odd sock bag.

'It's Finite Task Therapy Time: in the last 24 hours I've planted 24 tulip bulbs, dressed my Q.V. wig and cleaned three pairs of eyelashes—feel great.'

*   *   *

In June 1998 Prunella was the subject for one of a series of BBC programmes called *Funny Women*, made to recognize the skills and contributions of some of the leading actresses who, as the title suggests, have made a name for themselves in comedy. She gave a revealing interview about the way she views her work and how she approaches her characters. The programme managed to cover many areas, including extracts from some of her best-known television roles including Kate Starling, Sybil Fawlty, Miss Mapp, Sarah France, Queen Elizabeth II and Queen Victoria. There were comments from fellow actors, extracts from one of her teaching workshops and interviews with Timothy and Sam West. It's an absorbing programme, but underlines how challenging Prunella is to pin down—not least in half an hour of screen time—for as an actress she is often deliberately unrecognizable in a part, and plays classics, situation comedy, tragedy and farce with equal skill. The television clips naturally emphasized her high profile in situation comedy. But, as ever, her next part was different again.

At the end of February 1999 Harold Pinter's *The Birthday Party* went on tour to the Salisbury Playhouse, Birmingham Repertory Theatre, Newcastle Theatre Royal, Bradford Alhambra, Theatre Royal, Bath, and Richmond Theatre before going in to the Piccadilly Theatre in London on 26 April. Prunella and Timothy were both in it, but not as husband and wife. Prunella played Meg, the disorganized and daffy landlady of a seaside boarding-house; Meg's husband Petey, a deckchair attendant, was played by Barry Jackson. Meg decides to give a birthday party for their only lodger, Stanley, played by Steven Pacey. Enter unexpected guests Goldberg and McCann—Timothy West and Nigel Terry—whose appearance brings unexplained and unresolved menace. With an excellent cast, the notices were good.

When the play was over Prunella wrote to Timothy, who by then was away touring: 'Sardou failed to turn up for breakfast the day before yesterday—at about 9.00 a.m. muted mews from the front room revealed he'd been in there *all night*. He'd certainly left it very clean, but not a book opened, not a note played or a bar of music studied, hopeless case I'm afraid, howsoever endearing. Colman keeps coming in WET, even though sun be blazing outside. We suspect he's started bullying those neighbourhood kittens again, and that maybe they've bought a spray.' Prunella has always been extremely short-sighted, which can occasionally lead to some confusion. She writes to Timothy: 'The new handbag that Steffie gave me is exactly the same size and shape as Colman. I keep saying hullo to it in the morning before I've put my lenses in.'

Timothy and Prunella were together on stage again in *The External* by Rodney Clarke, which toured in the summer of 2002. Timothy played Sir Edgar Naseby, a leading academic and distinguished public figure who behind his intellectual façade is a drunken philanderer with an eye for attractive young female students. Prunella played his loyal and intelligent secretary, a much older woman whose self-sacrificing love has just managed to keep his career on the rails and save him from disgrace. She says she enjoyed the part because of the sensitivity of the writing. She liked the fact that 'although an older woman, she had strong sexual feelings and I enjoyed pretending to be in love with my own husband, it was quite fun. Although it's worth saying that your own private relationship with someone with whom you are acting has very little to do with what you bring to the stage.'

12

'See you Thurs.—or else'

'26 March 1988. 6.30 p.m. Gatwick Airport.

'Gatwick a horrendous mess of litter and passengers—our flight delayed 40 minutes by loaders' strike—but once aboard I feel guilty but relieved at having come business class and having room to stretch legs.

'I rate "Ordinary" in the In Flight Magazine Trivia Quiz. Disproportionately galled by this, SIX POINTS OFF EXCELLENT. Quite nervous about the whole expedition and cravenly choose champagne instead of orange juice when they come round. There's a lot of banging about on the tarmac underneath us—angry loaders throwing luggage out?

'4.00 a.m. (Having put watches on two hours, to Harare time). Lome, in Togo. We made a detour to pick up some Euro MPs. Couldn't even find Togo on the map.

'7.00 a.m. Flying South east, a staggering sunrise through the window, and a great grey-green greasy river below which I think must be the Congo. We're going to be about 40 minutes late in Harare.'

*　　　*　　　*

Prunella was flying out to visit Joe, who was spending part of his gap year teaching in Zimbabwe. Sam and Joe had been educated at Alleyn's School in Dulwich,

212

a co-educational independent school; in spite of their parents' strong Labour affiliations and their wish to educate the boys in a state school, because of three stabbings at their local school in one term, one of which was fatal, they decided to settle for somewhere less violent. When Sam finished school he went on to read English at Oxford. Now Joe, waiting to go to Manchester University, was spending part of his gap year teaching science and religious knowledge at St James's School, Zongoro, for an organization called Schools Partnership World Wide.

*   *   *

'28 March 1988. 9.00 a.m. Manica Hotel, Mutare. Yesterday the longest day of my LIFE—my luggage the last off as usual. Waited half an hour by the carousel, thank god for crochet, then trundled through customs to find Joe, in a beard, holding a large card saying MA.

'Drove with Joe to Marondera. We sat round chatting until alarmingly late in the afternoon, Joe seems to be coping well. He likes the week best, but finds the weekends a bit lonely, and is ludicrously pleased to see me. Afraid I let him drive back to St James's, it's not exactly illegal, but if there were an accident he's not covered. Picked up several hitchhikers who were all utterly charming. Got to the house and unpacked all the goodies which were greeted with whoops of joy. Joe and his friends still sleeping on the floor, which I find pretty disgraceful, but are coping with huge resource and cheerfulness. I got back here about 11.30 feeling I'd been awake a week.'

'29 March 1988 6.24 a.m. Manica Hotel. "I am

213

Mr West's Mother," I say. I sit on the verandah with my tapestry and the children come and look at me and giggle and smile. One nubile girl said, "I don't think so," when I told her I was Mr West's Mother, I said that was very kind of her, which I hope it was. I wash up and cook and am treated with respect, well it makes a change. The boys are quite stern with the kids, like a lot of prep school masters. It's sweet, you can practically tell exactly what the men who taught *them* were like. It seems to work, though I haven't seen a class yet. New teacher turned up yesterday, Reuben, a Zimbabwean, to teach Agriculture, Science and English. He and Joe both had baths here yesterday evening and it's taken two sachets of shampoo and eight sheets of that brown Kleenex they give you to get the ring off the bath. Just as well I brought a nail brush.

'7.00. Room boy has just brought me tea which I didn't order, asked how I spent the night and if he can please call me again. Cheeky, but obviously cheering for Mr West's Mother. Incidentally she leaves a fairly hefty ring round the bath too, the water is so absurdly soft here the boys have to leave their washing out in the rain all night to rinse it properly.'

'30 March 1988. 1.00 p.m. St James's Secondary School, Boy's House. I've been up since 5.45 a.m. and I feel like a pioneer wife. The Africans call me Mummy. So. Yesterday morning I bought chicken legs and onions at Omar's supermarket and drove out to Zongoro in time for the morning break. Went back to the school with them and sat in on two of Joe's classes. He's a wonderful teacher, I think, clear and rigorous and funny, but the schoolmaster acting is hilarious, he even cracks schoolmaster *jokes*.

'Some actual beds arrived in the afternoon, so I

214

drove back into Mutare to buy mattresses and pillows, lovely lumpy cotton things, incredibly comfortable after concrete. Today we've been to the river to collect water in buckets to do the washing—school tap on the blink. They've now got a charcoal-burning Tso-Tso stove in the wash house and can achieve constant hot water in an iron bucket on top of it. Afraid I bought them the bucket, also a primus lamp and small hurricane lantern, hope that wasn't overdoing it.'

'31 March 1988. Manica Hotel. Yesterday not nearly so nice, drove Joe and Al up to Juliasdale where there's a horrible hotel, Godalming by the swimming pool, cretonne everywhere and a *Casino*. Absolutely delicious toasted sandwiches, however. Drove back to Mutare, met Lucy, Adam and Nick and everyone came back here for showers, then we went to the White House Inn out on the Vimba road and had a delicious dinner. I took Joe and Al back home. Had been going to doss them down and take them back early this morning, but we decided the deception and the drive not worth it, so lent them the car I'm afraid and prayed for the best. Joe is driving quite well now, and it has been nice to have a night alone to recover—did you find being with them all the time a bit of a strain? For them too, I think, though at the house it's OK because one slips into the role of mother, bottle washer and water carrier, like Wendy with the Lost Boys.'

'1 April 1988. Zimbabwe Airport. 9.30 p.m. The second longest day of my life. Yesterday *nearly* a disaster. Nick, Joe, Lucy and I set forth at 4.30 in a car for Masuingo, 297 K to the south, to see the acclaimed ruins. One hour later on a delightful banana lined road littered with baboon families ushering each other across, the tarmac gave out and I got a blast of setting

sun in the driving-mirror—"why are we going EAST?"
I enquired nervously—"Not for long," chirruped Joe,
map-reading by my side. Twenty minutes after that
Nick said "Could I have a look at that map Joe?" by
which time the sun had practically plopped and we
were still climbing. "Oh," said Nick. "Well, we're on
the way back to Mutare. Quicker to go on and start
again really." Which we duly did, narrowly avoiding
the Mozambique border and arriving back at the
Manica at twenty-five to seven. Everybody pretty
good-tempered about it really, though Joe naturally
rather subdued. We set out again at 7.00, Joe driving,
had to stop for torrential rain and lightning, but I took
a Pro-plus and the wheel at thingy Bridge, (once the
longest suspension bridge in the world, v. impressive),
and we hit the Griel Zimbabwe Hotel at 12.08 this
morning. Sandwiches and beer, Joe, Lucy and I kipped
down in the vast bed, Nick on the floor of our chalet,
all slept like logs and ate huge breakfast at 8.00. The
kids loved it and have stayed on for the Easter
weekend. Bit touristy I thought, but the ruins are
wonderful, and I'm very glad we went. Melancholy and
knackering drive back to Harare on my own, listening
to *Little Dorrit* on Radio 1 and giving the odd lift. Hit
the airport at 8.00ish, where my knickers fell off. I
stuffed them in my bag with huge dignity, changed in
the Ladies, and here I am really.

'Felt like an astronaut coming into Heathrow: the
sun which I'd watched set on my left driving North to
Harare, had swapped places with the moon (last seen
rising on the right last night). And I'm still travelling
North.'

*   *   *

During Joe's gap year in Zongoro he had several visits from his parents. He found the whole experience of teaching in Zimbabwe fascinating. During his nine months there he managed to travel through Zambia, Malawi, Tanzania and Zanzibar. 'I always wanted to train as a teacher, and was thrown into teaching a wide range of classes of extremely well behaved children from the age of 10 to 21. Independence had come in 1981 and some of the older boys had been nine and ten then and had not gone to school because they were fighting. Everyone seemed to be working very well together. You gradually begin to understand what is going on.'

Prunella's experiences in Zimbabwe gave her some useful background when four years later, in March 1992, *Some Singing Blood* opened at the Royal Court. In it Prunella played a formidable mother, Iris, who follows her daughter, Alison, out to Zimbabwe in order to try to stop her marrying her father's best friend, played by Anton Rogers. The critics found the plot somewhat unbelievable, though they applauded Prunella's performance. Indeed, *Time Out* thought 'the play would sink without a trace without the arrival of the cavalry in the shape of Prunella Scales as Iris, Alison's mother, conventionally determined to prevent her daughter marrying somebody who qualifies for a bus pass. With her bizarre observations and her extraordinary outfits, she is the kind of mother we all hope to avoid.'

*   *   *

In 1996 Prunella filmed *Stiff Upper Lips*, which was set in the early 1900s and aimed to send up the whole Jane Austen, Merchant Ivory, BBC costume-drama

217

scene. The classics were being mined for good plots: the BBC had just made a very popular adaptation of *Pride and Prejudice*; Merchant Ivory had made *A Room with a View* and *Howards End*. Jane Austen's *Emma* was about to be filmed, and Gaskell's *Wives and Daughters* was being planned. *Stiff Upper Lips*, made in 1996, was to be a somewhat bawdy parody of the Edwardian costume drama. The idea was that if millions loved the big classical productions, they'd also flock to something that made gentle fun of them. It was filmed in the Isle of Man, India and Italy, though, as the budget was modest, the exotic locations consumed a large portion of the finances. Written by Paul Simpkin and Gary Sinyor, and directed by Gary Sinyor, the story concerns an aristocratic English family who travel to India and Italy to see the world. The young hero, Cedric, played by Robert Portal, is ultra-repressed and formal, his friend from Oxford, Edward, played by Samuel West, embarrassingly dim. Peter Ustinov plays an eccentric great-great uncle who falls for Aunt Agnes, a spinster aunt played by Prunella.

It was a very ambitious shoot, and the schedule was horrendous. Between the Isle of Man and flying out to India, Prunella had only twelve hours at home. Her almost daily faxes to Timothy record the progress of cast and crew through the disparate locations. It is possible the faxes are rather more entertaining than the finished film turned out to be, and they are a brilliant view of the trials and tribulations of a working actress—seen through Prunella's eyes.

* * *

'Isle of Man. Thursday 3rd March 1996. Attached is a

218

random polaroid of my first day's shooting [photograph of Prunella dressed in corset, stockings and a safety harness]. No, it's not really that kind of part, it's the harness for my shot up the ladder. Rather hairy scene, actually, specially in a long skirt. Got to do it again tomorrow for the wide shot, we lost the light this evening. I was terrifically brave.'

'4th March. 6.10 p.m. Horrid day, shooting sunny tea-on-the-lawn scenes in the FREEZING cold and a too-tight corset, with pages and pages of dauntingly unmemorable text. Sammy is being lovely, very good in the part, and hearing my lines with exemplary filial charm and firmness. It's very strange seeing so much of him suddenly. I see my father more and more in him—to look at I mean, it's almost creepy. It's a very good cast and a lovely unit so far.'

'Wednesday, 13th March 1996. The Nunnery, Isle of Man. I've been offered Miss Bates in *Emma*. Haven't seen script or heard about locations etc., but it looks possible. So things are looking up. They'd better, mind you, it's fucking FREEZING up here.'

'Isle of Man. Thursday, 14th March. (I think) 1996. 7.00 a.m. Two horrendous days filming in roofless hovels with 48 extras in period bowler hats who had to be told not to look at the camera on *every shot*. Actually they looked wonderful, and there was a lovely blind man (who of course didn't have to be told) with a guide dog called Winston, who also didn't have to be told anything except when he was off the lead, when he was glued to a crate of chickens, with a sort of puzzled frown on his forehead as if they were a mathematical problem. We worked until 8.30 p.m. (non-Equity contracts you see).

'It's the wedding scene today and tomorrow, more extras but at least the church will have a roof. Well, won't it? . . . There's something about corsets that stops you getting warm, however many thermals you wear over and under them. Wardrobe say cheerfully that it's the compression of the blood vessels, and are assiduous with sympathy and hot-water bottles, but I don't think I've ever been so cold ever—teeth actually chattering—v. corny.'

'March 16th 11.30 a.m. It PISSED with rain yesterday, and again today, hope I'll make Huddersfield, let alone get back. My second wig wasn't made for me, so it has to be STRETCHED on the pin-up, and is agony at the end of two hours, not to speak of ten. Everyone pretty good-tempered on the whole though, it's going to look beautiful and may even come off. Heigh ho. Peter is in very good form and an angel of patience.'

*   *   *

'29th March 1996. 10.12 a.m. Indian time, mid-air. Rather hairy take-off, pilot told us there would be slight delay as cabin communications unit was faulty and had to be replaced. We all drank some champagne. The Heathrow stores didn't have the necessary unit, another had to be removed from another plane. More champagne. "Right, ladies and gentlemen, we do apologize for the delay, we'll be moving off now, so seat-belts fastened please . . . ah." All the lights go out. But ALL of them except the seat-belt signs. Pause. "Sorry about that ladies and gentlemen. The generators *have* been under a strain during the delay, once we get the engines running the lighting *will* be restored . . ." Men with torches and luminous braces scamper up and down the aisle hissing "turn your ovens off." Cabin staff chorus, "We haven't got them on . . ." We are towed to runway in pitch blackness. We start to taxi down the runway—how? Are they still towing us? It's the latest of the range aircraft, Boeing 747.400, can they *jump-start* it? Do they know what they are doing?'

'30th March 1996, Savoy Hotel, Ootacamund. Four hours, across the plain and then into the mountain up well-metalled road, with fourteen (numbered) hairpin bends, and about a hundred (unnumbered and infinitely more scary) blind corners. The technique at blind corners, is that if you are behind anything—to overtake it while *sounding your horn*. On the straight parts you overtake without sounding your horn. About half way up there was a sharp gust of wind, a violent cloudburst and a tree fell down across the next hairpin bend. Cavalcades of vehicles ground to a halt in both directions. Everybody got out and moved it, very impressive.

'The vegetation changes from tropical to semi-tropical to sort of Wales, and then on the top here it's coolish and very beautiful tea country, still quite feudal and prosperous. The hotel is mahogany Colonial, most of the unit are here and they love it. I have room No. 2, which is a sort of 5-roomed flat with three single beds, the bathroom even darker than the others, even with the light on. Food lovely, when it arrives. The hairdryer in the bathroom plays you a tune while in use, it's very kind of it, but I can't help wishing it would save its energy. General temperature v. pleasant, coolish at night, no mosquitoes yet. My bedroom has an open fireplace with one of those nursery fireguards with a brass rim they used to hang the socks over to dry. We're all drinking gin and tonic, haven't had it since I was seventeen. Indian wine is revolting and French costs about £25 a bottle, so we're

221

on the beer and gin. It'll be solar topees next. I find I sustain separation very ILL these days. Love, love, love, love and things.'

'31st March 1996. Ooty is rather wonderful, company cheering up no end. Today we went first to the highest peak in the area, Doddabetta, with absolutely staggering views and crawling with Indian tourists—in the wake of the Raj I expected abuse, but there's a sort of tolerant matiness which is rather a relief. Whole thing Clovelly with saris really. Tamil Nadu is the home of vegetarianism and they cook brilliantly, so most of the unit are eating veggie—a couple of those who aren't have had the most horrendous trots, so Sam's beaming.

After lunch today Sam had organized four of us to go to Avalanchi (we should have known) which actually requires a four-wheel drive. Horrendous road most of the way, with totally unexplained stretches of good tarmac at random intervals, culminating in what the tourist guide promised would be ravishing lake, fishing and forest. We got out and walked over the worst bits, and eventually arrived at the lake, which is currently a sort of beautiful puddle set in acres of red earth banks because of the drought. The wild life parks are closed also because of the drought, only hope the monsoon sorts things out. We had a paddle and a wander and the guide gave me a rose from the garden there and we all felt better.'

'1st April 1996. Ah. Spoke too soon. Sam and Bertie ill this a.m. They've both gone back to bed. This afternoon I thought it would be jolly to go for a forest ride: Sam and Bertie not well, Sam doesn't like riding, so in the end it was Jess and Christine (the camera assistants) and me. Reception arranged for a man to come round with his two sons and a very old toothless

222

guide and three ponies called Goldie and Sweet Lady and Mumtaz. I had Sweet Lady, she was 8 and only trotted if you kicked her. Had a really ravishing wander through the woods above Ooty . . . First day's work tomorrow.'

'4th April 1996. It was quite a hard day yesterday, about two hours in the bath with Peter, *plus* the bottom spanking scene and two others. Bath scene was hilarious. They had imported massive period bath which would take me *and* Peter with space for enough foam to cover the embarrassing bits, and then of course had to fill it with bacteria-free bottled mineral water, crates and crates of it, because Peter has to put his head under. So then they had to heat it (very inadequately, four electric elements lashed together to a piece of wood and lowered into the bath on a line), then the mineral water wouldn't bubble properly, so Props put a pulley block on his battery power tool and spun it in the water, and Wardrobe and Make-up sculpted the bubbles in artistic mounds over my boobs (yes, I did have a bra on, strapless with about a ton of padding each side, quite effective really). Poor Sparks are having a frightful time with Indian equipment and personnel, but the location, Fernhill Palace, is magic. Built by a local Maharajah c.1890, the light fittings alone are worth a visit. The loo in my bathroom has shallow cast iron white painted cistern and polished brass down pipe—after that it's the paper-thin plastic contemporary seat as usual.'

'5th April 1996. 5.10 a.m. I'm being collected at 5.20. We wrapped at 8.30 last night having been called at 8.30 a.m. Not going to pull Age and Status because I wasn't used till 6 p.m., so got a lot of sleep in during the day, and we're pushed etc., etc., etc., but you can see the sort of thing. *I've* got the squitters this

223

morning, too, and it's not because I have to play polo on a baby elephant at 11.00 o'clock either. Honestly.

'Call sheet reads:

ART DEPARTMENT: As per script to include Parasol/fan, Polo Equipment, Pimms, Pistachios, Cashew nuts. Roped area for tea. Swing for extras. Hole in Fence. Breakaway Fence for Elephant to break through.

ANIMALS: 1x Large Elephant, 2x Small Elephants c/o Vishal Sood. Venkatesh to stand by from 6.45 to translate into Kanataka.

RIGGING: Elephant Mounting Platform to stand by from 6.45 for all cast.

UNIT NURSE: Nicky Jarvis to stand by on set from 7.00.

SAFETY MEETING re: Elephants on front lawn. All cast and crew to attend.

UNIT NOTES: Please don't wear perfume, cosmetics or anything alcohol based today as this will make the elephant very angry!!

CATERING: Lunch: Numbers 110 approx. Please keep taking your Malaria pills.

'Promise you—I'll bring it home to frame if I survive. I wasn't at all frightened until I read the schedule. I mean they might have found some elephants that speak ENGLISH for God's sake. No, apparently it's the *drivers* who only speak Kanataka. The big elephant is nine feet tall and called Badhur. The babies are only about seven feet with furry heads and are called Indira and Pretty. (Well that's what the head driver told us.) Indira has just done a massive crap—I know how he feels—and peed copiously on top of it through a fairly evident and uncompromising cock. I've had to construct myself a nappy out of loo paper and a plastic bag from wardrobe—"if I shit in my pants my enemies will say it was from fear . . ."

'Later 11.50 a.m. Well, it *was* a bit hairy: the elephant people hadn't brought anything for us to sit on, so they roped a bit of sacking over Indira and Pretty and we held onto that. Peter *very* scared to begin with, but enjoyed it in the end. Sat sideways on with his legs sticking straight out before him, wielding his stick like a croquet mallet. Gary put me up first and required me to sit side-saddle, facing forward, legs to the left, stick in right hand. Cannot describe the pain in the *hips* after ten minutes or so. Wardrobe had been *promised* proper seats, so didn't bring a split skirt for me. After the seventh or eighth take I said, *fairly* quietly, Gary, I've been on this elephant for nearly one hour and I've got dysentery—and they let me down. Sam had to ride Badhur—he's a circus elephant and rides a bicycle and is 31. He behaves like a very camp old actor, crossing his legs and waving his trunk around and looking at his fingernails. Apparently he has to be back over the border before nightfall.'

'10th April 1996. Craigmore Plantations India Pty Ltd. 6.45 p.m. Arrived here yesterday lunchtime— ravishing tea plantation, actually lower than Ooty, though the journey through the mountains felt as if we were climbing. The light outside is magical and every buzz track sounds like a BBC nature programme— about 36 different bird calls per second, and (for once in India) hardly any traffic. As Peter said, you expect a David Attenborough voice any minute.'

'11th April 1996. 8.30 a.m. I'm sitting on the verandah drinking fresh orange pekoe off the estate, with dew on the grass and a positive roar of birdsong. We've seen hoopoes and red-cheeked bul-buls, and now the school children are cheering the unit buses as they drive up through the village from Ooty. Day

225

began with the muezzin at dawn, about 5.30, followed by amplified pop music as the workers (about 40% of local population apparently) leave for the plantations, then toll from the Christian Mission Church. Wonderful moment yesterday during rather difficult scene on the lawn at Woodlands. Richard said, right, very quiet everyone, hold the work, roll sound— whereupon there was a monstrous clap of thunder and helpless corpsing from the entire cast.'

'Sunday, 14th April 1996. My last Indian day with any luck. Another time I'll bring an UMBRELLA. All the Indians carry them everywhere, looks very strange with bare feet and dhotis. They're usually black with big wooden crooks like City gents' umbrellas, and have a beautiful spoke structure inside quite different from the British ones. The heavens opened again on Friday, our one day off. I've never SEEN such rain, the downpipes from the gutters on the verandas were washing out over the top, and thunder quite deafening though couldn't see any lightning. Apparently it's called the Mango Monsoon, helps ripen the mangoes, and the real monsoon comes in July and sweeps away lots of people's houses.

'Never told you about the tea. I expected sort of cotton fields—rows of brown chest-high bushes with lines of saried pickers moving through them, I'm an ignorant cow. The tea bushes are between 2 and 4 feet high, rounded with green shiny leaves rather like small rhododendrons. Some of the bushes are 100 years old and they grow all over the hillsides as far as the eye can see, interspersed with palms and fir trees. The leaves are picked selectively every ten days, and pruned by hand annually.'

'Monday 15th April 1996. 9.20 a.m. Well. I'm finished! The BA flight leaves Bombay at 1.00 a.m., so

226

I'll have many hours in the Business Lounge. Never MIND, I'm coming HOME, can't wait. I'm sort of terrified of this journey today, but at least we'll avoid that ghastly Cambatore road.'

'16th April 1996. In the air. Bombay-Delhi. Earplugs (not issued on this flight) desirable less for drowning engine noise than to mitigate the piercing tone of the inevitable crashing bore sitting behind you. Why does he always have such a penetrating voice, such banal ideas and such a compulsive need to impart them to his neighbour? There's a really nice American sitting next to me, but he's hardly uttered. I think he's feeling sick.

'Bombay airport rather hairy, all the signs in Hindi and you have to walk miles to identify luggage, and I haven't travelled ALONE for ages, it's rather melancholy. Feel better now I've started writing, just waffle really but at least I'm not keeping anybody awake.'

'Delhi Domestic 8.45 p.m. Ah, I've been sitting alone for 1/2 hour in a very rude courtesy bus, which refuses to leave for Delhi International until 9.00 p.m. Flight for London doesn't leave till midnight, but I've got to change tickets etc., and could have been sitting in a courtesy *lounge* by now having a DRINK (no alcohol on an Indian Domestic flight). There's actually a power cut at the moment, emergency lights only—I suppose all the technical stuff is still working, but it's incredibly difficult to identify luggage on a carousel by the light of one small T.V. screen. Hope I've got the right bags.

'8.55 p.m. Lights have come on again, also two more passengers. I want to go to the loo. Was horribly sick again yesterday, dodgy omelette at breakfast, but O.K. now I HOPE. Wish everything didn't

227

FRIGHTEN me so much. We're off. I hate Indian driving.

11.35 p.m. Down to the departure lounge in the Maharajah Club Class lounge where I was having a nice double brandy and a slight kip, they call the flight every ¼ of an hour, so I got nervous in the end and came down to Security.'

*   *   *

'Monday 29th April 1996. Latina, Italy. Things are looking up. Two amazing days in Rome and they've given me a little trolley in my room to put things on. (Thinking of setting up a business. "Consult the Sybil: don't let your hotel be a Fawlty Tower—she'll cost you £500 per hour and she'll save you thousands.")

'Yesterday went and got blessed by the Pope in the pissing rain and then watched Rome draw against Juventus in a rather dull match, but the occasion and the stadium were amazing, and in between did the Sistine Chapel and had another beautiful lunch. They get upwards of 100,000 people through the Chapel per day (or did I get that wrong), it's agony, you walk for *miles* through amazing anterooms and when you finally get to Michelangelo, you're so tired you would really rather buy the book. Thought it would be like wandering in King's Cambridge, but it's more like the Marathon. Loved the Cathedral though—beautiful and friendly and alive, a mass going on in good spoken Latin, the staff much more relaxed than in the Chapel. I thought it was rather moving. Bernini's circus a sea of coloured umbrellas (this is the Umbrella Job, isn't it) some people just staring, some devout, lots singing. Stood next to a local "Romana"—she said, who sang and shouted and prayed and pointing to this tiny little

228

Pope up in a side window, told me it was *"Gesù sulla terra"*. Got today off, catching up on letters and things.'

'3rd May 1996. From the window, just to the right of the car park, there's a good view of a large factory building labelled "ARSOL. INDUSTRIA MANGIMISTICA." Don't wish to know what Mangimistica means, the rest says it all.

'The Anzio location is ravishing—a villa where Coriolanus is supposed to have stayed, lovely village, lovely food, lovely Italian crew, and at last lovely *weather*. If only we were staying here, instead of at awful Latina. Never mind—trains to Rome outside the door.'

'Friday, 3rd May 1996. 9.05 a.m. Sort of double day yesterday—two lunches and we wrapped at midnight. I'm most unpopular person with the management now because (at the request of the rest of the cast and unit), I insisted on the 10 hour break, and am being picked up at 11.00 instead of 9.30, but lots of Brownie points from the unit. Coming back on 16th. There are so many lovely things about this job, the locations, Sammy, great cast, lovely unit, just wish I had more faith in the Product, but all may yet be well. Look after your darling self and love to the seeds and Colman and the fish.'

'7th May 1996. Bugger it, the weather is now wonderful and I've got one of my colds, trying desperately to avoid laryngitis, and Nicky nurse is being wonderful, but REALLY. Had quite enough of this job, it's really peculiar having no mate in the unit (except Sam, who of course has all the kids). I'm the oldest person, and people are quite prepared to treat one as a STAR, in fact they'd probably be happier if I did all that, but I can't, so there. We saw the trailer they've cut together for Cannes the other night. It all

229

looks rather good and quite funny, though the voice over was awful—a bit coy and pretend grand but rather "common" really, you know? We tried to persuade them to redub, but they said no, too late. Heigh ho.'

'Saturday, 11th May 1996. We've got the day off, *and* tomorrow, the unit could do with it, but since they're now keeping me until Thursday afternoon 16th, I feel cross and under-used and exploited and I've had this movie up to here. However, if you're going to have time on your hands, Rome's the place to have it. We had a magical day yesterday doing the "Bernini walk" out of Sam's very good guide book, and today we're going to do the Pantheon and more Bernini in the Villa Borghese. The *Emma* script is v. disappointing but I'm committed to it now. Perhaps I shd. give up and just do gardening. I love you enormously much, be good, see you Thurs. or else.'

13

Finding Victoria

'God knows how much I want to be taken care of'

*   *   *

Prunella had met Katrina Hendrey and her husband, Richard Burnett, when they were working with the Prospect Theatre Company, initially with a production called *The Grand Tour*. This led to other shows, including, in the mid-1970s, an anthology of children's writing compiled by Katrina. Musical accompaniment was by the pianist Richard Burnett, with songs performed by the lyric tenor Ian Partridge. In 1974 Prunella had been to Canada with *The Hollow Crown*, a history of England using the words of the monarchs themselves, originally devised for the Royal Shakespeare Company by John Barton. Prunella's favourite piece was Queen Victoria's account of her coronation. As background reading Prunella took with her (out of the Westminster Public Library) the three published volumes of Queen Victoria's diaries. 'I was absolutely knocked out by them: they are so funny, intelligent and quite indiscreet.'

When Katrina said she would like to write a show for Prunella, Richard and Ian, because they got on so well together, Prunella suggested a programme based on the diaries. Katrina agreed, and *An Evening with Queen Victoria* was devised. Richard Burnett, an expert on ancient instruments, chose all the period music for the show, including pieces written by Prince

231

Albert. Prunella plays Queen Victoria from the age of thirteen to eighty-two, using minimal make-up, and a costume and wig indicative of the Victorian era. We meet Queen Victoria as she changes from an impulsive young girl refusing to be overwhelmed by her royal inheritance, through her joy in her marriage, to total devastation at the early death of her beloved Albert, and finally the transformation into the implacable matriarch of her later years. Interspersed between these changes, music of the period is played and sung by Richard and Ian. The show, entirely based on Queen Victoria's diaries and letters, views her life through her own eyes.

The first two performances, in September 1979, were at Katrina and Richard's house, Finchcocks, in Kent, in their museum of music and musical instruments. They followed this in the New Year with a Sunday evening performance at the Old Vic. Nicholas Curry, then a company manager for the theatre, has stayed with them ever since as director, agent and administrator. The production came to the attention of BBC 2, who recorded it live at the Lyric Theatre Hammersmith on 26 May 1981. The *Daily Mail* commented, 'Prunella Scales shows just what a delightful, many-faceted artist she is. [With] movements lilting or laborious, and just the odd flick of a shawl, Miss Scales grows younger or older at will. You can imagine the magic working for a theatre audience, but to succeed in camera close-ups is nothing short of a miracle.' Sylvia Clayton in the *Telegraph* wrote of 'a bravura performance, using no make-up, minimal props and agreeable music of the period. Prunella Scales [is] a clever, observant actress.' Leon Radic agreed, 'Miss Scales performs with consummate skill, helped in no small degree by her two partners.' Since then they have played in every possible venue, and have given more than 400 performances in concert halls, town halls and parish halls, in night-clubs, arts centres, churches and every size of theatre. *An Evening with Queen Victoria* has become an intermittent source of work for Prunella and the rest of the cast which they fit in between other engagements. Over the years they have travelled to countries on four continents, from New Zealand to Bermuda, Brunei to the USA—where they opened in the Library of Congress in Washington. Recorded by Decca in 1984 and nominated the best spoken-word recording of the year, as a stage show it is just as much in demand today.

Their first Australian tour was at the beginning of 1983. Prunella wrote to Timothy from Melbourne on 30 January: 'I have punishing publicity programme tomorrow and Tuesday (when we open): they originally wanted me from 8.30 a.m. to 3.30 p.m. on Tuesday for TV and radio. Nick has said 3 hours only starting at 10.30. All this publicity effort means of course they haven't sold next week as well as they hoped. This week OK apparently. God, I hope we're going to be all right. Australia could easily hate it, I suppose.' Australia didn't hate it—they had to put extra seats in the aisles every night. She tells Timothy that 'the drought is v. serious, Victoria pale brown all over and the corn harvest ruined'. The next day, 'Well, we've opened. The Victorian Arts centre people amazed by the show, they've got awful posters up saying "You *will* be amused"—but I don't think they expected to be really.' From Melbourne they went to Canberra for a week, where the show was praised as 'a rare and lovely entertainment', then on to the Festival of Perth, whose directors had organized

233

the tour. At one performance in Perth the cast had to compete for attention with a man in the audience listening to the election results on his transistor radio, which he turned up for the benefit of those around him.

After two weeks in Perth, they took the show on a ten-day whistle-stop tour round the outback, performing in ten different country towns. Actors, management, luggage and props all piled into a minibus for a tour arranged by the Arts Council to take theatre to the bush. It was quite an experience. At their first venue there was an enthusiastic turn-out. 'Posters in every window, newly tuned piano, laughter, breathless attention, rapturous applause and huge whiskies at the thrash afterwards. They couldn't believe we were there—farmers, teachers, housewives, dentists, schoolchildren, all saying it was the best thing they'd ever seen or heard.' Later in the tour, in another small town, the reception was very different: 'Full house, sat like stones for the first three-quarters of an hour except for applauding the songs. I worked heroically and got them going by the interval, whereupon they produced a baby, two brilliant coughers and a lady with a heart condition who had to be taken out ten minutes before the end. Afterwards we were given a lot of cold quiche and sandwiches and a choice of tea or milky coffee. Bruce [the driver] had found me a glass of vin rosé and I'm afraid they thought I was the most frightful tart.' She suspected some of the promoters were waiting for 'Basil Fawlty meets Her Majesty'.

At the end of the tour Prunella returned to Wandsworth 'for 10 days of knicker-washing and sleep before we leave for the US of A', as she wrote to her school friend Veronica Conyers in America. Veronica had invited her to stay for a few days, but Prunella told her, 'I haven't really got "a few days"—just the one travel day, which if Australia is anything to go by, will also be occupied in wig-dressing, frock ironing and further knicker-washing. We are supposed to be a "portable" show, which is a euphemism for "do it yourself". However, I do enjoy it, and it's quite refreshing to do it yourself occasionally, specially on stage, and I'd love you to see the show. Have to do Albert's lines myself, in GERMAN, so you could give me some notes!'

After ten days at home, in January the cast were off again for a performance at the Bermuda Festival on 21 January. By April 1983 she told Timothy she was delighted to have met up with Veronica and her husband in Charleston, 'which was beautiful and warm. It has been sort of lovely, in that I've remembered how much I like America and Americans—you must go to the Deep South one day—it is extraordinary. Want to play Savannah sometime, like Ellen Terry.'

From there they took three plane journeys, Charleston—Atlanta—Chicago—Saginaw, and were 'properly met in Saginaw by nice people with lots of station wagons, and the show is sold out tonight, and then ensued this drive into Midland, which is remarkable only for a vast chemical works'. In Midland they were taken to 'a dreadful hotel. Minute rooms dominated by a vast colour TV (which in my case doesn't work), no coffee shop, just a sprint across the tarmac to a sort of passage behind reception for orange juice, coffee and doughnut (that was breakfast) and it is PISSING with rain, but PISSING. And Nick has got my cold and Ian is coughing. Heigh-ho.' The tour was deemed a success, but they were all glad to

235

get home.

Two years later they were invited to take part in the Sydney Festival. Heading off to Australia in the New Year, Prunella's first letter to Timothy reads, typically: 'I've done five interviews this a.m. so hope bookings are picking up.' On 6 January she tells Timothy, 'I'm missing you a *lot*. Enjoying the show though. Three down, 32 to go. Perhaps it's early days to say.' And by 7 January: 'We're the hottest ticket in the Festival. 280-seater theatre, you see. Awful actually. You either have the airconditioning off and fry the audience, or have it on and get laryngitis trying to be heard. Still liking the show though. The Melbourne Age asked me if we were bored with it yet. I said that after our 104th performance Ian P had come into my dressing room and given me six notes, so we probably weren't yet.' From Sydney they went on to Melbourne and then for a return visit to Perth.

There was other radio, television and stage work in between the evenings with Queen Victoria, but the show and its offshoots continued to keep Prunella busy. One associated programme, *A Victorian Christmas*, also written by Katrina Hendrey, was performed at the Albert Hall in 1984 to complement an exhibition on Prince Albert at the Royal College of Art. The cast included Prunella, Joss Ackland and Anton Rogers.

In early 1987 *An Evening with Queen Victoria* toured to the Far East—to Brunei, Taiwan and the Hong Kong Festival. Her letters home start with her account of their horrendous flight to Bahrein: 'bumpiest I've ever known, convinced last hours had come, Ian's hand *blue* with bruises from me clutching it, and a woman was sick all over Richard.' Before the show was allowed to be shown to the public in Brunei, which is strictly Muslim, the censors insisted on seeing it to make sure it contained nothing offensive. Prunella tells Timothy: 'The censorship preview was really very funny. There were five censors, four male, one female and we rather assumed that once they had seen me clad from head to toe in opaque white cotton, they'd OK it instantly—but they let us go on and on and ON: three quarters of the way through the first half we were cutting CHUNKS of music and text and getting very giggly: I kept hands clamped to sides in the quadrilles so not a smidgeon of ankle showed. I think perhaps they couldn't believe it was so boring and were waiting for some sort of dénouement. I resisted almost uncontrollable urge to rip Ian's trousers off at the end of *Schmerz der Liebe*, and we lumbered to end of act one. I then suggested that perhaps we shouldn't waste any more of their valuable time, as there was no further change of costume; the two who were asleep woke up, the others put away their watches, and the main one came up to the front, shook our hands and said it was "very great".'

When they went on to Hong Kong they played the unlikely venue of the Hilton Hotel discothèque, much to the bemusement of some of the guests. A Hong Kong paper reported that 'a kindly old sport must have found the erstwhile Mrs Basil Fawlty to be the woman of his dreams, because he spent the majority of the first act snoring in heart-felt appreciation of her theatrical efforts'.

They reached Taiwan at the end of February, and stayed at the Hilton in Taipei. Prunella tells Timothy that 'One of the customs girls at Hong Kong airport yesterday asked to see inside my wig-box and nearly *died*—she thought it was a sawn-off head.' They were billed to appear in the Tiffany Room, which advertised

237

itself as the Disco of the 90s, 'an experience in light and sound, the place in Taipei to see and be seen, Disco the hours away every night from 9 p.m.' Booked to do three nights of dinner theatre, posters for the show were up on easels sporting a picture of Queen Victoria which was subtitled 'Yes, but can she write?' The blurb read: 'She has all the right qualifications, over 63 years managing and ruling a country, wife and mother of nine, hostess to leading international figures—she even had a period in history named after her. She looks great on paper, but can this woman write?' Prunella writes to Timothy: 'Not sure that many of its regular clientele will be spending an evening with Queen Victoria . . . In order to avoid meeting the audience, we were instructed by Mr Yu to make our way backstage via the kitchens of adjacent Golden China restaurant, so at 7.55 we duly processed in full costume and orderly British fashion through roomful of diners, only to be repulsed at the kitchen doors by restaurant manager and several waiters wielding trays of soup. We retraced our progress with as much dignity as we could muster to the door of Tiffany's, where Mr Yu firmly propelled us back through the restaurant (inscrutable smiles of diners by this time giving way to undisguised hilarity) and finally into the kitchen, to pick our way through hordes of steaming woks and emerge through the fire exit at the side of the stage in full view of the assembling audience. All 36 of them. After that the show was rather well received.'

From Taipei they went to Queensland in Australia, where they stayed at a hotel called Waltzing Matilda in Redcliffe, then a rather dreary suburb of Brisbane. Queen Victoria played to disappointingly small audiences at the beginning of the week, but picked up well by the end, and Prunella was invited to launch a 'Beer off the Wood' campaign at Carlton Brewery. She gave Timothy a summary of proposed events. 'They say the chairman will give a speech for forty minutes after which the bung will be drilled—apparently P. Scales is to stand by and at 11.21 pull the first beer. Chairman will ask guests to join him for "one off the wood" (another 20 minutes), after which bush band strikes up and I imagine everyone gets pissed. Still it's an outing.'

The last leg of the tour was to New Zealand. Because of the international popularity of *Fawlty Towers*, at every stop the reporters noted, with obvious surprise, how unlike Sybil Prunella was. She was forced to tell an interviewer, Peter Shaw, that the character 'follows me around like a shadow'. Peter Shaw went to the show: 'Prunella Scales' performance is charming. She held the audience through a long solo performance to such an extent that they were responding to all the subtleties of her playing. It is a rare pleasure in Christchurch these days to be able to enjoy the performance of one so professional and skilled.' She had told him, 'It's a challenging programme for all of us, refreshing and stimulating. So far it's never been routine . . . well-written parts never are.'

Just before Christmas 1990 Prunella went once again to Western Australia with *An Evening with Queen Victoria*. Timothy planned to join her when his play had finished so that they could spend Christmas together in Sydney. She described her hotel room to him. 'I have another flock and velvet suite, overlooking the car park, wherein you will be more than welcome. No bath and no shower caps, double indignity.' From Perth they went straight to Bunbury, which 'is so quiet that I actually heard a man on a bicycle *belch*, quite clearly from the other side of the street. The two farmers and their wives rather quiet too, last night, probably felt a bit lost in the new Entertainment Centre, which has 800 seats and is to be opened by Prince Philip next week.'

By the end of November 1990 they were back in Perth. 'Show settling in and it's lovely to be back in the Playhouse, just like Salisbury or somewhere.' Two days later she told Timothy, 'Well we're winning, I *think*. Houses small and mystified, but improving.' She described the attitude of a few of the press towards the performance. ' "Of course you've been doing this show for eleven years," say the media. "Oh come on," I say, "it's a chamber work. You wouldn't say to a string player, look you've been playing that Schubert quartet for eleven years now, isn't it time to give it a rest." Actually the media, as usual in Oz, are v. nice and supportive and have all been to see us.' *An Evening with Queen Victoria* had its twentieth anniversary on 13 January 2000 in a Millennium performance at the Wigmore Hall.

The long-running success of the show was the inspiration for the BBC's two-part drama/documentary *Looking for Victoria*, shown in November 2003. In contrast to the stage show, in the BBC dramatized version Prunella played Queen Victoria only as an old woman looking back on her life. For the documentary part of the BBC version, she travelled to places of moment during Victoria's life, where she interviewed various experts about events that had shaped Victoria's long reign. Prunella was delighted to play Victoria in full costume and prosthetic make-up, but with her chameleon-like need to portray someone other than herself on screen, she

240

was not happy with the idea of being identified as the interviewer, even though the 'ad lib' section was scripted. She admitted, 'I'm very interested in Victoria herself and have learned a great deal about her, but I don't like talking to camera. I don't mind talking to people. Talking to camera feels slightly immoral—slightly self-regarding.'

As this was one of my chances to watch Prunella working, I was given permission by the director, Louise Osmond, to sit in on some of the filming of the BBC production of *Looking for Victoria*. The drama section was made first.

*   *   *

19 January 2003.
I spend the night at Wandsworth as the next day is a 6.10 a.m. start. We are up very early. The car arrives and we set off for Syon House, near Richmond, which for the next two weeks will stand in as the home of Queen Victoria. Arriving in the cold, rainy dark, we find the front door still locked, so traipse off through the stables looking for an entrance. We are met by Luke Barclay, Prunella's personal minder for the duration of the filming, who leads the way up to Prunella's dressing-room on the first floor, a large room with deep, comfortable armchairs and a view over the park. Her costumes hang on a rack but before being dressed she must go across to make-up. Walkie-talkies crackle 'Prunella is travelling', and with Luke leading the way, followed by Prunella, June Nevin, the wardrobe mistress, and myself we travel for what seems like miles, down the red-floral-carpeted stairs, across a wide hall into the servants' quarters in the basement. As we sweep along the long, cold, stone-

241

flagged passages, high above us on the wall hang rows of bells, once used to summon servants. At the end of the passages another flight of stairs leads to a small flat, now housing make-up, wardrobe and a green room. It is here Pauline Cox, Make-up, will transform Prunella into Queen Victoria.

First her hair is scraped back with a centre parting and gelled down. Pincurls keep it in place, with a stocking top over the pincurls to hold it firm. Unlike Prunella, Victoria's nose was prominent, so prosthetic gelatine noses have been made, one of which must now be attached. This is a slow and painstaking process, but once done the effect is startling. Prunella, vivacious and pretty, is transformed by the nose into a dour, bad-tempered woman with a down-turned severe mouth. The director, Louise, comes to talk over the day's schedule with her. While they talk, the long wig is pinned into place and coiled into a soft chignon at the back; lastly a minimum of make-up is applied. Victoria, herself, would have worn none.

With make-up and hair completed, we retrace our steps to the room where the costumes hang ready. Here Prunella, who is small and slim, is transformed into Victoria, who was small and very fat. Over a camisole she puts on padding to fill her out, over the padding a corset to pull her in and tame the fatness to Victorian curves. Over the fatness and the corset, two bustles to accentuate her backside. Then two petticoats and an overskirt to cover her up, a long-sleeved jacket and over it all, a beautifully worked cape. After Albert's death, the Queen retired into perpetual mourning, so all is black. Rings on her fingers, bracelets and earrings, and Queen Victoria, with minions in tow, sails forth from the dressing-room, down the red-carpeted stairs, across the echoing

242

marble hall, and sweeps into the vast anteroom where the filming is to take place. The transformation has taken two and a half hours.

Inside the anteroom grey-green marble pillars frame the vast space. The dark walls, inset with intricate gilded panels, are brightened by life-size gilt statues which loom over the beautiful Adam floor. In the dim lighting a low armchair is set before the open fire. The Queen sweeps in and takes her seat, making the candles flicker in the winter gloom. The crew stand motionless, waiting. The old Queen begins to read from her journal and we listen in rapt silence as she recalls the pain of Albert's death. The words fall out of the shadows and the hairs tingle on the back of my neck. The year is 1872 and we are listening to Queen Victoria.

All day the filming continues while I stand absorbed, huddled in overcoat and scarf as a buffer against the intense cold. Victoria remembers the day when Albert was thrown from his horse and how she panicked when she thought he might have been seriously hurt. The furniture is moved—and she recalls her eighteenth birthday, and the day she learnt she was Queen. A cut, a scenery change and she talks of her affection for John Brown, then a change of mood as she rages against being summoned to open Parliament when still in mourning. There are minor problems with the nose; it seems the humidity caused by Prunella's breathing is softening the adhesive. Pauline fixes it and the filming goes on.

When the wrap is called at 5.50 Queen Victoria is escorted upstairs to disrobe. Layer by layer the costume is removed and hung up. Then to make-up, where her wig is carefully removed and placed on a wig stand for tomorrow. The Queen's nose is peeled off; Prunella cleans the adhesive from her face, then sets to work to put her own make-up back on. All through the next few days of filming, the change from bare face, to Queen Victoria, and back to Prunella, will be constant. For the next three days I watch enthralled as Prunella shifts through a variety of ages between forty-one to seventy-nine. This is achieved partly through make-up, partly through the adding or shedding of fat suits, but mainly through Prunella's acting. It is wonderful to watch.

In the final production the historical drama scenes are intercut with the modern documentary sections shot in a variety of locations including Parliament, Westminster Abbey, Buckingham Palace, the Victoria and Albert Museum and Kensington Palace. There is to be a lot of travelling for Prunella, as the crew will also film in Germany, the Isle of Wight, Sidmouth, Windsor Palace, the Scottish Highlands and at Balmoral.

*   *   *

8 April 2003.
Today it is Westminster. There is some confusion about which gate we are to go through at the Houses of Parliament. Security is tight and we are stopped by police, who search the car thoroughly. The BBC have been lent the Speaker's flat, where Prunella can talk to Lord Healey about Victoria's intense dislike of Gladstone, and also the attitude of the government to her self-imposed exile during her time of mourning.

The flat is sumptuous. Wooden panelled walls are hung with bewigged portraits of generations of speakers. Hogwarts School crossed with Gilbert and Sullivan. The crew move in and set up the equipment;

244

we wait for Lord Healey. He arrives in an ebullient frame of mind, pleased to meet Prunella. The interview progresses entertainingly, albeit somewhat erratically, with a number of interruptions. Eventually they decide they have enough material.

Westminster Abbey will not be available until after Evensong at six o'clock. Louise and the crew go off to look for locations for linking shots, Prunella stretches out on one of the yellow sofas in the Speaker's drawing-room and puts her feet up for a power kip. She has the ability to lie down in the most unlikely places and almost immediately drop off to sleep. She may only sleep for ten minutes but it is enough to recharge her energy. Watching her work these fifteen-hour days, sometimes even longer, these naps are probably the only way in which she can keep going.

Before we go to the Abbey we gather for a pizza. It is a long day for Prunella, who is always in front of camera as speaker and interviewer; she is picked up early and must do her own make-up and hair before she leaves. At Westminster Abbey there will be no vestige of a mirror, so Prunella, who never complains, goes into the ladies' room in the restaurant to repair her make-up and hair: for continuity reasons she needs to keep the same image all day.

We get to the Abbey before Evensong is finished, and huddle in the porch trying to find some shelter from the blistering wind. Once allowed in, the crew get set up and eventually filming starts. For the first shot, Prunella walks slowly towards the altar speculating on how the eighteen-year-old Queen Victoria must have felt when she came here to be crowned. It would have been very daunting for a young girl. To keep out of shot we hide ourselves away in a small vestry area underneath the organ loft and sit on the floor. At least

245

it is warm in here. For the last scene of the day the cameraman wants to use the whole length of the abbey. The massive doors at the west end are opened, admitting an icy blast which whistles up the nave. Prunella, entering through the doors, is buffeted by the wind as she walks slowly towards the altar. There are six takes. It is hard work and very cold—you have to be tough to be an actor.

We finish at 7.15 and Luke, her 'minder', takes Prunella home. They will fly to Aberdeen early tomorrow for two days' filming at Balmoral.

*   *   *

Tuesday 16, Wednesday 17 April.
Up early to be collected by Luke at 6.20. Because the BBC has not provided a make-up artist for this part of the programme, Prunella has been up since 5 a.m. to do her hair and make-up. Today it is to be Kensington Palace, where Victoria spent a miserable childhood under the constant supervision of her mother and her governess, Baroness Lehtzen.

We drive through the park, at this hour almost completely deserted with low mist hanging under the trees. By 7.45 we are all standing inside Kensington Palace in the Cupola Room, where Victoria was christened. At first sight the vast, high-ceilinged room appears to be ornamented with fluted pillars and intricately carved panels. On closer inspection all is *trompe l'œil*; the 'fluted' pillars are painted on planks of flat wood. Reality and illusion exist in life as well as on camera. By ten o'clock we have to be out of the way for the day's visitors, so Prunella goes home, but has no time to rest; she has work to do and lunch to prepare for Timothy. We return to Kensington Palace

246

at 4 p.m. after the tourists have gone home, and then work until after 8 p.m. Timothy is playing *King Lear* at the Old Vic and won't get home until after 11, but Prunella wants to keep awake until then to give him supper. It is a very long day.

The next morning up again before 5 for Prunella. She must be tired, but it doesn't show. Back to Kensington Palace once more, this time to talk to the historian Tristram Hunt about the influences on the young Princess Victoria. They walk from Victoria's bedroom through the vastness of the presence chamber into the painted Cupola Room. Numerous takes—filmed from every angle, talking and walking. While the camera is rolling everyone else must stand motionless and silent. The old wooden floors creak at every step and every sound is picked up by the microphones. Before the doors open to the public, Prunella and the crew load into the cars and move on to Windsor Castle.

*   *   *

23 April 2003.
Up at 5.30 for a morning in the Victoria and Albert Museum. Filming starts at 7.15. Prunella and Tristram Hunt enter the sculpture gallery, talking as they wander through the figures. Tristram tells Prunella about Victoria's interest in nudes and how her awakened sexuality revealed itself in the nude figures which she gave to her beloved Albert. It requires a number of retakes, but all is progressing well until the silence of the museum is shattered by the contract cleaners coming into the area where the BBC are filming. They vacuum, move rattling rubbish skips, set up the queue lines by the main desk, and bring in a

hydraulic tower lift to change the light bulbs. The cleaners have to be finished before the museum opens its doors at 10—but so do the film crew. A compromise is reached: during the rehearsals the cleaners will work, but they will stop during the actual filming. By 9 no one has had any breakfast, but deadlines loom, so they push on. At 10 a.m. we all move on to the next location, St Luke's Church in Sydney Street.

Prunella arrives before the rest of the crew and is keen to get set up. Time is short; when filming finishes today, they must drive down to Devon. We are shown into the oak-panelled vestry, crowded with large gothic chairs and a massive table. Prunella begins to set out her make-up on the table. This vestry represents the actual dressing-room she will use before the filming of extracts from *An Evening with Queen Victoria*. It is this scene which is the starting point for the BBC's documentary.

According to the schedule, she is to put on her stage make-up, then the wig, while talking to camera about why she became fascinated by Queen Victoria's diaries. This is ostensibly filmed just before she goes on stage to perform. She has brought her own make-up, and the wig and costumes she uses for the show. Wearing the pink gingham dressing-gown she has used for the last twenty years, she sits at the table to check her make-up. There is a ritual in this preparation, manifested by the familiar dressing-gown, the systematic laying out of the make-up, the use of the same well-used bags for the shoes and the battered old wig box. In a touring show, often played for only a few nights in venues ranging from vast theatres to tiny church halls like this one, the pre-show ritual provides a reassuring continuity.

The BBC crew arrive and unload. Because they want to create a hazy, timeless atmosphere, a smoke machine is brought in, but when tested it sets off all the vestry smoke alarms. There is a hiatus while a church official is found who is prepared to authorize their disconnection. The cameraman decides the lights around Prunella's make-up mirror are too bright, and dims them down with grey gel; now they are so dim that Prunella can't see her face properly. She is not at all fazed by the smoke and alarms, but is worried that she can't see herself in the mirror.

They start to film. Smoke billows from the machine—when it begins to clear Prunella talks to camera about how the show was devised. It is decided that the table is in the wrong place, so filming is halted while the heavy old vestry table is moved into the centre of the room. This involves most of the crew and means taking everything off the table. It is reset and they resume filming. For this scene Prunella is putting on her wig. 'Cut' is called. Again the table has to be moved, but this time only six inches to the right. They drag it. The wig is taken off and put back on the wig block. They start again. She begins to put the wig on, talking as she secures it with pins. This section has not been scripted, which, as Prunella explains to the director, may present a problem. As there are to be several takes of the scene, including close-ups, a script is essential for continuity. There is an enforced pause while an agreed speech is hastily written out—and Prunella learns it. Learning a new script on demand is frustrating for the actor, and can be confusing. An actor with less experience might find it impossible. At midday filming recommences. The wig is put on. Wig off again. The table has to be moved a further twenty inches to the right. 12.20. More smoke—another take.

Wig on. 12.30. Sound reports that the steadi-cam harness is creaking as the cameraman moves. Consultation. He will work without the harness; the camera is very heavy. They do pick up shots from every angle. Close-ups. Wig on—wig off—wig on. They want shots of her putting on make-up while wearing the wig, but Prunella is worried about this as it's the wrong sequence—make-up is always applied before the wig. They compromise and ask her to touch up her lipstick. There are numerous shots of her putting on lipstick. Each time she has to wipe it off so they can film from another angle. Between each take, Prunella tries to repair her own make-up in the dimmed-down lighting.

After lunch the director wants to record Prunella's thoughts as to how her performance has been changed or enhanced by some of the new information on Victoria's past garnered during the making of the documentary. She is to voice her thoughts to the camera, as though this is being filmed after an actual performance of *An Evening with Queen Victoria*. Prunella, who has been amazingly patient and calm throughout the long day, is not happy with this. She argues, justifiably, that she has no idea how her performance may have changed until she has actually played the show again in front of an audience, and feels she can't talk truthfully about something which hasn't yet happened. It is eventually resolved that the post-show interview will not be filmed until after the production at Beckenham in a few weeks' time.

The last scene for today's filming is of Prunella in costume, ready to go on stage for the opening scene. Because she's not happy with the state of the wig, Prunella stipulates that she must only be shot from the back as she makes her entrance on to the stage. She tidies the wig as well as she can and checks her make-up in the dim mirror. Putting on her white dress for the first scene, and wrapping the black shawl round her shoulders, she waits for the cue. Lights stream through an open door, silhouetting the tiny figure as she walks up the steps and out on to the stage.

*   *   *

May 2003.

I go to St George's Church, Beckenham, where scenes from a public performance of *An Evening with Queen Victoria* are to be filmed as part of the documentary. The company arrive at the church in the middle of the afternoon, and begin to set up for the evening. A wide, shallow stage has been built half-way up the nave in front of the Rood Screen. About four feet high, with two sets of rather rickety wooden steps to provide entrances and exits at each end; it is not ideal. The acoustics in this church are notoriously bad, but that is one of the hazards of taking a show 'that you can perform anywhere' on tour.

First the furniture is set, then the props are taken out of a much-travelled trunk. At one end of the stage is a grand piano for Richard Burnett, beside it a chair for Ian Partridge. Centre stage is Prunella's armchair and to the prompt side of that another upright chair and a desk covered with writing materials. This is where the Queen writes her diary. When I get there the stage is almost set, but the car sent to collect Prunella was late, so she has only just arrived, which has obviously fussed her; she hates to be late. The camera crew are hovering, looking for shots, and follow the rehearsal.

When finished, the cast break for a rest before the

251

show, which is due to start at eight o'clock, but the BBC team need shots of Prunella arriving at the church with her costumes, and then shots of her getting ready for the show. This cuts into her normal preparation time, but she is very patient. Eventually, when it gets to about seven o'clock, she asks them to go. She needs time to dress, and to get her make-up and wig on. They all go off to get something to eat, and Prunella is left in peace.

I sit in the audience and wait: there is lots of chatter as they start coming in and slowly fill up the rows of very hard pews. Those in the know have brought cushions and sit near the front where the acoustics are better. There is a smattering of younger people, but the majority of the audience are grey-haired. The film crew weaves in and out, filming from every angle. The church is packed. The lights go down, the noise dims, and in a burst of applause the actors walk on to the stage. The BBC crew disappear—the play has begun.

*   *   *

Prunella still enjoys doing *An Evening with Queen Victoria*, and likes to keep it on the go. 'If you leave it too long it feels like a big number when you have to do it again.' I saw a performance in Sydney in 2004, towards the end of her gruelling eight-week tour covering every state in Australia and parts of New Zealand; it was a hot December evening, and the new purpose-built 850-seat Sydney Theatre was packed. The contrast with the setting in St George's Church in Beckenham could hardly have been greater, and only served to highlight how versatile the show is. The Sydney audience were wildly enthusiastic, the *Sydney Morning Herald* calling it 'an acting masterclass'.

Prunella says, 'It's wonderfully useful artistically as it's a big part and quite demanding one way and another, and to have that demand and challenge every now and then, and not to have to wait for someone to offer you something, is a huge blessing. The play goes through a lot of ages and a lot of emotions which is quite satisfying when it goes well. At a time when I'm playing a lot of old bags to earn the mortgage, it's lovely to have something that stretches one a bit. It is a lovely show. It's kept me sane really.'

14

Passing it on

'If you want to be an actor find out about life. Broaden your experience. Get a degree or take a year out, and *then* go to drama school. Acting can be learnt, but it must be constantly practised to grow and succeed. The equipment must be cared for, especially the voice and the body. Everything must be in top condition so there is a strong base to work from.'

*   *   *

Prunella is a member of the accreditation panel for the National Council for Drama Training, which entails visits with colleagues to the drama schools to sit in on classes and assess the training. In *Contacts*, the professional directory for the acting profession, there is only one page listing the twenty-odd members of the Conference of Drama Schools controlled by the National Council of Drama Training—about twenty-two schools qualify. After that there are seventeen pages of non-accredited schools and teachers. Prunella says, 'It's obscene how many people are making money out of people's ambitions and aspirations.' She herself has been teaching since she was twenty-one; she started at LAMDA, but now she teaches privately, gives workshops at the Actors Centre and also, occasionally, a masterclass or a workshop for drama students.

Timothy tells me how times have changed. 'What

has happened in our business during our lifetime is a flowering of incidental activities. Like talking books, commercials, voice-overs, corporate junkets for which acting talents are employed; and the enormous growth of television of course . . . the possibilities for an actor now are considerably more varied. In my father's day he was either a "touring actor" or a "repertory actor" and later he became a "West End actor". Or you were in films which was a very separate thing, or in radio of course. They were a bit compartmentalized; it is very good now that you can work in every field. Another thing is how actors have been differently perceived during the time we have been working; we're more accepted members of society now.'

Prunella once told an interviewer, Peter Shaw, that the theatre had 'treated her well, but I would never recommend it to anyone because the frustrations are so painful when you haven't got work, or you don't get the part, or if the part isn't going well. I would do as much as possible to dissuade people from becoming professional actors, because there isn't nearly enough work and it's an extremely tough, disappointing and harrowing job.' In spite of this she will do everything she can to help those who are determined to enter the profession. In 1991 she worked with young actors at the National Theatre, directing a rehearsed reading of Chaucer's *The Franklin's Tale*, which played for two sell-out performances in the theatre. The following year she was asked to repeat the process but with *The Nun's Priest's Tale*. These readings were primarily aimed at teachers and students studying Chaucer and included a post-show discussion. Not only were they helpful to students, but they gave some of the actors in the company, who were only playing small parts and understudying, a chance to work on substantial pieces

255

of text. She thinks it is probably quite useful for the actors to work with 'a jaded old hack like me, who is supposed to be quite good on text. I can on the whole get the laughs in a classical text, so they are likely to trust my ideas about phrasing—which are extremely rigid.'

She still believes there is a desperate need for classical texts to be brought alive. 'Often in class students study the text in isolation; they don't even read it out loud and almost never get on their feet. We're very good at encouraging children to express themselves in their own words, but not so good when it comes to expressing themselves in other people's words. So the whole tradition of the spoken word, the experience of reading a text and speaking it at the same time—which is the quickest way of learning it— is neglected as a teaching aid. All drama was written to be spoken aloud, and phrasing is all important. There should only be one major stress in each sentence. Let subordinate clauses work for themselves. Don't colour. Don't waste energy. English audiences from birth know how to listen to Shakespeare. Don't push it at them, they'll get it all right. Otherwise you're insulting them, you're saying, "I'll explain it to you." A comma is a licence to breathe. With a full stop, you can stop for ever.'

In November 2003 Prunella gave a masterclass at the Theatre Royal, Haymarket, which runs a series of classes to encourage and inform young people who are curious about the theatre. The classes provide a unique chance for students to meet and work with well-known, successful actors; people with a vast store of knowledge and experience who are more than happy to pass it on to others. Officially provided for young actors and acting students between the ages of sixteen and thirty, anyone with a legitimate interest can in fact, book themselves a seat and go along as an observer, which is what I did.

*   *   *

I collect my ticket and information about today's set pieces from the table in the foyer; on the way down to the theatre I pass a knot of girls in the downstairs bar area. They have that kind of starry-eyed innocence of would-be drama students. The class will be conducted on the set of the current play, *A Breath of Air*. Looking around we seem to be a motley collection. Lots of students here, some school students with a teacher, but most are older. There's a buzz of noise. The class starts in five minutes and the stalls are filling up. A dapper young man comes in with suit and rolled umbrella and sits on my right. Two rows in front and to the left, two fruity-voiced women wonder when it will finish—they let it be known they are going on to the National Gallery later. The stalls are almost filled; we move our belongings from unoccupied seats to make room for the late-comers to shuffle into the spaces.

Prunella comes on stage looking very small, wearing a neatly fitting grey trouser-suit over a pink silk shirt, and boots with dizzily high heels. Introduction and applause. We sit back to listen. She seems very comfortable in the role of teacher and makes immediate contact with the audience.

This is to be a workshop with the emphasis on 'how to get the laughs with the words'. Three young actors have prepared pieces taken from classical texts. The first piece is from *The Country Wife* by William Wycherley. In it Margery Pinchwife, the wife, is

257

writing to Mr Horner, the man with whom her husband has forbidden her to correspond because he supects they are having an affair. She is writing the letter furtively while her husband is out of the house. The actress performs the piece intelligently, but it is too generalized. She uses no props, and stands on the bare stage, miming the letter-writing.

Prunella makes no comment until she has finished, but then asks her standard question: 'Who are you? How old are you? What are you doing? What do you want?' She waits for answers. Slowly, as she makes the actress focus on each change of thought, the scene begins to come alive. She gets her to set the scene more explicitly; to sit down and draw up a table to write on, and to find some paper and a pen. One major obstacle she must face in the scene is her need to write the letter quickly before her husband comes home, another, the physical difficulty she has in writing (she has only just learnt). She must remember her aversion to her husband, while thinking of her growing love for Mr Horner. Prunella emphasizes that the actor must not 'colour' the words. Because she is alone, she should play some of it as though to herself. When she hears her husband at the door there must be real panic. Always, always play the truth. 'Trust the text. Let the words and action work for you.' She makes us realize that if the actor has a monologue it cannot just be performed to a generalized audience, because an audience is too big a target. The actor must select, or invent, a person. They must find a character to talk to.

Prunella is a very positive teacher. She explains points well, doesn't demonstrate, and gives examples to clarify her meaning. For those of us watching, there is a marked change between the staginess of the first performance and the reality and humour of the worked-on piece.

With the second piece, from *The Importance of Being Earnest*, very similar changes take place. Again the first playing is too stagy and unfocused, but once the actors are told to use the obstacles and the reality of what is happening, not only in the scene, but also in their lives, it becomes believable and funny. In the first run-through we are observers; by the end of the rehearsal, we have become involved.

She tells the actors, 'In acting, clarity, variety and speed are all important. They create the reality of the scene. Timing can make a scene very funny (or not).' By the end of the hour and a half the audience are taking in every word and beginning to appreciate just how much work is needed. Acting is a job.

*   *   *

Prunella says the acting profession is a great leveller because all actors can experience the dole queue, and frequently do during their lives. 'When you're out of work and you don't know where your next job is coming from, it's scary; it is good to have somewhere to go to hone your skills.' She enjoys teaching. 'It's something we have to offer. My generation can pass on to the next generation things about acting that the previous generation knew and did. A good actor will know how to adapt to the medium he is working in, and indeed, to the *building* he is working in. What are you doing when you are running a theatre? You are trying to get people in to it. There's a generation of kids now who are not used to going to the theatre. But they'd go perhaps to see an actor who they've enjoyed on television. If you want to work in the theatre it

259

helps to have been in a successful television production. It helps to sell the show.'

She feels the experience of playing things live is vital. 'The differences between one audience and another; the way you can develop a performance, and what successive live audiences teach you about the part and the play and the philosophy of the whole thing, is terribly important. Nowadays kids very often haven't seen their A-level plays acted live. For example—Timothy and Sam were once playing Falstaff and Hal in Shakespeare's *Henry IV Parts I and II* with the English Touring Theatre, and were coming out of the stage door after the performance, when they were accosted by two fifteen-year-old boys who in tones of surprise said, "Hey, that was really great—who did the translation?" '

On another occasion she tells me: 'In this country—this is a preoccupation and passion of mine—because of the compact nature of our geography, we have the inestimable advantage of being able to work in all four media, if necessary, all on the same day. I think our training should, and in most cases does, equip us to deal with that. Why does the Arts Council or the Government not *invest* in this priceless geographical privilege we have? We work in the most widely spoken and understood language in the world, with arguably the richest dramatic and literary heritage. Why don't we invest in it? Musicians are brought up on the classics, but our children, nowadays, aren't reared on classic dramatic literature. They should be reading, playing, seeing and being provided with responsible touring productions of the classics—as they always used to be.

'I don't think that there is enough emphasis on trying to express yourself in someone else's words,

260

which is not only useful psychologically (reading aloud can be a form of role playing, of putting yourself in another person's place), but if you try and express yourself in words from another era, it can be an invaluable way of apprehending the ideas and philosophy and atmosphere of an age different from your own. Every word of literature written before the advent of general literacy in the late nineteenth century was designed to be read aloud, sometimes in quite large spaces.'

Timothy West says: 'Pru has something to show people, and has this huge thing about teaching. She feels that doing it right in performance has got a kind of educational value, both for audiences and for possible practitioners. So she feels that she has something to give in that area and would be very frustrated if she weren't allowed to do it. She is an extraordinarily good teacher.' He thinks Prunella has been influenced by many widely different areas in her life. This has been a great advantage, 'but it does mean that throughout her life people haven't known how complex a person she is. This has done her out of certain parts, and certain kinds of companies, because she's been typecast in their minds. What we all try for is to do interesting work and interesting writing. Not just interesting parts, but parts in interesting plays. The writing is of paramount importance. One is more interested in reading the script to see what the play is saying, and how it's saying it, than whether it's giving us a meaty part.'

Prunella agrees. 'Not only is the writing of paramount importance, but also one should entertain the eyes of people as well as the ears. To sell the play or the writing—and in an ideal world one hopes to believe enough in the writing to want to sell it hard—you must be as watchable and listenable-to as possible. One should be conscious of the "shape" one is, and the "shape" the character should be. You must be visually and aurally compelling—and that doesn't mean doing acrobatic acting or vocal fireworks. Of course it must be consistent with truth, and with the situation of the character and so on, but repetitive gestures, for instance, are meaningless and take away from what you are saying. In the same way over-stressing makes a nonsense of the meaning.'

*   *   *

The Actors Centre in Tower Street, off Shaftesbury Avenue in London's West End, is an association for the use of Equity members, offering classes, including masterclasses, and gives showcase possibilities to younger, less experienced actors. I sit in on two classes Prunella gives there. The first is 'How to Get the Laughs with the Words', the second is 'Big Stuff: Reading the Score.' There are limited numbers in each class and each actor has brought in a prepared speech. As members of the Actors Centre they are all professionals, usually between jobs, keen to maintain their skills for the next opportunity that comes along. The actors in this class have picked pieces from Wilde, Shakespeare and Sheridan. Very different classical writers, but some basic principles apply to them all.

Prunella watches the pieces, and then works with each actor. In most cases the initial playing is too vague, so that we, the audience, are not drawn into the scene. She suggests the basic questions for them to ask when working on a scene:

Who am I (character)? What are the circumstances—physical and non-physical (hot, cold,

262

am I scared—whatever)? What do I *want* in this scene? What do I want to achieve? What are the *obstacles* to what I want—physical and non-physical? Given the person I am, given the circumstances, given the obstacles, what do I *do*? In the end the only thing you must play is—what do I do? The *action*.

After each piece, Prunella asks the actor about their character. If the answer is generalized, she says, 'That's not good enough. You must be specific. Where did you grow up?' They establish the exact age of the character, and where he or she has lived. The location is important, as it will affect the voice and accent, and the attitude of the person played. For an actor in search of employment, specific accents indicative of status are an essential skill, especially in classics such as the plays of Oscar Wilde, when it is important to be aware of the subtle class differences of pronunciation. Prunella observes that young actors will take endless trouble to acquire a working-class accent, but they are often unaware that there is almost as much variety in 'posh speak' as there is in working-class and regional dialects. 'There is still the vexed question of RP [received pronunciation] or, as it used to be called, Standard English. I don't like either term very much . . . and I often find a resistance in drama students to acquiring RP on the grounds that it sounds snobbish. However, it is important to emphasize two points. Nobody expects, or should expect, an actor to alter his native speech in private life unless he wants to, and RP is not the same as "posh" English which, for the actor, is a dialect like any other and varies according to character, background, age and period, and should be studied as carefully as any other dialect.

'I wish we had, as the French do, a standard pronunciation that indicates not class, but a concern

263

for the language. A robust, flexible, serviceable speech, carrying no special social or regional connotations, but useful for working in translated plays—or in the older period texts, where if we spoke as the characters of the time did we should frequently be incomprehensible to a modern audience. It's hard to find the right term to describe this. "Actor's English" suggests the Edwardian throb of an actor-laddie; "Educated English" carries overtones of academicism . . . There ought to be a form of speech that conveys education and culture without sounding prissy or academic or exclusive in any way . . . People are not snobbish about pronouncing Italian in the right way, so why are actors snobbish about pronouncing English in the classical form?'

This is something she tells all her students. 'We actors in this country are lucky enough to have probably the richest dramatic and literary heritage of any nation in history. The English language has a wonderful diversity of dialect and accent within it, both regional and historical, and the connotations of those individual variations are an incredibly useful resource to the actor, and a valuable tool in communicating with audiences.

'The way a character pronounces words—in English perhaps more than in any other language in the world—gives a distinct clue, not only to the area the character comes from, but also to age, background, history and predilections. The first thing I ever want to know about a part, a character, is not usually how they look, but how they speak, and this is dependent on age, health, where they were born, their education, and the influence of various people in their lives. That's why it is lovely to work in plays you believe in, but even if it is a writer for whom you don't have an enormous amount of respect, you still, ethically, have to do your best for that author, and for the people who've paid on that night.'

At the Actors Centre, once the actor begins to establish who their character is, Prunella asks them to do the piece again. Already there is more focus. Next questions: 'Ask yourself, where am I? What does the author want in this scene? If it's a period play remember what you are wearing, this will obviously affect the way you move, especially how you sit. Don't play the quality of your emotion, such as happy, sad, etc., otherwise it becomes a self-indulgent, demonstrated performance. It's crucially important to keep trying different approaches—but don't play anything but the *action*.'

On another occasion she tells me: 'We have to be fully audible without bombast, lucid without being academic, sensitive without being precious, varied without being flashy, accurate without being dull, faithful without being stuffy. It is, I suppose, a tall order . . . Acting is pretending to be other people, it's not projecting yourself. Acting is using what God gave you, and using what you've acquired in terms of skill and versatility and physique to deliver that person [the character], to those people [the audience], and the less there is of you in the middle the better. Of course you must use *yourself* to do this, you haven't anything else, but the less there is of you in the end, the more you can give the person you are playing to the audience. That's the morality of acting to me. It's using yourself to deliver the writer to the people who have paid their money.

'The approach to playing comedy and tragedy is the same. What the actor has to think about is the character. If you play it truthfully, it will be sad or funny according to the author's intention.'

At the end of the morning Prunella gives each actor her printed notes on the principles of stress.

Some Principles of Stress in Spoken English

A. Observe these principles for the sake of a) clarity, b) variety and c) speed.
B. Ignore them, often, for the sake of a) sense and b) character.
1. Assume there is only *one* main stress in every grammatical sentence.
2. Stress nouns before adjectives and verbs before adverbs. When in doubt go for the *noun*.
3. Don't colour 'colour' words, e.g. 'red', 'brilliant', 'rolling', 'pomp', etc.,—they should work for themselves.
4. Don't stress negatives—they should also work for themselves.
5. Don't stress personal pronouns and possessive adjectives—I, me, mine, you, your, his, her, etc.,—they are strong and don't usually need help.
6. Let subordinate clauses ride without stress or emphasis, also phrases in brackets or any form of parenthesis. Also look at the possibility of saying them all on one note. This will allow you to take them as slowly or as quickly as you like.
7. Don't stress prepositions, conjunctions or particles unless playing newsreaders, sports reporters, or any other users of media-speak.
8. In compound verbs, go for the main verb, not the auxiliary. E.g. don't say 'Much HAVE I travelled in the realms of gold', or, 'I WILL arise and go now . . .' (except when arguing or playing users of media-speak).
9. Don't make heavy weather of titles, formal

phrases of introduction, vocative phrases such as 'Good my lord', 'Nay, I protest, madam', or casual oaths such as 'Pox on't', 'for Christ's sake' etc. Often they are there only as courtesies, rhythmic aids or to draw attention to the speaker. In Restoration comedy, particularly, it is often useful to take whole phrases on the upbeat (like anacrusis in music).

Some Extra Points in the Speaking of Verse

1. Observe contractions, e.g. 'smil'st', 'cunning'st', 'splitt'st' etc. The poet intends the unusual sound and it is wrong to correct it or re-expand it to 'smilest', 'cunningest', 'splittest', etc.
2. Look out for adjacent consonants, 'led to', 'like cousins', 'and down', etc. Often to mark them will sound affected or academic, but sometimes the poet may intend the distinction to be made.
3. Don't be afraid to breathe at commas, as well as at full stops.
4. Look out for lines of monosyllables: 'and slew him thus', 'I do not know why yet I live to say this thing's to do'—*sometimes* it can indicate that each word is to be stressed, or a specially measured delivery.
5. Don't insert 'ah's' and 'oh's', or sighs or gasps into the text: poets usually provide any they want, and to add extra ones would spoil the rhythm.
6. Enjambment (run-on lines in verse). Before an enjambment, breathe well at the beginning of the sentence, then take it steadily, not rushing round the corner, letting the word at the end of the line have its due weight, but *not* 'lifting' it to indicate the enjambment. It also helps to hit the first words of the second line quite hard.

267

Two Sophisticated Points

1. Lists. When you have lists of words or phrases, separated by commas, be aware that to lift the inflection on each creates an expectation of further words or phrases in the list, i.e. it will sound literary and prepared. If you want it to sound spontaneous, repeat the inflection you would use on the first word if it stood alone.
2. Antithesis. In general, don't anticipate the second statement: it is more elegant to deliver the first statement as if it were going to stand alone, then pick out the sense of the second. (Also it gets a bigger laugh.) E.g. 'From me far off, with others all too near.'
Or—'Ninety-nine per cent of the people in the world are fools: and the rest of us are in great danger of contagion.' Don't lift the inflection on 'fools' at the end of the first statement, thus anticipating the joke. Not—'Marriage is a bribe to make a houseKEEPer think she's a houseHOLDer.' But—'Marriage is a bribe to make a housekeeper think she's a houseHOLDer.'

Her son Sam, who also teaches, calls these notes 'Ma's principles of stress; or, if you can phrase properly, you will earn more money.'

15

'One thing has to pay for the other'

'Last day of the Tesco shoot. Spent the morning being wheeled round Gerrards Cross by John Rutland, who is lovely and eighty next birthday. Bit hazardous, as in the ad he's blindfold after a cataract operation, and I've got one foot sticking out ahead of the wheelchair in bandages after an ingrowing toenail op. Both of us in dressing-gowns. (Second time on TV I've had an ingrowing toenail, am I getting type-cast?) Citizens of Gerrards Cross supremely indifferent. Nice crew, jolly job, wish it wasn't a commercial—we've spent three days shooting sixty seconds, it's obscene. We worked until 3 a.m. on Sunday, because Tesco's won't let us have the store [Bracknell] on a shopping day. "Do they realize what this will cost them in overtime?" I asked naïvely. "Darling," the producer riposted, digging her toes in a hot footwarmer, "they take a million per working day in a store this size, what's a couple of grand in overtime?" I must go and do something to atone.'

*   *   *

Prunella tells me that she is often cast 'as very unattractive eccentrics'—but this is probably because she is so good at playing them. Sam thinks eccentrics are the best parts—what the English specialize in. But he thinks Prunella may have been padding up for rather too many years and began playing middle-aged women a bit earlier than she should have done—because, as he says, she is extremely attractive.

One of Prunella's eccentrics is Dottie Turnbull, the mother and mother-in-law from hell who promoted Tesco's supermarket. There is so much truth and humour in Prunella's portrayal that Dottie and her family have made the Tesco's commercials fun to watch. Prunella, who has played Dottie since 1995, emerged in a 2004 survey as the celebrity who appeared in the most successful British advertising campaign. Hamish Pringle, author of *Celebrity Sells*, says the secret of her success is her engaging, chatty manner. I would suggest it is also because Dottie has been created by Prunella with so much attention to detail that she is both recognizable and believable as a character. When so many commercials are celebrity-based, few are character-based.

*   *   *

Nearly ten years after Dottie's first appearance I go up to London to be taken to watch the making of a Tesco's commercial at the Bracknell store, and to stay overnight at Prunella's house, as we have to be up at 5.30 the next morning. It is February and still dark when the car arrives to collect us—the wind is biting. When we arrive at the store Prunella greets the crew like old friends; many of them have worked with her for many years. Universally liked, Prunella is also warmly admired for her professionalism. She is always on time, on cue, and word perfect.

We have breakfast in the comfortable caravan which is her base during the day before she is called to the make-up van to be transformed into Dottie. First they pin up her hair in preparation for the wig. Next

270

she is carefully made up. Because of Dottie's character, the eye-shadow is very blue, the lipstick a little too red and the nails deep crimson. Once made up and with the wig on, Prunella begins to look more like Dottie. Back in Prunella's van the clothes, the glittery jewellery, handbag and glasses are waiting. Before long the transformation is complete. Dottie is ready to take on Tesco's.

Prunella tells me about Dottie's background. She comes from the north of England, knows a bargain when she sees one, but likes to be thought genteel. Because she tries to keep up appearances her make-up is a bit over-the-top. She is domineering, self-opinionated and believes herself to be always right, constantly embarrassing her long-suffering daughter and bullying her much put-upon son-in-law in the process. Prunella has created the character with as much care as she does for every part she plays. When Tesco approved their advertising agency's idea that Jane Horrocks and Prunella were to be a mother-and-daughter combination, Prunella went to Manchester and met Jane to discuss their respective characters and how they wanted to play them. Jane tells me that as she didn't particularly want to play the daughter, Kate, with her own northern accent, and Prunella didn't want to play the mother with her RP accent, they proposed a role reversal. Jane would be an educated, upwardly mobile schoolteacher; Prunella an overbearing council-house widow. Kate, the daughter, is trying to better herself, so her outspoken north-country bargain-hunting mother is a continual source of embarrassment to her. The grandchildren came into the storyline later, when Jane became pregnant, and her husband, played by John Gordon-Sinclair, later still. Jane says in the early commercials the

271

children's ages varied quite a bit; one was four one minute and fourteen the next, but later they were more consistent and the parts were usually played by the same child actors. The family has never grown beyond two children. There was an addition to the family one Christmas when Dottie's twin sister arrived—also played by Prunella.

While Prunella is waiting to be called, I go over to the store, which is bustling with activity. The areas to be included in the filming have been carefully prepared the night before, false counters have been built where needed and stocked with groceries or produce. I'm told that the visible parts of the store are sometimes repainted overnight to suit the commercial. When the filming is finished, everything will be restored so that the store can open for business as usual the next day.

The fifteen background artists, who will provide the non-speaking customers, are sitting on chairs at the back of the store and have been carefully chosen as representatives of the Tesco clientele. They are a cross-section of characters of every age and race; a mother and child, an elderly couple, a student, a businessman, a young couple and an old woman with a stick. I ask Pam, a frail white-haired lady with a beautiful face, how long she has been in the business. Most of her life, she says. Originally a ballet dancer at Covent Garden, she has always worked in theatre and is a member of Equity. Now she is happy to take any work which helps to eke out her pension. The last job she had was as a dead body in *The Bill*. When the scene is shot with the extras in the background it must be carefully choreographed. Actors are placed in strategic positions and walked through their moves, starting off from behind racks of newspapers, hidden behind notices, or in out-of-camera-shot aisles. Once in place they stand silent and still, waiting to be set in motion on the cue 'action', then off they go, criss-crossing the aisles, trying to make the pre-ordained path look like a random choice. On 'cut' they stop. When the scene is re-shot they all go back to their starting places and wait to be set in motion once again—like clockwork trains on a fixed track.

Prunella has a stand-in, Anne Ford, who walks through Dottie's part for her so that the cameras can plot shooting angles and focus before she comes on set. It also gives the other actors and extras a chance to rehearse before the actual filming starts. Anne tells me Prunella is universally liked; she shows a genuine concern for her fellow actors and always telephones Anne to thank her for her help. On one occasion when the weather was particularly foul and the shoot ran very late and was going into the next day, Prunella refused to let Anne drive home, saying it was too dangerous; she insisted on taking her back to Wandsworth with her in the car, and gave her a bed for the night.

Eventually Prunella is called and filming begins. Each advertisement is carefully scripted, with a central promotional theme. The theme this time is to extol Tesco's in-store service. In today's story the assistants fall over themselves to help Dottie. They fetch things for her, offer to wrap the flowers she has just bought and ply her with free tastings. Dottie, in her contrary way, instead of being grateful for the helpful service, becomes more and more suspicious of their motives. She thinks they are trying to buy her favours.

The day's filming—at least fifteen hours will be spent to film the forty seconds of the commercial—has its lighter moments. At the cheese counter, offered a free tasting by the keen young sales assistant, Dotty takes a piece and sweeps past, declaring loudly that she 'won't be bought'. After about ten takes, Prunella has eaten a lot of cheese. On the eleventh she has had enough—as she sweeps past, she grabs the whole plate and bears it away, to the visible astonishment of the actor playing the sales assistant—we all collapse with laughter.

Later in the day I get a chance to talk to David Garfath, the director. He says that when he took over as director, quite early on, he was surprised when Prunella said she wanted to meet him. This was unusual for an actor in a commercial. They had lunch together and she told him all about the character of Dottie, giving him an outline of her life and her relationship with her daughter. David found this very interesting, as he realized that to Prunella it was very important that he knew all about the character she was playing. Sometimes when she sees the script she says to him, 'No, I wouldn't say it like that'—she knows Dottie's character so well, and it has to sound right. He's noticed that when she's called to come on set, as she leaves her caravan her walk changes, her mouth turns down, and by the time she has reached the store she has become Dottie. He tells me that to date they have together made over eighty commercials, and he likes to think that making them gives Prunella the freedom to do less well-paid but more challenging work. For her part, Jane Horrocks says doing the commercial has given her the financial freedom to pick and choose work.

Part of Prunella's earnings from Tesco's is in the shape of vouchers. Once, recently, on holiday, having selected what she wanted to buy at the local Tesco branch, she presented her vouchers to the girl at the checkout. The assistant wouldn't accept them and said rather officiously, 'I don't think we can take that many, I'm afraid you will have to clear these with the manager.' Prunella said gently, 'Well, I do work for you, you know.' 'Oh yes,' queried the assistant, 'which department?'

I ask Timothy West how he sees her involvement with Tesco's. He says, 'She's been able to steer a path, where she manages to get jobs that subsidize other jobs. This is the ideal way in which to live as an actor, obviously, because very often the well-paid jobs are not things which you think are desperately valuable, and nearly always the things which you think are valuable are also frightfully badly paid. One thing has to pay for the other.' Prunella herself tells me, 'Commercial work can be very enjoyable if the scripts are well-written—then it can be great fun. The advertisers have huge budgets and they do pay well, which helps to subsidize my work on stage which I love so much.'

Soon after she began to play Dottie, Prunella wrote to Veronica to tell her how the money she was earning from Tesco's 'financed Timothy and Sam in their Arts Council funded tour of *Henry IV Parts I and II*. I tell critical socialist chums that it's my method of obliging Industry to fund the Arts.'

*   *   *

One low-budget part the money from Tesco's allowed her to do was Clarissa in *Too Far to Walk*—very much the sort of challenging part she looks for, where she can play someone quite different from the public's expectations of her. Written by Mary Morris, the play was directed by Lucy Skilbeck and performed at the

275

King's Head Theatre in London in November 2002. In the play, Clarissa has been institutionalized in mental hospitals in the north of England for nearly fifty years. She is the younger sister of Olive, played by Gillian Axtell; their mother died when they were small. Their father couldn't cope on his own and both girls were committed to children's care homes, but because of a chronic lack of places Clarissa had to be placed, temporarily, in a state mental home. There she was to remain, abandoned and forgotten, for the next fifty years. With no education or outside stimulus, Clarissa slowly began to assume the ways and habits of her fellow inmates, but stuck firmly to the belief that she had an older sister, Olive. She won't shift from this, even though she can't make anyone believe her. When a more enlightened management takes over and a young social worker, played by James Livingstone, investigates, he discovers that Olive does exist. She had been sent out to Australia with a boatload of orphans and, when interviewed, has no recollection of ever having had a sister. The play concerns the reuniting of the pair in Australia, and explores the problems caused by their very disparate backgrounds. As part of my research I have permission from the director to watch a rehearsal.

*   *   *

4 November 2002.
Climbing up three flights of peeling red cement stairs, the entrance to the rehearsal room, a large airy gym painted in institution cream, is through scuffed doors. Basketball hoops are suspended at each end; there's a vaulting box in the corner, and one wall is covered with mirrors. The acting area is marked out on the

276

floor with black tape. Prunella arrives at 11.30 a.m., half an hour early, but the rehearsal is behind schedule so she will not be needed for a while, and goes off immediately to run lines with Becky, the stage manager. Apparently her part is complex and fiendishly hard to learn.

She is needed for a telephone interview with a newspaper at 2 p.m. as part of the publicity for the play. Two o'clock comes and goes, no phone call. At 2.15 Becky phones the paper, as they need to get on with the rehearsal. It seems they have forgotten—they will phone back. Prunella starts to pace up and down, irritated by the waste of rehearsal time. Twenty minutes later the phone rings and the interview takes place. They eventually start the rehearsal at 2.45.

Prunella is normally cheerful and animated, and to watch as she transforms herself into Clarissa is riveting. She seems to grow physically shorter and becomes shut in on herself. Her walk changes. She hides behind her hair, watches other people with caution, relating to them with difficulty; it seems she has been badly treated. Although ignorant, she has a strong native intelligence. Her speech and language are uneducated and pithy; she speaks in short sentences, with a strong northern accent. The scenes are run many times to build on motivation for the moves, and consolidation of the dialogue. Prunella is fussed because she is having trouble with the lines, which is unusual for her, and they open in a week's time. For the actual performances she will wear a wispy grey wig, but it has not yet come. She is anxious, as she needs it for rehearsals to get into character. Physical disguises such as prosthetics and wigs are always important for her.

The last thing they work on is a stage fight between

Clarissa and Olive. It has been carefully choreographed but is full on and very physical. At six o'clock they call it a day, we pack up props, put away chairs and head for the Underground.

*   *   *

12 November 2002.
I go to the preview at the King's Head Theatre. Situated behind a pub, the theatre is very small with an exposed stage. Most of the space is filled by long benches softened by red velvet cushions, standing between cloth-covered tables. Somehow it feels more like a courtroom than a theatre, although apparently it was once a boxing ring. When the play starts, the lights come up on the two elderly sisters, together with their younger selves, played respectively by Susan Harrison as the young Clarissa and Annie Rowe as the young Olive. Until she speaks, Prunella is almost unrecognizable. The play unfolds like a macabre dance. The two sets of sisters intermingle, echoing each other's movements and speech and passing the story from the past to the present, through their childhood, their separation, their reunion and the eventual catharsis which is the climax of the play. Prunella creates the pathos of this woman lost to the world for fifty years, wrongfully kept in care, who has battled so fiercely to retain her identity. She is also, surprisingly in view of the subject matter, very funny. One reviewer described her as 'decrepit but pigheaded'.

*   *   *

The reviewers were enthusiastic, though all of them

felt that the play needed to be longer. Fiona Mountford wrote: 'Its potentially intriguing and troubling story line should be both broadened and deepened to serve to best effect the issues it aims to lay bare. Lucy Skilbeck's production skilfully interweaves the past and the present. It also boasts an outstanding turn from Scales, virtually unrecognizable in her old-age make-up. She delivers her sharp lines with dry humour ("Praise the Lord and send us sausage!"), and almost manages to convince us that she can forgive her sister for never having tried to liberate her.'

Susannah Clapp wrote in the *Observer*, 'In the tiny confines of the King's Head the chance of disguise for an actor is slight, but such is Prunella Scales's transforming skill that in the opening moments of *Too Far to Walk* you find yourself wondering where she is. Then you see her usually quick face trapped inside another one—that of a bloated, dull-eyed figure, drugged, depressed, torpid as a beached whale.' Michael Billington in the *Guardian*: 'Within its domestic limits the play has an authentic pathos. And the image I shall carry away from Lucy Skilbeck's production is of Prunella Scales as the aged Clarissa. Under a wild mane of white hair, Scales' features acquire the innocent curiosity of a young girl; and the highest tribute I can pay to her compassionate performance is that I was reminded of Deborah, in Pinter's *A Kind of Alaska*, waking up to a new world with a sense of bewildered wonderment.'

*　　　*　　　*

9 December 2002.
When I see Prunella the day after the play finishes, I

ask her if she did any special background work for the part. 'This time I didn't actually feel the need to do much research, somehow the writing illuminated it, and I also used what I had done, met, and seen over my whole life. There was enough there to feed the characterization. Of course there are all sorts of parts where you have to do specialized research, but in this particular instance, I think, perhaps I knew enough. Mary Morris tells you an awful lot about her past in the opening dialogue, and her background is beautifully covered by the writing for the young girl.

'Clarissa has a formula for speech, probably learnt from "our Mam", a set of polite replies. "Very well thank you," "Yes, thank you," "Very nice, thank you," and when she is under sedation, these are the phrases that come out. It's only at the end, when she swears at her sister and they have a fight, that she does get more articulate. She lived in Australia for six months before she was granted citizenship, and before she went out there she had been living in a more open mental home in England and so could get out a bit. She had no education. The social worker was the one to get her passport and ticket for Australia. The words only come to her when she has been out in Australia for some time.

'The first question an actor has to ask himself according to my philosophy and training is "Who am I?" If you are a professional actor, people you have known who are remotely like that, or any experience you have had, comes back to you automatically. Part of being an actor is that you can draw on your experiences of life and people. Certain things stay with you, and, as an actor, your craft calls on those things. All the people you have ever met in your entire life— everybody is there—I use an amalgam of people.'

16

'I have no wish to slow down'

'If you're lucky enough to be given a part in a popular television series and are being interviewed, try to avoid the words I, me, my, or mine. DON'T talk about "my career". This means that person is not interested in the play, they're interested in themselves. It puts me off if I hear an actor I quite respect say "In my career", "what I've found in my career", "for me". The most important thing is to deliver what the author had in mind to the people who have paid that night. You are the least important thing about that.'

*   *   *

In spite of numerous tours with various productions, and many trips overseas, Prunella is, by inclination, a home person. She has been heard to say that she doesn't even like opening the front door to put out the empty milk bottles. On the other hand Timothy loves to travel, and, ingeniously, they have discovered a way in which they both get what they want, by spending holiday weeks exploring canals and waterways in their narrowboat. They first borrowed one from some friends when the boys were about six and eight, and loved it so much that they bought a half share in it. In about 1978 they sold their share and had one built for themselves by a friend in Banbury. The boat is sixty feet long and painted in blue and red, the interior lined with pine. It is a wonderful means of getting away, and can be used, and has been, as a place to live while performing in any part of the country reachable by canal. It also provides a good meeting place. Joe remembers that when they were younger just the four of them would go away together at Easter, and occasionally in the summer. They were great holidays and seemed to him like a kind of game; they did a lot of exploring. He says there was a clear distribution of roles, though Timothy was usually at the tiller. The decision about where you were going to, and when, depended on the placing of the locks. The children wore lifejackets and Joe can remember at one lock he fell in. 'I was desperately trying to tread water and keep my arm up because I had been told my new watch wasn't waterproof and I must keep it dry.'

Prunella and Timothy love the narrowboat and find it a wonderful way to escape. Prunella says, 'On it, I feel rather like a snail with my house on my back.' She can travel around the waterways without losing the sense of security of still being at home. 'I don't want a place in the country, because if I did I would want to do it properly and keep hens and grow vegetables and so on and that wouldn't leave time and energy to be an actor. Waterways are wonderfully relaxing, as is the discipline that travelling at 4mph puts on you.' Joe thinks the boat agrees with Prunella and Timothy as an economically sound second home. 'Tim loves it because it is mechanical. Pru loves it because she has things to do, she has a finite task. She hates having nothing to do.'

*   *   *

Politically active, Prunella has always been a strong Labour supporter and campaigns locally for the party.

282

She has always encouraged good, safe, clean public transport and always uses it herself in preference to driving.

She is a member of an organization called Arts for Labour. 'Under the present Labour government there isn't nearly enough money devoted to the arts and I'm constantly campaigning for this. Regional theatre is severely under-funded, as is regional touring and overseas touring. When Timothy and I were younger we went all over the world with full-scale productions of Shakespeare plays with the Prospect Theatre Company and the Oxford Playhouse Company, funded by the British Council. Nowadays you can't get the funding for a two-person recital tour, and I think that's crazy. I think live theatre should be cheap, which does mean subsidy. I believe that, like libraries and museums, live theatre should be widely available to everyone because it can really enrich people's lives.'

As a popular actress Prunella is constantly being asked to support this and that, to open worthwhile events, and to donate proceeds from various special evenings. More than happy to do this when she believes in the project, her help is very seldom publicized. She has been a member of the Howard League since the 1980s and feels very strongly about the lack of positive rehabilitation programmes in prisons, something the Howard League would like to rectify. She is an intermittent prison visitor, but her working life is so busy that her time is very limited. She says she feels guilty that she is not doing more. But looking at her overlapping schedules of work commitments, my sense is that she has been very generous with her time and energies.

In August 1997 Prunella went with a group of six children and their carers from Time2Care for a long weekend at a twenty-first-century theme park near Poitiers. She has been patron of the charity for many years; its aim is to provide desperately needed breaks for children who would otherwise not have them and to give every child in residential care a week's holiday. When Prunella performed *An Evening with Queen Victoria* at the Wigmore Hall on 13 January 2000, the proceeds went to Time2Care. She is also a patron of the Voices Foundation, an organization which helps children who have no access to instruments to learn about music through singing.

*   *   *

The tall, thin house in Wandsworth has been their family home since Joe was born in 1969, and Prunella can't envisage ever leaving it. Here, with both Prunella and Timothy almost constantly in work, but always at very different times, it is essential that they have a personal assistant/cook/manager to oversee the smooth running of their lives. As Prunella says, 'What I need is a wife.' During a typical week when I was spending a lot of time with her, she was filming *Looking for Victoria* one day, starting work at 6 a.m.; taking a class at the Actors Centre the next; flying to Majorca to make a Tesco ad another day, and working in a radio play for the rest of the week. In between, she was attending to her mail and giving interviews. One of the down sides of being well-known is the vast amount of mail which arrives every day asking for donations, interviews and assistance with charity appearances; in fact, this is one of the main reasons why they employ a PA.

I asked Prunella about the practicalities of being married to another working actor. For much of April

2003 she was filming *Looking for Victoria* during the day, including several days away on location. At that time Timothy was playing *King Lear* at the Old Vic every night except Sunday, and twice on Wednesday and Saturday. He was on call for publicity interviews in the mornings, recording a book on tape, and working on a play he was about to direct. Prunella's work got her up very early, Timothy's work kept him up late, and, as Prunella always likes to have supper with him when he gets home, sometimes the days could be very long. Prunella admits to being an early morning person and likes to go to bed early; she says she is very bad at doing things in the evening, though if she is in a play she will get to the theatre early and have half an hour to an hour's sleep before the show. Timothy likes to get up later but is happy to stay up in the evening. The time when they are both functioning well is lunchtime. Prunella says when they have rows it's because Timothy gets irritated when she doesn't finish her sentences, or she walks out of a room while still talking. Like many couples they have 'who gives the directions in the car' rows, and she admits to being obsessive about routes. She has enormous energy, and seems to be able to keep going almost indefinitely with the aid of short power naps. Sam says that as children they were always kept busy. 'We have always been ultra busy—a family illness!'

Resting and working are synonymous for Prunella. Sam believes her life is very bound up with acting: her principles, her interests and her enthusiasms are those of the profession. Reading and gardening are recreations she enjoys. She likes growing things, influenced perhaps by the war, and remembers she couldn't grow much at their Barnes house because the garden there was too small. For her, one of the

285

attractions of the house in Wandsworth was its garden, even though when they moved in half of it was a vegetable patch. She is a passionate gardener, and when Aunt Freda died, the whole of her £500 legacy was spent on landscaping. She asked the designers to create a place where she and Timothy could entertain their friends, where they could grow some fruit and where the boys could play. The garden is not very large—a central lawn with fruit trees, surrounded by flowerbeds, and a small summerhouse at the far end—but looking after it is one of Prunella's favourite occupations. 'If you lead a creative life and you're not working, then to grow things is a relief and satisfaction. A sort of substitute for creative work.'

An early riser, she spends a lot of time pottering about outside before the rest of the family are awake. 'I like all the boring things like weeding, planting out, cutting the grass. I like getting my hands extremely dirty.' Not only a keen gardener but also a compost enthusiast, she makes it in such quantity she can share it with the neighbours. She is also an avid recycler, saving paper clips, elastic bands, bits of string and the ribbons from gift wrapping; the latter she stores in a bulging plastic bag kept under the bed. Thriftiness with such bric-a-brac, it must be noted, is a habit common to most children brought up during the war, when shortages were so acute that absolutely everything was saved. She still mends her clothes and wears much-loved pairs of old shoes until they fall apart. She confesses she keeps clothes for ever: 'I've had some for thirty years.' This has nothing to do with necessity, and everything to do with habit. She admits to being a bag lady—Timothy once likened her handbag to a camel's stomach. 'Inside the main bag are a number of subsidiary ones called the Bank, the

Office, the Dispensary, the Dressing-table and Eyes and Teeth.' Her diary is always in her bag or beside her, it regulates her life and keeps it in some kind of order. Without it she would be in total confusion. At one meeting she says, 'My idea of hell is a very cold place, where I'm changing handbags for all eternity.'

One day while we are going through some of her boxes of photos, Prunella tells me firmly, 'Always name and date photographs when they come back from the developers.' As many of the pictures I'm looking at are neither named nor dated, I wholeheartedly agree with her.

In a newspaper interview Prunella revealed that her idea of perfect happiness is a day in the garden, with the family at home—and lots of work coming up. Her greatest fear is of being alone, and her favourite word is 'sorry'. John Cleese says, 'I tease her terribly about saying "sorry" a lot. And sometimes at the beginning of the evening I give her a certain number of minutes when she can apologize and another number of minutes when she can put herself down. I time her, then I say, "You have had four minutes of apologizing and you have to stop now." It comes, I think, from an excessive desire to behave decently, and if somebody is not happy, it bothers her. I think that Pru does worry excessively about whether she is doing the right thing—had done the right thing—will do the right thing. This may not be a bad thing from other people's point of view, but it probably causes her worry that she doesn't really need to undergo. She wants things to be good, she wants things to be happy, she wants people to enjoy themselves. I think she really loves what she does, and I think Tim is the same. She is a perfectionist in all things, she'd worry about making a salad, but not so much as she would about her latest

287

performance. There is a real desire for perfection. No compromise.

Prunella taught Joe how to cook, how to make sauces, how to cook a steak, how to produce the perfect poached egg. She told him, 'This is the way these things are done,' and he says she has great respect for certain processes or disciplines, they must be correct. I ask her if her need for perfection is why she always likes to check interviews before they are printed. She admits, 'I always ask the interviewer to fax me the quotes. "Not that I don't trust you," I say, but I speak so fast that very often people mis-hear what I say, which is my fault; but also if I do see the quotes I very often think of something more interesting to add. It worries me when anyone punctuates badly. You see, I think of punctuation in terms of delivery. You can breathe at a full stop. By examining the punctuation you can find out how quickly the person is supposed to think and how quickly they are supposed to talk, and so on and so forth.'

*   *   *

What does she consider the highlight of her life? 'I don't think of life in terms of highlights. I do think that I have been incredibly lucky and that I've been married for over forty years to the most remarkable person whom I simply adore. That's an abiding good fortune. I've kept pretty steadily in work, most of which has been extremely interesting. I haven't achieved workwise—yet—a lot of things I would like to achieve but it's important also to still have a goal.

'I would like to be given the opportunity to succeed, to satisfy myself and other people, in a major classical part. There aren't many left when you're a woman and get to my age, but I'm quite professionally envious of Tim that he has been able to play King Lear—I think it is three times now—and has probably got another two in him. I haven't myself had that kind of classical opportunity—maybe for reasons of incapacity, possibly because I've been fortunate enough to be successful in situation comedy on television, which in the eyes of many producers and casting directors shuts you out from the classical scenes. It makes me so angry that there is a tranche of perception in the public and the media which separates sit-com from the classics. Or Shakespeare from enjoyable situation comedy. It's absolute rubbish. I want the people who have enjoyed seeing me in *Fawlty Towers*, or *Marriage Lines*, to come and see me in some Chekhov and both laugh and cry.'

Timothy tells me, 'Pru is fanatical about acting and getting it right. She is a perfectionist and totally professional. She thinks acting is the most important thing in her life. It is the only thing we don't quite agree on. If she's not working and with no prospect of work, she's less of a person. She'll probably never retire. I don't know if she actually needs the physical outlet, or whether she needs to be wanted. I don't know the answer to that. It's to do with self-esteem. She still has a lack of self-confidence. Lack of self-confidence is perhaps not such a bad thing because it makes you try harder, and not blindly accept people's adulation.'

I ask Prunella how she feels about public adulation. She says she never wanted to be famous or recognized in the street, in fact she is sometimes embarrassed by it. 'Of course I want people to come and see what I'm doing. Of course. I've always wanted to be an actor and it's the most wonderful thing—to hear people laughing, or being very, very quiet and listening to what you're saying on stage, and to know that you're bringing the author to the people sitting out front. It's a tremendous and very complicated buzz. When Tim and I are walking along the street one of two things happens. They either come up to Tim and say, "Thank you for all the pleasure we have had from your wonderful classical work." Then they turn to me and say, "Of course we've seen you too, you do more the comedy, don't you?" Or they bounce up to me and say, "Thank you for all the pleasure you've given us in those wonderful comedy shows." Then they turn to Tim and say, "Of course you do more the Shakespeare, don't you?" Over the years I've played different parts and attracted considerable notices for classical productions, but in the public's mind I'm more remembered for the good fortune of having been successful in situation comedy.'

*   *   *

I ask her if she ever suffers from stage fright. 'Everyone has stage fright to a certain extent. You have to be able to deal with it and if possible use it—depending on the circumstances one is more, or less, successful. After about the first two or three weeks it goes and I really begin to enjoy the show.'

*   *   *

Prunella says she is not interested in retirement. 'I never thought of giving up acting, I've no wish to slow down. The parts can get more interesting as you get older. I hope to continue working as long as I keep my health, strength and memory. I'd like to die on the eighth curtain call—which would suggest the play was a success. Just hope I'm fairly near the middle of the line-up and had a good part—I'd keep sinking down and down—then they'll pick me up and carry me off!

'Let's not talk about me.'